Frederick Warren

A primer of French literature

Frederick Warren

A primer of French literature

ISBN/EAN: 9783337204938

Printed in Europe, USA, Canada, Australia, Japan

Cover: Foto ©Paul-Georg Meister /pixelio.de

More available books at **www.hansebooks.com**

A PRIMER

OF

FRENCH LITERATURE.

BY

F. M. WARREN, Ph.D.,

Associate in Modern Languages in the Johns Hopkins
University.

———oo;◦;oo———

BOSTON, U.S.A.:
D. C. HEATH & CO., PUBLISHERS.
1889.

TYPOGRAPHY BY J. S. CUSHING & CO., BOSTON

TABLE OF CONTENTS.

	PAGE
PREFACE	V

CHAPTER
I. INTRODUCTION 1

PART I.

MEDIÆVAL LITERATURE, TO 1327 9–61
   II. First Period, to 1150 9
   III. Second Period, 1150–1250. Epic Poetry . . 17
   IV. Second Period, 1150–1250. Narrative Poetry . 31
   V. Second Period, 1150–1250. Didactic and Lyric
      Poetry. The Drama. Prose . . . 40
   VI. Third Period, 1250–1327 52

PART II.

PRE-RENAISSANCE LITERATURE, 1327–1515 . . 62–89
   VII. First Period, 1327–1422 62
   VIII. Second Period, 1422–1515 73

PART III.

RENAISSANCE LITERATURE, 1515–1601 . . . 90–121
   IX. First Period, 1515–1549 90
   X. Second Period, 1549–1601 101

PART IV.

THE SEVENTEENTH CENTURY, 1601–1718 . . 122–17

CHAPTER
- XI. First Period, 1601–1659 12
- XII. Second Period, 1659–1689 14
- XIII. Third Period, 1689–1718 16

PART V.

THE EIGHTEENTH CENTURY, 1718–1801 . . . 174–19
- XIV. First Period, 1718–1750 17
- XV. Second Period, 1750–1801 18

PART VI.

THE NINETEENTH CENTURY, 1801– 198–23
- XVI. First Period, 1801–1848. Poetry. The Drama . 19
- XVII. First Period, 1801–1848. Prose 21
- XVIII. Second Period, 1848– 22

INDEX 23

PREFACE.

THE following outline of French literature is based on lectures given in the Johns Hopkins University, and has therefore certain definite needs of instruction in mind. The original notes have however been worked over, enlarged, and separated into paragraphs — not always happily — and can, by omission or expansion, be made to serve as a statement of facts for any period desired.

Certain defects of execution are evident. The attempt to modernize all names and titles previous to the sixteenth century has sometimes failed through habit or inadvertence. The substitution of the English definite article for the French has led to many absurdities, and seems now to have been unwise. In the first chapters, intended for specialists or for extended commentaries by instructors, the necessary conciseness has at times led to obscurity for beginners. The least satisfactory period is that of the Eighteenth Century, both in division and matter. A serious omission is the dramatic work of LOUIS-SÉBASTIEN MERCIER (1740–1814).

The most available reference book for Mediæval Literature is: *La littérature française au moyen âge*, Gaston Paris. Paris, 1888. 16mo. This manual has served to revise the whole period. Its Bibliography is an important feature.

For Pre-Renaissance Literature review articles and lectures at the Collége de France by Gaston Paris on the poetry of the fifteenth century have furnished the larger part of the material. The history of the stage previous to the Renaissance is fully treated in the *Histoire du théâtre*, L. Petit de Julleville. Paris, 1880–1886. 5 vols. 8vo and 16mo.

On Renaissance Literature the standard authority is: *Le Seizième Siècle en France*, A. Darmesteter and A. Hatzfeld. Paris, 3d ed., 1887. 16mo. The first volume of the *Geschichte der französischen Litteratur seit Anfang des XVI. Jahrhunderts*, A. Birch-Hirschfeld, Stuttgart, 1889, 8vo, furnishes many additional facts on the first part of the century. A more general treatise, which has been of much use in the remaining centuries also, is the *Leçons de littérature française*, L. Petit de Julleville. Paris, 1884. 18mo.

The best work on the Seventeenth Century is the *Geschichte der französischen Litteratur im XVII. Jahrhundert*, F. Lotheissen. Wien, 1877–1884. 4 vols. 8vo. For the novels of the century consult the *Geschichte des französischen Romans im XVII. Jahrhundert*, H. Koerting. Leipzig, 1885–1887. 2 vols. 8vo.

The Eighteenth and Nineteenth Centuries are extensively treated in the *Geschichte der französischen Litteratur*, G. Bornhak. Berlin, 1886. 8vo.

The Index, mainly of proper names and anonymous works, is designed to supplement the chapter headings.

F. M. WARREN.

BALTIMORE, Nov. 1, 1889.

PRIMER OF FRENCH LITERATURE.

CHAPTER I.

INTRODUCTION.

1. Race; Language. — The territory of the French language has varied but little since its formation. The Celts inhabiting Gaul were completely Romanized. But slight traces of their tongue are to be found in the Latin of the country when the barbaric invasions took place. The Gallo-Romans assimilated then their Teutonic conquerors more or less completely, according to the number of settlers. Their territory was pushed back from the Rhine to its present limits by the end of the fifth century. In the interior of the country there soon appeared a general linguistic difference which separated the Romance-speaking region into two nearly equal parts, on a line running from the Atlantic, just north of Bordeaux, east almost to Lyons, then bending to the southeast and reaching the Alps, after passing near Grenoble. To the south of this line Germanic influence scarcely penetrated. An independent language and literature, the Provençal, developed freely. — On the contrary, the region north of this boundary was strongly penetrated by the foreign manners and tongue. The vocabulary received new terms, such as those relating to feudal institutions, to war, to seafaring, to natural scenery, to dress, household utensils, and even to mental and moral conceptions. The spirit of the invaders is also reflected plainly in the literature. — About the same time the original Gallic domain was further circumscribed by the immigration of the British Celts who, fleeing before the Anglo-Saxons, settled the Armorican peninsula in the fifth and sixth centuries, established there their language and customs and preserved their race traditions. To compensate for these losses, the Norman conquest, in the eleventh century, brought England under the sway of French thought. When the English, in their turn, had absorbed the invaders, South France was restored in the thirteenth century, through the decay of Provençal literature.

2. **Dialects; Centres of Early Literary Activity.** — Already in the tenth century there appear linguistic differences in Northern France, and the subsequent literature shows the presence of four leading dialects — the Burgundian, Picard, Norman (including Anglo-Norman), and the French proper. With the political predominance of the Isle-de-France and the extension of the influence of Paris, French becomes the standard idiom, and prevails from the time of Philip Augustus (1180–1223). — The various sections of the country present also different kinds of literature. The heroic epic flourishes best in the northeast, the center, and the northwest. The Arthurian legends prefer Champagne and Picardy, as does also lyric poetry. Historical and didactic works are produced mainly in Normandy and its dependencies.

The drama is best maintained in the wealthy communes of Picardy and Flanders.

3. Characteristics of the Age; Attitude of the Educated Classes; Value of the Literature. — All literatures are at first orally transmitted. Their primitive form is poetical, as best suited to singing. Later, when the poems are intrusted to manuscript, a class of readers is implied for whom prose can be written. In mediæval France this natural order was followed. Little prose is found previous to the last quarter of the twelfth century. Up to that time epic and lyric poetry, the amusement of the nobles, prevailed. — On all the spirit of feudalism is plainly stamped. It was taken for granted that the social fabric had always existed as it was, and would continue unchanged. Hence the distorted and curious view of antiquity, transformed into mediævalism in all imitation of Latin authors (Greek authors were known only by Latin translations), and that sense of self-satisfaction, which precluded all curiosity in regard to the future. Society felt no longings, gave no tokens of a desire to progress. The demands of art were satisfied by the useful. The beautiful was almost unnoticed. The portrayal of feudal passions on the one hand, on the other the new relations of the sexes, consequent on the real and assumed rise of woman, constitute the distinctive features of the literature of these centuries. Yet, in opposition to the prevailing factitious and conventional style, we find in certain works that common sense, malicious wit, and airy grace, which became later the leading qualities of the matured literature. — The principal reason for lack of art can be attributed to the hostility of the professional classes to the vernacular. Preferring a perfected language, though dead, to a rough and changing tongue, the best minds of the time looked with contempt on the national literature and abandoned it to the needy talents of the undisciplined. The consequences were, absence of individuality, of style, and of standards of taste. The most attractive subjects, reposing on the broad base of popular tradition, were diluted by succeeding generations of hack writers, to suit the passing fashion. Therefore the literature of feudal France is valuable mainly for the study of the manners and thought of the period. It is also the repository for the material which modern times have artistically used. The knowledge of it is essential to the understanding of the other literatures of Western Europe.

4. **Independent Development of French Literature.** — The cause of the literary leadership of mediæval France is mainly due to the originality of its literary development. In this it most closely resembles the literature of Greece. It produced spontaneously epic, lyric, and dramatic poetry. No foreign influence is perceptible before the last part of the twelfth century, and even then lyric poetry alone is affected in its outward form. — No less remarkable was the ease with which French poets seized on every subject which was furnished by the decay of antiquity, the conflicts of new peoples, the rise of Christianity, the superstitions of heathenism still surviving, the nondescript fragments caused by the collision of primeval mythologies, historical religions, savage customs giving way to civilization, the drift-wood of vanished nations drawn in on the wake of the Crusades —

all of which, misunderstood, perverted, they twisted into their notion of utility and ran into their unyielding groove of insipidity.

5. **Versification.** — Inasmuch as the mass of literature took a poetical shape, the structure of the verse assumes importance. In common with that of all Romance nations, French versification is based on accent. The quantity of vowels is never brought into question. A line is made up of syllables, even in number if the last syllable is masculine, uneven if feminine, though the accent in all cases comes on the last syllable, if masculine, on the next to the last, if the last is feminine. — The origin of this accented verse is probably to be found in the rhythmical versification of the Latins, crowded out of classical literature by Greek influence, but which survived among the people. — For rime, the earliest epic and lyric poetry, being sung, is assonanced — an agreement in sound between the tonic vowels, and not necessarily between the consonants following them. The earliest poetry is also not strophic, but is found in long tirades ending with the same tonic vowel. Later, through the introduction of reading, ordinary rime was employed. — The cæsura occurs in verses of more than eight syllables, also occasionally in the latter.

6. **Oldest Monuments.** — The oldest specimens of the French language do not belong to the domain of French literature, properly speaking, yet show somewhat the national influence. — The earliest French preserved is in the oaths taken at Strassburg in 842, in French and German, by the armies of Louis and Charles, and recorded by NITHARD in his Latin history. The lan-

guage wavers on the border-line of Latin and French. — To the tenth century belongs a fragment of a homily on *Jonah*, delivered evidently in French, but taken down half in French, half in Latin, partly in ordinary characters, partly in Tironian notes. — A sequence on Saint Eulalia, modeled on a Latin sequence, relating the martyrdom of the saint, is perhaps as early, and is the first poem in French. — The *Vie de Saint Léger*, somewhat later in the century, offers however the first regular French verse — forty strophes of six octosyllabic verses each, riming in couplets. — The influence of the clergy seen in adapting these edifying subjects to the vernacular was sufficient also to preserve them in monastic libraries, grafted on Latin manuscripts, while the many popular and national poems of the epoch do not appear, in their present form at least, before the last half of the eleventh century.

7. Periods of the Mediæval Literature. — French literature, from its beginnings to the advent of the Valois, can be considered as roughly divided into three periods.

The First Period, ending about 1150, is characterized by the formation of the national heroic epic, the beginnings of the liturgical drama, and the commencement of didactic treatises both in poetry and prose.

The Second Period, embracing perhaps a Hundred Years, from 1150 to 1250, is marked, at first, by the predominance of the Breton epic (the Arthurian legends) and of historical poetry; later, by the flowering of lyric poetry under Provençal influence, by the appearance of *romans d'aventure*, — precursors of a type of modern novels, — by the rise of allegorical and symbolistic poetry, representing the finical side of French character, and of satirical and jocose poetry, embodying its practical and rough side — the *esprit gaulois*. This is the brilliant period of the mediæval literature, in which prose also attains a high degree of excellence.

The Third Period, extending from 1250 to 1327, is one of decay in the branches of poetical literature previously cultivated — save the allegorical, which chokes in the end lyrical expansion; and the dramatic, which gains among the people ever-increasing favor. Prose holds its own in legal and historical works.

PART I.

MEDIÆVAL LITERATURE. TO 1327.

CHAPTER II.

FIRST PERIOD. To 1150.

1. **Epic Poetry.** *Roland*, a. 1060; *Roi Louis*, XI c.; *Pèlerinage de Charlemagne*, XI c.; *Charroi de Nîmes*, XII c.; *Chevalerie Vivien*, XII c.
2. **Didactic Poetry.** *Vie de Saint Alexis*, a. 1050; *Vie de Saint Grégoire*, XII c.; *Voyage de Saint Brendan*, a. 1125; Lapidaries. Bestiaries. PHILIPPE DE THAON, a. 1110–a. 1135.
3. **Lyric Poetry.** *Cantique des Cantiques*, XII c.; *Romance; Pastourelle; Chanson de croisade*.
4. **Drama.** Latin plays. *Sponsus*, b. 1150.
5. **Prose.** Psalters of Oxford and Cambridge, a. 1100–a. 1120.

1. **Origin of the National Epic.** — "The French heroic epic is the product of the fusion of the Germanic spirit, in a Romance form, with the new Christian civilization of France" (G. PARIS). — The ancient custom of the Germans to sing their heroes' deeds was turned to the advantage of the Roman Church as early as the baptism of Clovis. Throughout the Merovingian epoch the Latin chronicles are full of poetical allusions to the more

noted kings, which are evidently the echoes of popular songs both in German and Romance. The French poem, *Floovent* (XII c.), preserves, without doubt, the traditions concerning Dagobert (620) and his title (Chlodovinc). — Under the Carolingian dynasty existing songs were gradually transferred to Charles Martel, Pippin, and Charlemagne, and the epic material was vastly increased by their conquests. The reign of Charlemagne saw the greatest development of the national poetry. It diminished under Louis I. and his successors, and rose again under Charles the Bald, to celebrate victorious feudalism. By the middle of the tenth century the original epic matter was complete.

2. **Spirit of the National Epic; Confusion of Subject.** — Based on historical events (with a slight admixture of Teutonic mythology) and preserved by popular tradition, the epic poems tended to center about one person, Charlemagne — confused with Charles Martel and Charles the Bald — and to present a single theme, the struggle of Christian Europe against the Saracens — who finally included all the enemies of the Frankish monarchy. — Many songs, however, remained independent. These generally extol local heroes and wars, either against the sovereign or between vassals. Some are popular stories of adventure or are made up by the minstrels on epic commonplaces.

3. **The Minstrels; Divisions of the National Epic.** — The songs at their beginnings were by eye-witnesses of the events, and lyric. As the events receded they became more and more narrative and finally fell into the hands of professional singers, the *jongleurs*. Traveling from

place to place, already in the ninth century they amalgamated and fused the numerous local traditions, developing and increasing their material. — The various *chansons de geste* they thus formed (sung to the *vielle*) they tried to separate into three cycles — the **Cycle of the King**, relating the deeds of the royal family and the national wars; the **Cycle of Garin de Monglane,** called also of **Guillaume d'Orange,** or of **Guillaume au Court Nez,** which recounts the struggle in Southern France against the Saracens; and the **Cycle of Doon de Mayence,** in which the vassals overcome the monarch. — Including independent poems, the total number of epic songs still extant is about one hundred, while others are preserved in translations.

4. **Cycle of the King.** — The three oldest epic poems (1050–1100), and the only ones in the first finished form, belong to the cycle of the King. — *Roland,* the earliest and most celebrated, having some four thousand decasyllabic verses grouped in assonanced tirades, is founded on the Spanish war of Charlemagne. In the year 778 his rear-guard was cut to pieces by the Basques at Roncesvalles, and Roland, count of the Breton Marches, killed. The song in his honor, expanding in true epic style, made him the nephew of Charlemagne, changed the Basques into Saracens, and explained the defeat by the treason of a Frankish ambassador, Ganelon. With Roland die his friend, Oliver, the archbishop Turpin, and the remaining Paladins. Various portents and marvels accompany the fight. Charlemagne returns to punish the enemy, and Ganelon is put to death. — The poem presents the feudal ideal in its loyalty, its sense of honor

and of religious duty. Pathetic incidents are not wanting. Patriotism is seen in the invocations of "dulce France."— The epic spirit is shown in the use of dialogue, in the action before the eyes, in the frequent repetitions. The style is simple, energetic, noble, but scarcely poetical. The success of the poem was immediate and extensive, as is seen by the German translation of KONRAD (a. 1133). — The *Roi Louis* is a fragment of some six hundred and sixty assonanced octosyllabic verses. It has its origin in the victory of Louis III. over the Normans (here Saracens), at Saucourt (881) (the German *Ludwigslied*). A traitor is introduced. — The *Pèlerinage de Charlemagne*, composed of about eight hundred and seventy verses of twelve syllables, — the earliest example of the Alexandrine, — is rather mock-heroic. It is made up of separate traditions devoid of historical basis. The Teutonic love for stories (*gab*) is shown, and the introduction is borrowed from an Eastern tale. The object of the poem is to amuse the crowd at the Lendit fair at Saint-Denis, and to magnify the relics of the abbey. Half serious, half comic, it has little of the spirit of *Roland*, but much of the later *gaulois fableaux*.

5. **Cycle of Garin de Monglane.** — After the eleventh century no poem of the national epic is preserved in its original form. The minstrels constantly renewed, expanded, and increased what was bequeathed to them. Most of the manuscripts belong to the thirteenth and fourteenth centuries, and none are earlier than the middle of the twelfth. — Rewritten are all the poems of the cycle of Garin de Monglane. The first trace of them is in a fragment of a Latin poem (X c.). The hero of the

cycle is Guillaume of Toulouse († 812), who profited by the deeds of homonyms. — The *Charroi de Nîmes* (XII c.) relates the transfer of Guillaume, under Louis I., to the South, and the capture of Nîmes by introducing his warriors, hidden in wine-tuns, into the city. — The *Chevalerie Vivien* (XII c.) is based on a battle lost near Arles, and is important for its sequels, *Aleschans* (the Roman cemetery near Arles), translated by WOLFRAM VON ESCHENBACH, and *Foulque de Candie*, which popularized the whole cycle in Italy under the title of the *Nerbonesi*.

6. **Didactic Poetry; Lives of Saints.** — The mediæval writers made no distinction between didactic, religious, and moral literature. It was all viewed from the standpoint of utility. It proceeded from the clergy, generally in translations from the Latin. Its poetical form in French is the octosyllabic couplet. — The Latin lives of saints offered a fruitful field. The *Vie de Saint Alexis* (a. 1050), composed after epic models in assonanced decasyllabic strophes, is, in its origin, a Byzantine tradition. Its success is seen in many later revisions and translations. — The *Vie de Saint Grégoire* (XII c.), also very popular, is a version of the story of Œdipus, where the crimes are absolved by repentance. In octosyllabic verse it was often translated. — The *Voyage de Saint Brendan* (a. 1125) is a translation from the Latin, by the monk BENEDICT, for Queen Adelaide. From Celtic sources it contains many Irish legends of the Atlantic, and became very popular, even entering into assumed discoveries of America.

7. **Lapidaries ; Bestiaries ;** PHILIPPE DE THAON,

a. 1110–a. 1135. — The treatises on precious stones and beasts are more scientific. Very numerous in Latin, they had incorporated both Eastern and Western superstitions, modified often by additions from the Bible and by allegorical explanations. — The French lapidaries were translated from the Latin of MARBODIUS († 1123). They enumerate as a rule the virtues of the stones, but also show, in their allegory, Church influence. — The bestiaries were much more symbolistic. To real animals many fabulous types from the Scriptures and from Oriental tales were added, and each signified some Church doctrine or belief. — The earliest known was dedicated (after 1121) to Queen Adelaide, by PHILIPPE DE THAON (a. 1110–a. 1135), a priest. He had already addressed to his uncle, chaplain to the Earl of Norfolk, a *Comput* (b. 1119), in couplets of six syllables, based on Latin sources, as the *De temporum ratione* of BEDE. It is a popular astronomy, containing a calendar for the use of priests.

8. **Lyric Poetry; Kinds.** — The only religious lyric of the century is a paraphrase of the *Song of Solomon* in assonance, popular in tone and of considerable grace. — The earliest form of the secular lyric seems to be the *romance*, called also *chanson d'histoire* and *chanson de toile*. In form it is lyric-epic — assonanced strophes of from four to eight octo- or decasyllabic verses with refrain. The subject is court-life, both in joustings and love-making. Concise in expression and charming in sentiment, the *romances* offer the most agreeable reading of the early literature. Among the best are *Rainaud*, *Orior*, and *Belle Doette*. — The *pastourelle*, undoubtedly of popu-

lar origin, is more artistic in the specimens extant. It is composed of rimed strophes of short verses, having a lively measure. A short introduction precedes a dialogue between a knight and a shepherdess. The scenes are rural. — The *chanson de croisade* is the earliest form of strophes having interlaced rimes. The *outrée* song of the first crusade is lost, but one of the second (b. 1147) still exists. It has a refrain, like all songs of popular origin.

9. **The Origin of the Drama; Mysteries and Miracles.** — Save certain elements of traditional comedy, kept alive by wandering buffoons, the mediæval theater grew up within the church. It developed either from the liturgical office, by constantly increasing interpolations, varied by the use of the dialogue, or from sermons, hymns, and devout narratives, thrown likewise into dialogue form. The interpolations, at first textual quotations from the Vulgate, were gradually changed into Latin metrical verse, then into rimed and accented poetry, until, about the beginning of the twelfth century, the vernacular appears, and profane elements mingle with the sacred. In the meanwhile the stage has advanced from before the high altar to the inclosure in front of the church. As a last change, the clergy cease to be the actors, though they support and control the play and keep it in connection with the office of the day. — The plays gather around two centers. Those of Christmas have their origin in the liturgy and canonical traditions and in a sermon, attributed to SAINT AUGUSTIN, made up of the Messianic prophecies. — Those played at Easter present two themes: the Resurrection and, later, the Passion. — The dramas

of both these cycles, Scriptural in their essence, were afterwards known as *mystères*. — The *miracles* were the development of songs in honor of saints and the Virgin, or of treatises on their lives. They were given on the eve of the saint's day. — The earliest play in which the vernacular rivals the Latin is *Sponsus* (b. 1150), a paraphrase of the parable of the Foolish Virgins, rather lyric in its nature. The French (of Poitou) is in decasyllabic verse, generally monorime.

10. **Didactic Prose; Psalters, a. 1100–a. 1120.** — The prose of the period is wholly didactic, and is the work of Anglo-Normans. It consists of two psalters, translated (a. 1100–a. 1120) probably at Canterbury, and called after their present localities, the *Psalters* of Oxford and Cambridge. The translation is literal and plain, and became the base of many subsequent renderings in prose and poetry.

Mediæval Literature. To 1327.

CHAPTER III.

SECOND PERIOD. 1150-1250.

Epic Poetry.

1. **National Epic.** Cycle of the King; *Mainet*, XII c.; Jean Bodel, a. 1200; *Couronnement de Louis*, XII c.; *Fierabras*, XII c. Cycle of Garin de Monglane; Bertrand, of Bar-sur-Aube, XIII c. Cycle of Doon de Mayence; *Renaud de Montauban*, XIII c.; Raimbert, of Paris, XII c.; *Girard de Roussillon*, XII c.; *Huon de Bordeaux*, XII c. Independent poems; The Lorraine cycle, XII c.; *Raoul de Cambrai*, XII c.; *Horn*, XII c.; *Ami et Amile*, XII c.; *Jourdain de Blaie*, XII c.
2. **Crusade Epic.** *Chanson de Jérusalem*, XII c.; Graindor de Douai, a. 1180–a. 1190; *Chevalier au Cygne*, XII c.
3. **Epic of Antiquity.** *Alexandre* by Albéric, of Briançon, b. 1125; Lambert le Tort and Alexandre, of Bernai, b. 1190. Benoît de Sainte-More, a. 1160–a. 1175.
4. **Breton Epic.** Nennius, X c.; Geoffrey of Monmouth, †1154. Lais; Marie de France, XII c. The Tristran cycle; Béroul, a. 1150; Thomas, a. 1170. The Arthurian cycle; Chrétien de Troies, a. 1160–a. 1180; Raoul de Houdan, b. 1235; *Guinglain*, XII c.; *Durmart le Gallois*, XIII c. The Grail cycle; Robert de Boron, a. 1200. Prose romances; *Tristran; Lancelot; Perceval; Saint Graal; Merlin.*

1. **The National Epic; Cycle of the King.** — The greater part of the epic poems were written in this period, which includes the reign of Philip Augustus (1180–1223) and ends with the Egyptian crusade of Saint Louis. They are not, however, in their original form. — *Roland* underwent, as the others, a rimed version (a. 1170) which crowded out the assonanced form. — In a second dress is also *Mainet* (*Maigne*), on the youth and exile in Spain of Charlemagne, and his marriage with a Saracen princess — an epic commonplace. The historical basis is found in the life of Charles Martel. The poem is preserved in fragments of monorime alexandrines, the verse which succeeded the decasyllabic tirade. — *Fierabras* (a. 1200), an expanded episode of a lost poem, which had great success abroad, relates the deeds of that giant who is overcome and converted by Oliver — a medley of legends. — The *Saisnes* (a. 1200), by JEAN BODEL, of Arras, an imitation of a previous poem, confuses the Saxon wars of Dagobert with those of Charlemagne. The enemy are often called Saracens. — The *Couronnement de Louis* is based on the transference of the empire to Louis I., confused with the succeeding Louis.

2. **Cycle of Garin de Monglane.** — The hero of the last-named poem is Guillaume d'Orange. — Another of the same family is seen in *Aimeri de Narbonne*, by BERTRAND (a. 1212–a. 1225), of Bar-sur-Aube, an imitation of lost poems, which contains the original of HUGO's *Aymerillot*. — A fusion of epic traditions appears in *Girard de Vienne*, also by BERTRAND. The historical basis is a siege sustained by Girard de Roussillon in Vienne. To this, the

poet added legends concerning Roland and Oliver, as their duel (reproduced by Hugo in the *Mariage de Roland*) and the meeting of Roland and Aude (the source of Uhland's *Roland und Alda*).

3. **Cycle of Doon de Mayence.**— After *Roland*, the most important poems are those which favor the feudal idea. — *Renaud de Montauban*, or the *Quatre Fils Aimon* — the events of which, occurring under Charles Martel in Aquitania, were enlarged by Rhenish traditions and episodes of the Crusades, — relates the conflicts with Charlemagne of Renaud (who has killed an imperial prince with a chess-board) and his brothers, aided by the enchanter, Maugis, and the horse, Bayard. The scene is laid at Montauban and Dortmund. Renaud finally turns monk, meets a violent death at Cologne, and is glorified by a miracle. Bayard, escaping the vengeance of Charlemagne, still wanders in the Ardennes. — The deeds of Renaud, attractive to the communes of Lombardy, availed to make him the chief hero of the Italian romances. The later prose form of the poem is still the popular chap-book of France and Germany. — *Oger le Danois*, by Raimbert, of Paris, is made up from previous poems, the *Enfances Oger* (his early deeds), and a narrative of his later exploits. The Lombard wars of Charlemagne are the basis, and Oger, count of the Danish Marches, profited by the renown of homonyms. — *Girard de Roussillon*, in Burgundian dialect, rests on the wars of Girard, duke of Provence, with Charles the Bald (in the poem, Charles Martel). The celebrity of Girard (who is always aided by his faithful wife, Bertha) gave rise to various Latin lives and French poems, as *Girard de Fratte* and

Girard de Vienne. — *Huon de Bordeaux* mingles the history of Charles the Infant († 866) with the magic of the Breton cycle, and introduces Alberich of Germanic tradition in the person of the enchanter, Oberon. The English translation of the prose version was used by SHAKSPERE, while the French, becoming a chap-book, and, appearing in the *Bibliothèque des romans* (1778), gave rise to the poem of WIELAND, which in turn inspired WEBER's opera, *Oberon.* — Dramatized as a *miracle*, it was played in France down to the time of MOLIÈRE.

4. **Independent Poems.** — The five poems relating the feud of the houses of Metz and Bordeaux, called the **Lorraine cycle**, are the most important of those which resisted the cyclic tendencies of the minstrels. Their interest is purely local. They present unchanged the ferocity and harshness of feudalism. — The same characteristics are seen in *Raoul de Cambrai*, killed in 943 by the house of Vermandois. A fine passage is the burning of the abbey of Ortigny, with its nuns. — *Horn* is a tale of adventure, from the Anglo-Saxon, which assumes in French the epic verse and certain epic commonplaces. — *Ami et Amile*, an Eastern story of friendship and mutual likeness, was artificially connected with the court of Charlemagne. — A sequel to it is *Jourdain de Blaie*, a clever transformation of the Latin form of the Greek novel, *Apollonius of Tyre*.

5. **The Crusade Epic; Development from History and Legend;** GRAINDOR DE DOUAI, **a. 1180–a. 1190.** — The poems relating to the first crusade are conscious imitations of the national epic. Based on Latin chronicles, they contain also Walloon traditions, arising from the

stories of the pilgrims, and borrowings from the national songs. They remain, however, rather historical than epic. — The poetical versions of the previous decades were worked over by GRAINDOR DE DOUAI into the *Chanson de Jérusalem* (a. 1180–a. 1190), which contains a purely romantic episode of the fights of French prisoners with monsters — the *Chétifs*. — The real or assumed historical account of GRAINDOR was introduced by a version of a mythological legend, probably Germanic, the *Chevalier au Cygne*, due to minstrels attached to the house of Bouillon. In it the origin of the house is related and the history of the swan-knight, Hélias, who later becomes the ancestor of Godfrey. — The German version, *Lohengrin*, was attached by WOLFRAM VON ESCHENBACH to the story of the Grail. — Before 1250 both parts of the epic were rendered into prose, to the great advantage of the legendary part, which became very popular throughout Northern and Western Europe.

6. **The Cycle of Antiquity; Poems on Alexander.** — In rivalry with the national epic, the clerks chose from among their Latin readings strange and wonderful adventures, adapted them to the vernacular and to the popular taste. — The first subject thus introduced was the legend of Alexander the Great. A narrative embodying his fabulous history and various Oriental superstitions, the *Pseudo-Callisthenes* (II c.), had its rise at Alexandria, and was later made known to the West by various Latin translations, as the *Epitome* (IX c.) and the *Historia de proeliis* (X c.). Other sources existed in the *Itinerarium*, the *Epistola ad Aristotelem*, and the late *Iter ad Paradisum*. — Based on the *Historia*, the first French version

was made by ALBÉRIC, of Briançon (or Besançon), in octosyllabic tirades, of which a fragment of one hundred and five verses remains. The purpose is to illustrate by Alexander's short life, the text: "Vanity of vanities." Curious is the transformation of the son of a magician into a mediæval Christian, surrounded by his *knights* (*milites*). Lively and poetical, the work had great success and was soon translated into German by LAMPRECHT (b. 1125). — It was also imitated in decasyllabic French in the lost version of a certain SIMON. — These French renderings, the fictitious Latin chronicles, the history of QUINTUS CURTIUS, and various popular beliefs gave rise to the poem *Alexandre* (b. 1190), in four separate branches, and due to at least three authors, ALEXANDRE, of Bérnai, LAMBERT LE TORT, of Chateaudun, and PIERRE, of Saint Cloud. The peculiar feature of the work is to magnify the knightly virtues of Alexander, and especially his largesses, for which he became the model. Its popularity is seen in the name, alexandrine, given to the already existing line of twelve syllables, which it adopted. — Among the sequels are the *Vengeance d'Alexandre* (b. 1191) by GUI DE CAMBRAI, and, later, by JEAN LE VENELAIS. — The Spanish and Dutch versions derive from the Latin *Alexandreïs* (b. 1179) of GAUTIER DE CHÂTILLON.

7. **Imitations of Antiquity by** BENOÎT DE SAINTE-MORE, a. 1160–a. 1175. — The octosyllabic couplet of narrative poetry is the verse of the other works on Greek and Roman themes, most of which are due to a poet of the English court, BENOÎT, of Sainte-More. — He dedicated to Queen Eleanor his *Roman de Troie* (a. 1160),

taken from the fictitious narrative of the Trojan *Dares* (V c.), from OVID and other sources, among them the forged account of the Cretan *Dictys* (II c.), translated into Latin and, together with the *Iliad*, the original of *Dares*. — HOMER, known only by a Latin abridgment, passed in the Middle Ages as a falsifier. — The *Troie* was probably suggested by the legend of the descent of the French from Francus, grandson of Priam. BENOÎT added to his material and expanded the episodes. He assimilated characters and events to the notions of his age. He refines the manners according to the prevailing view of "courtesy," and pleased his hearers by many descriptions of Eastern luxury. His most important episode is that of Troilus and Briseida, rendered in true romantic style, and which, through the Latin version (1287) of his poem by GUIDO COLONNA, suggested to BOCCACCIO the *Filostrato*. This in turn reached SHAKSPERE through CHAUCER and LYDGATE. The *Troie* was likewise translated into German (by HERBORT VON FRITZLAR) and into other languages of Europe. — The *Énéas* is probably by BENOÎT also. It adapts to mediæval notions a glossed text of the *Eneid*. Feudal combats and the childish love of Æneas and Lavinia are presented in the easy style and conventional manner which make BENOÎT the predecessor of the finical graces of the Breton cycle. It introduced "courtesy" into German literature through the translation of HEINRICH VON VELDEKE. — BENOÎT is perhaps the author of the *Roman de Thèbes*, based on a glossed text of STATIUS and expanded by new episodes. Its prose versions gave rise to foreign imitations, as that of LYDGATE, while in France various tales of adventure borrow from it the names of their heroes.

8. **Origin of the Breton Epic; Celtic Mythology and Historical Tradition;** Geoffrey of Monmouth, † 1154. — The poems of the Breton cycle find their historical basis in the wars of the Anglo-Saxon conquest (V–VI c.). From these a national epic was evolved which incorporated with it previously existing elements, mainly mythological. The traditions first appear in the *Historia Britonum* (X c.), ascribed to Nennius, in which Arthur is a *dux bellorum*, who defeats the Saxons in twelve battles. — Soon after the Gaelic minstrels and Breton bards make the legends familiar to the Anglo-Saxons and Normans, who introduce them into literature after the Norman conquest. — Geoffrey of Monmouth († 1154), making use of Celtic material, wrote the *Prophetia Merlini* (1135), which he later inserted in his *Historia regum Britanniae* (a. 1137), made up from Nennius, Celtic and Latin documents, popular tales, and his own invention. To this work is due the chivalric conception peculiar to the cycle and before unknown. — Translations into French verse followed. That of Geoffrei Gaimar (a. 1145) is lost, but that of Wace, dedicated to Eleanor, the *Brut* (1155) — so-called from the pretended ancestor of the Britons, Brutus, the grandson of Æneas — adds new legends, notably that of the Round Table. — The *Vita Merlini* (b. 1154), of Geoffrey, is a mixture of Breton and foreign traditions which influenced somewhat later poems.

9. **Breton Minstrel Poesy; the Lais;** Marie de France. — While the compilations of Geoffrey of

Monmouth attracted the attention of scholars to the Arthurian tales, they had no immediate effect on the subsequent French poems. The latter developed from the songs of the bards, who, traveling through England and France, recited to the accompaniment of the *rote* (a kind of harp) musical pieces, which they preceded by, an explanation of the subject — invariably a story of adventure which had lost its national setting. The French designated both the explanatory prologue and the song by the term *lai* (Anglo-Saxon *lag?*), and soon translated the best into narrative poems of octosyllabic couplets, of which some twenty have been preserved. — Most of these are due to a poetess, MARIE, of French birth, who resided at the English court, probably under Henry II., and who knew English and perhaps Celtic. In the fifteen lais which she imitated (evidently from the Anglo-Saxon) are visible the remains of an old mythology, misunderstood, and transformed after the life of the twelfth century. *Lanval*, a knight beloved by a fairy; *Eliduc*, the two-fold love of a knight, ending with veiling of the lawful wife; *Chevrefeuille*, an episode of the love of Tristran and Ysolt, are among her best, all rendered in a tender and passionate spirit. — Of the lais not by MARIE that of *Ignaure*, by RENAUD, modelled on the lost lai, *Guiron*, relates the story of the lover's heart fed to the wife.

10. **Divisions of the Breton Epic; Poems relating to Tristran, f. 1150.** — The French poems (all in octosyllabic couplets) of the Breton cycle are grouped around three centers, at first separate, and of which one is possibly not Celtic in origin: **Tristran**; the **Round**

Table; the **Holy Grail**. — The sources of the first two are in lais and Celtic legends, which went either directly into the French poems, or indirectly by means of Anglo-Norman versions, now lost. They are mainly biographical. — The poems on the Holy Grail are later and more complex. — The fortunes of Tristran (the earliest French narratives preserved) repose on lost lais of a mythological character, resembling strongly the story of Theseus. These were roughly joined together by an Anglo-Norman, BÉROUL (a. 1150), and connected with the Arthurian narratives. His poem, in fragments (imitated by EILHART VON OBERG), shows its Celtic origin (possibly in English translations) in its rude conception of love and its local coloring. — THOMAS (a. 1170) is more artistic in the fragments of his *Tristran*, embellishing with reflections and digressions the logical narrative, which he has formed from his material by selection and elimination. He attempts to refine the Celtic conception of love, after courtly models of the time of Henry II., and adds descriptions of luxury after the manner of BENOÎT. His poem was reproduced by GOTTFRIED VON STRASSBURG, and by English and Norse translations. — CHRÉTIEN DE TROIES wrote a *Tristran* (a. 1160), now lost.

11. **The Arthurian Legends**; CHRÉTIEN DE TROIES, **a. 1160-a. 1175**; **Provençal Influence**. — The tales of the Round Table, which represent the heroic epic and the mythology it absorbed, passed, as a rule, both through lais and Anglo-Norman versions before they reached their present state in the French of the continent. On the way a change of spirit took place. Entering the

domain of court poetry, they reflected in their chivalry and refined passion the ideal of the age. — This change became complete in the poems of CHRÉTIEN DE TROIES. Resident at the court of Champagne, protected and influenced by the Countess Mary (1164–1198), daughter of Eleanor of Poitou, CHRÉTIEN came into contact both with the metaphysical love poetry of the Provençals, and the Breton legends brought to Mary from England. Beginning his career with a translation of OVID's *Ars amoris* and imitations of the *Metamorphoses*, CHRÉTIEN is the first French poet known to have followed in his lyrics Provençal versification. — The Celtic material given him by Mary was in a very mutilated form. The mythological basis — the abduction of a wife by the god of the dead, and her rescue by the husband — had been obscured and fused with historical events and characters. It persisted, however, in certain commonplaces, as the "island of glass," the "country whence none return," the "sword bridge." The husband, identified in NENNIUS with Arthur, was replaced, perhaps in the Anglo-Norman poems, by Lancelot. CHRÉTIEN accentuates the biographical element by which the knights are made the heroes. After *Tristran* he writes *Érec*, followed by *Cligès*, an Eastern story (attached to the cycle), of the voluntary abduction of a wife. — Returning to Breton subjects, he dedicates to Mary the *Conte de la charrette* (a. 1170), the rescue of Guinevere by Lancelot, mounted on a cart. This poem is noteworthy for the first presentation of the unlawful love of Lancelot for the queen, due no doubt to Provençal influence and to that of OVID. — His next work, *Ivain*, or the *Chevalier au lion*, is followed by *Perceval*, or the *Conte du graal* (a. 1175), from a poem given to CHRÉTIEN by Philip of Flanders. — The success of these poems was great. Though the subject is often indefinite and the solution of the plot deferred, the form, in spite of monotony and prolixity, is the best of the age, and the language the model of the century. The expression is delicate, the sentiment graceful, the descriptions are brilliant. In CHRÉTIEN is seen best the ideal of mediæval society : the cultivation of love as an ennobling virtue, having a code designed to make a perfect knight. Imitations and translations of his poems abound.

12. **Biographical Poems**; RAOUL DE HOUDAN. — The biographical poems of the imitators of CHRÉTIEN have as a constant actor Gawain, second only to the particular hero of the tale. — RAOUL DE HOUDAN († b. 1235), the best known of his followers, and also an allegorical poet, is probably the author of *Méraugis de Portlesguez*, a succession of commonplaces, and of the *Vengeance de Raguidel*, where Gawain avenges a dead knight. RAOUL is celebrated for his style and his fondness for rich rime and overflow. — *Guinglain*, or the *Bel Inconnu*, by RENAUD (XII c.), of Beaujeu, concerns the son of Gawain, who frees an enchanted maiden by the kiss given to her serpent form. It is well written, and its popularity is seen in the English translation, *Lybeas Disconus*, and the German imitation of WIRNT VON GRAVENBERG (1203–1205). The Italian poem *Carduino* rests on an earlier version. — *Durmart le Gallois*, imitating the style of CHRÉTIEN, is one of the best poems of the cycle. It attempts to unite the chivalric and Christian moral, and begins with

an allegory — a tree bearing burning candles, having the Christ-child at the top. The marvelous is almost absent, the plot is logical, and it has unity of action.

13. **The Holy Grail**; ROBERT DE BORON, a. 1200. — It is uncertain whether the third center of the Breton cycle, the Holy Grail, is of Celtic or Christian origin. The Grail first appears in the *Perceval* of CHRÉTIEN, left unfinished by its author. His continuators also stopped short of the solution. But their successors, among whom are MENNESSIER (a. 1220) and GERBERT DE MONTREUIL, extended the poem to over sixty-three thousand verses, in which the Grail becomes the cup of the Last Supper, given to Joseph of Arimathea. — ROBERT DE BORON (a. 1200), probably of Northeastern France, proposed to attach this notion of the Grail to the Arthurian legends in a trilogy of poems: *Joseph d'Arimathie*, from the gospel of *Nicodemus* and local traditions; *Merlin*, the connecting poem, based vaguely on GEOFFREY OF MONMOUTH and popular tales; and *Perceval*, which ends with the death of Arthur. The last, preserved only in the prose version, soon gave way in the series to the prose *Lancelot*.

14. **The Breton Epic in Prose; Religious Mysticism Predominant.** — The prose romances of the Breton cycle seem to have superseded the poetical in favor from the beginning of the thirteenth century, a result due to their excellent style and language. Of these prose versions, all anonymous, *Tristran*, based on the *Tristran* of CHRÉTIEN, and the source of the *Tavola Ritonda* in Italian, alone escapes the mysticism of the Holy Grail. The prose *Lancelot*, derived from various poems (among them

the *Conte de la charrette*) and from GEOFFREY, relates the history of all the Round Table from Lancelot's birth to its final ruin. Its substitution for *Perceval* necessitated connecting narratives in the series of ROBERT DE BORON. Hence a sequel to *Merlin* and a *Quête du saint graal* later united to the *Lancelot.* — These narratives, all having reference to the Grail on the one hand, and to the love of Lancelot and Guinevere on the other, — two centers connected by the failure of Lancelot to find the Grail on account of that love, — were worked over and enlarged many times until they reached their fixed form (a. 1250). The *Joseph* of ROBERT DE BORON became known, in its prose form, as the *Saint graal*, and in the *Quête*, made up from the other works, Percival is displaced by Galaad. — The popularity of the Breton epic, both poetry and prose, gave rise to many translations. In Germany the *Ivain* and the *Érec* of CHRÉTIEN were translated by HARTMANN VON AUE, and his *Perceval* imitated by WOLFRAM VON ESCHENBACH. — An abridgment of the prose versions, made (a. 1270) by RUSTICIANO, of Pisa, was rendered later into Italian and occasioned new poems. — In England, MALORY's *Morte Arthure* (a. 1470) is based on a similar compilation which contained several poems lost in French. — To the Breton romances was due in great measure the long-prevalent conception of the chivalric society of the Middle Ages.

Mediæval Literature. To 1327.

CHAPTER IV.

SECOND PERIOD. 1150-1250.

NARRATIVE POETRY.

1. **Romans d'aventure.** Of Breton origin; *Ille et Galeron*, a. 1157, by GAUTIER D'ARRAS; *Galeran de Bretagne*, by RENAUD, XIII c. Of Breton and Byzantine origin; *Guillaume de Dole*, a. 1200; *Guillaume de Palerme*, XII c. From life; *Châtelaine de Vergi*, XIII c.; *Gui de Warwick*, a. 1250. National; *Robert le Diable*, XIII c.
2. **Greek and Byzantine Romances.** *Éracle*, a. 1160, by GAUTIER D'ARRAS; *Floire et Blancheflleur*, b. 1170 (?); *Parténopeus de Blois*, XII c.; *Comte de Poitiers*, XII c.; GERBERT DE MONTREUIL, b. 1225.
3. **Popular Tales.** In Eastern framework; *Sept Sages*, XII c. Fableaux; *Richeut*, a. 1156; HENRI D'ANDELI, XIII c.; *Housse partie; Vilain mire*. Animal fables; *Romulus;* MARIE DE FRANCE; *Isopets;* *Isengrimus*, a. 1148; *Roman de Renard*, XII–XIII c.
4. **Historical Poetry.** GEOFFREI GAIMAR, a. 1150; WACE, a. 1100–a. 1175; BENOÎT DE SAINTE-MORE; GUILLAUME DE SAINT-PAIR, a. 1170; JOURDAIN FANTOSME, a. 1183; AMBROISE, b. 1200; *Vie de Guillaume le Maréchal*, a. 1220; PHILIPPE MOUSKET, a. 1200–a. 1243.

1. **Romans d'Aventure; Origin and Significance.** — The *roman d'aventure* is a tale of love and adventure, a

novel in verse. In style and spirit they resemble most the lyric *romances*, which may have been their model. They are the favorite literature of the nobility, whose manners and life they portray, and are cultivated by a class of professional writers desirous of reputation. Those preserved, some sixty in all, averaging six or seven thousand octosyllabic verses, are often expanded lais and popular stories in local setting. They may be considered, with the Breton prose narratives, the precursors of the romances of chivalry. — They can be divided into those presenting Breton themes, those confusing Breton and Byzantine stories, those due to events of the age, those based on national history or tradition. The dividing line between the *romans d'aventure* and the poems imitated from Greek novels and tales is not always visible.

2. **From Breton Sources**; Gautier d'Arras; Renaud. — The first known *roman d'aventure* is *Ille et Galeron* (a. 1157), dedicated to Beatrice, wife of Frederick Barbarossa, by Gautier d'Arras. It is a version of the lai *Eliduc*, preceded by the story of the persecuted orphan, Ille. — *Galeran de Bretagne* by Renaud (XIII c.) is a development of the lai, *Frêne*, of Marie, — the story of a foundling who recovers finally her lover. The poem, natural and spirited, imitates the style of the *Énéas* of Benoît.

3. **From Breton and Byzantine Sources.** — *Guillaume de Palerme* (XII c.), dedicated to Yolande of Flanders, mixes Greek novelistic elements with notions of the were-wolf, as in the lai *Bisclavret*, of Marie. The scene is laid in Sicily, and the poem may be due to the Nor-

mans. — *Guillaume de Dole*, dedicated to Miles de Nanteuil († 1235), is one of the best *romans d'aventure*. It unites an account of knightly intercourse between French and Germans with the story of the hidden birthmark (from which the poem is also called the *Roman de la Rose*) and of the persecuted woman. The insertion of some forty well-known lyrics into the narrative (an innovation of the author, much copied) gives it variety and naturalness. The poem has also unity of action and describes vividly feudal life.

4. **Poems based on Events of the Time, and on National History and Legend.** — The *Châtelaine de Vergi* (XIII c.) is based on actual events, and contains no foreign elements. A tale of love, having a tragic end, it shows keen analysis and delicacy of feeling, and is nearest of all to the modern novel. — *Gui de Warwick* (a. 1250), from the Anglo-Saxon, is reproduced in English translations of the next century. — *Robert le Diable* (XIII c.) is a story of sin and repentance, here arbitrarily attached to a Norman duke. — The *romans d'aventure* were widely imitated and translated.

5. **Poems reproducing the Plots of Greek and Byzantine Narratives**; GAUTIER D'ARRAS; GERBERT DE MONTREUIL, b. 1225. — To Greek tales and their Byzantine imitations are due the plots of many French poems, epic, as *Jourdain de Blaie*, didactic, as the lives of the saints, and narrative. — Of the latter, the first rendering known is *Éracle* (a. 1160), by GAUTIER D'ARRAS, a youth endowed with the knowledge of precious stones, of horses, and of women, who becomes Emperor, and wars against Persia. — The charming tale of *Floire et Blanche-*

fleur, in two versions of the twelfth century, may have reached France through the Crusades. In the French a chivalric element has been introduced which pervades also the imitations, of which BOCCACCIO's *Filocolo* is the most artistic. — The form of the story, known as *Aucassin et Nicolette* (a. 1200), in prose and seven-syllable tirades (hence called *Chantefable*), is the most attractive literary work of feudal France. — *Parténopeus de Blois* (XII c.) is the story of Psyche with the parts reversed. In plot and structure it shows superior talent. — The *Comte de Poitiers* (XII c.) and the *Roman de la Violette* — by GERBERT DE MONTREUIL (b. 1225) — have the same plot as *Guillaume de Dole*. In the *Comte de Poitiers* the innocence of the woman is the object of a wager. The *Violette* further follows *Guillaume de Dole* in inserting lyric songs as well as epic tirades into the narrative. Many variants exist, as SHAKSPERE's *Cymbeline*.

6. **Folk Lore in Mediæval Literature; its Eastern Sources.** — Many of the romances already mentioned are simply popular stories amplified, embellished, and adapted to the refined tastes of the nobility. Undeveloped, nearer to nature, are the tales which circulated among the lower classes. Their love is coarse, their adventures often buffoon. The source of most of them is Eastern. They were transmitted to France in writing, or orally through traders, quacks, or pilgrims. Their Indian origin is seen in the Buddhistic notions of transmigration, in polygamy (often misunderstood), and in the strategy invariably assigned to woman. They had at the start a moral application, lost in the transmission. Written down at first in Sanscrit, they reached Europe through Persia,

Syria and Constantinople, or through the Arabs. — The latter touched Europe in Spain, and the first Latin translation of Eastern tales known is the *Disciplina clericalis* (a. 1106), by a converted Spanish Jew, PETRUS ALPHONSUS, after Arabic originals. These instructions of a dying father to his son were afterwards twice rendered into French verse, as the *Chastiement d'un père à son fils* (XIII c). — Before the translations of collections, many separate tales which show no literary influence had found their way orally to France. — Other stories are due to the fables of ESOP, and others are indigenous or are the inventions of their narrators.

7. **Stories in Eastern Framework; the Sept Sages, XII c.** — Tales derived from Oriental collections are invariably in the form of a loosely connected series. Such a series is seen in the *Sept Sages*, in poetry (XII c.) and prose (XIII c.). Beginning in India, this collection made its way through Persia, Syria, and the Arabs. In Greek it was worked over and became the source for the Western versions. — A Latin form, the *Dolopathos* (XII c.), by JEAN DE HAUTE-SEILLE, substitutes many new stories (as the swan legend), changes the scene to Rome, and makes VERGIL the preceptor. It was translated into French (b. 1223) by HERBERT. — The imitations of this series are numerous.

8. **The Fableaux.** — An ordinary form of popular stories is the *fableau*. It is a poetical narrative, generally in octosyllabic couplets, of a definite and common event. It is usually jocose, often satirical, frequently coarse, and belongs to peasant or citizen life, using the vocabulary and idioms of the people. The plot is generally

the deceit practised by the crafty wife on her boorish husband or on her pretentious clerical lover. Some two hundred fableaux exist, varying from thirty to several hundred lines in length and dated from the middle of the twelfth to the beginning of the fourteenth century. They are mainly anonymous. — *Richeut* (a. 1156), the earliest known, is a description of courtesan life taken from nature. — *Aristote*, by HENRI D'ANDELI (XIII c.), is the Indian tale of the power of love over the wisest, here attributed to the mistress of Alexander and Aristotle. The attitude of the sage, bridled and carrying his subduer, is a frequent subject of literary reference and artistic representation. — The *Housse partie*, by BERNIER, is also Indian, and teaches filial respect. — The *Vilain mire*, the revenge of a wife on her cruel husband, is later the theme of the *Médecin malgré lui* of MOLIÈRE.

9. **Esopic and Animal Fables**; MARIE DE FRANCE. — The animal fables of ESOP, in which the moral is the object, were known through the translation of PHÆDRUS. — Of these, one in prose, the *Romulus*, absorbed (a. 1000) Oriental tales affected by Christianity and mediævalism. Translated into Anglo-Saxon, this collection was rendered into concise French verse, the *Isopet* of MARIE DE FRANCE, containing one hundred and three fables. — Other *Isopets* of the period are based on versions of *Romulus* in Latin distichs.

10. **The *Roman de Renard*, XII-XIII c.** — Besides the Esopic fables, animal stories without morals, derived from shrewd observation, circulated among the people. Many of them referred to the struggle between the cunning fox and the heavy wolf. These, forming a group,

attracted the Esopic fables, rid of their morals. The species were individualized. A proper name, Raganhard, was given to the typical fox, and Isengrin to the typical wolf. Around them and their wives, Richild and Hersind, were gathered the animals of Western Europe and others borrowed from the literary part of the cycle, as Noble, the lion. This process went on, probably in the eleventh century, on the Flemish border, and is first mentioned in a Latin chronicle (1112). — The poem *Isengrimus* (1148), by a Fleming, in Latin distichs, is composed of twelve main episodes, most of which are found in later French versions. — A lost French compilation, of sixteen episodes, is preserved in *Reinhart Fuchs* (a. 1180) by HEINRICH DER GLICHEZARE. — The French *Roman de Renard* is an artistic union of some twenty-six episodes, giving a connected narrative of the lives of Renard and Isengrin. The episode, *Pèlerinage de Renard*, and others belong to the twelfth century. The greater part are of the thirteenth. Among the authors is PIERRE DE SAINT CLOUD. — The most popular episode, the *Jugement de Renard*, is the source of the Flemish *Reynaert de vos*, in turn the original of the German *Reinke de vos* (1498), imitated by GOETHE. — The merit of the episodes varies with their age. An observation, keen and ironical at first, passes into a parody on society and ends in fastidious allegory, the animals typifying men. The style is natural, and the best scenes are realistic.

11. **Historical Poetry; Anglo-Norman Accounts;** GEOFFREI GAIMAR; WACE; BENOÎT; GUILLAUME DE SAINT-PAIR; JOURDAIN FANTOSME. — The Latin chronicles of the first crusade went into epic poetry, excepting a mon-

orime translation of BAUDRI DE BOURGUEIL (a. 1190). The second crusade passed without popular notice. It is therefore to Norman history that the first narratives in the vernacular belong. They are mainly in octosyllabic couplets. — GEOFFREI GAIMAR wrote the *Histoire des Anglais* (1147-1151), beginning with the Argonauts, translating GEOFFREY OF MONMOUTH, outlining Anglo-Saxon history, and stopping with the death of William Rufus. The fragments of his work have but little historical value. — WACE (a. 1100-a. 1175), of Guernsey, canon at Bayeux, after his *Brut* and various didactic poems, composed the *Rou*, or *Geste des Normands* (1160-1174), in monorime alexandrines and octosyllabic couplets. He follows Latin chronicles, but adds popular stories and traditions, stopping with 1107. His work is of historical worth. His style is clear, simple, and concise. — WACE, of the old school, was supplanted in the favor of Henry II. by BENOÎT DE SAINTE-MORE. The latter's *Chronique des ducs de Normandie* made use of WACE's sources and WACE himself, and contains romantic developments in the flowery language of the *Troie* and *Énéas*. — The *Chronique du Mont-Saint-Michel* (a. 1170), by GUILLAUME DE SAINT-PAIR, is local history, rather edifying than scientific. — JOURDAIN FANTOSME, attached to Westminster, relates the Scottish war (1173-1174) of Henry II. in monorime alexandrines.

12. **The Third Crusade; English History;** PHILIPPE MOUSKET, a. 1200-a. 1243. — The *Histoire de la Guerre sainte*, by AMBROISE, a minstrel of Richard I., is a record of the third crusade. — The *Vie de Guillaume le Maréchal*, Earl of Pembroke († 1219), of over nineteen thousand

lines, is valuable for history and sociology. — PHILIPPE
MOUSKET (a. 1200–a. 1243), of Tournai, attempted a history of the French, from Priam to the year 1242. The historical value of his long poem is limited to the thirteenth century, but it has a literary importance in the numerous extracts from epic poems (some of which are now lost) relating to Charlemagne.

Mediæval Literature. To 1327.

CHAPTER V.

SECOND PERIOD. 1150-1250.

Didactic and Lyric Poetry. The Drama. Prose.

1. **Didactic Poetry.** Narrative: Legends and lives of saints; *Épître farcie de Saint Étienne*, XII c.; *Vie de Saint Nicolas*, by Wace; *Vies des Pères*, XIII c.; *Barlaam et Josaphat*, by Chardri, XIII c., and Gui de Cambrai, b. 1225; *Purgatoire de Saint Patrice*, XII c.; Garnier de Pont-Sainte-Maxence, XII c. The Virgin; Herman de Valenciennes, a. 1150; *Miracles de Nostre Dame*. Devout tales; Jacques de Vitri, †1240; the *Ange et l'Ermite*. Moral; Influence of Ovid. Satirical; *États du monde;* Étienne de Fougères, †1178; Guiot de Provins, a. 1170-a. 1220; *Évangile des femmes;* André de Coutances, XIII c. Sermons in verse. Hortatory; Hélinand †a. 1229; Reclus de Molliens, a. 1150-a. 1230; *Poème moral*, a. 1200; *Débats; Dits;* Guillaume le Clerc, XIII c. Allegorical; Raoul de Houdan; Huon de Méri, XIII c.; Guillaume de Lorris, XIII c. Translations of Scripture and holy writings. Scientific treatises; *Image du Monde*, 1245, by Gautier de Metz.
2. **Lyric Poetry.** Of French origin; Audefroi le Bâtard, XIII c.; *Motet; Lai; Rotrouenge*. Of Provençal origin; *Chanson; Jeu parti;* Conon de Béthune, †1224; Gace Brulé, a. 1200; Blondel de Nesle, a. 1200; Guide Couci, †1201; Gautier de Coinci, 1177-1236; Thibaut de Navarre, 1201-1253.

3. **The Drama.** Mysteries; *Adam*, XII c.; *Résurrection*, XII c. Miracles; JEAN BODEL. The Puis.
4. **Prose.** Translations; *Quatre Livres des Rois*, XII c.; The Bible, 1235; *Turpin*; Ancient history, a. 1225; JEAN DE THUIN, a. 1240. Chronicles; GEOFFREI DE VILLEHARDOUIN, a. 1160–a. 1213; ROBERT DE CLARI, XIII c.; ERNOUL, 1228. *Description de Jérusalem.* Laws; *Assises de Jérusalem; Coutumiers.* MAURICE DE SULLY, † 1195.

1. **Legends of Greek, Latin, and Hebrew Saints**; WACE. — The church office of saints' days gave rise to interpolations of Scripture, after the style of the liturgical drama. The story of Stephen's martyrdom became a favorite, and poetical paraphrases in the vernacular of the text of the Vulgate are numerous. Of these *Épîtres farcies*, one of the twelfth century, in monorime decasyllables, shows much skill and addresses the audience like an epic poem. — WACE wrote, for his patrons, lives of saints, as those of Saint Nicolas, his first poetical effort, and of Saint Margaret — both frequent subjects of poems. — The Eastern compilation, known in French as the *Vies des Pères* (XIII c.), containing forty-two tales of piety, was very popular. A Western pendant was the *Dialogus* of GREGORY I., rendered into French prose and verse, the latter by ANGER (1212), of England.

2. **Pagan and Celtic Legends**; CHARDRI, a. 1200; **Mediæval Saints**; GARNIER DE PONT-SAINTE-MAXENCE, a. 1173. — The absorbing tendency of French literature is seen in *Barlaam et Josaphat*, the story of Buddha. Three versions exist, those by the Anglo-Norman, CHARDRI (a. 1200), and by GUI DE CAMBRAI (a. 1225), being best known. — CHARDRI versified also

the legend of the Seven Sleepers (*Sept Dormants*), and wrote the *Petit Plaid*, a discussion between an Epicurean youth and a pessimistic old man on the goods and ills of life. — The Celtic visions of Tungdal and Owen were rendered into French from the Latin, as by MARIE DE FRANCE, in the *Purgatoire de Saint Patrice*. — A favorite subject of Latin and French writers was the death of Thomas Becket. The *Vie de Saint Thomas le Martyr* (1173), in strophes of five monorime alexandrines, by the clerk, GARNIER, of Pont-Sainte-Maxence, is one of the best poems of the age. His narrative, rather historical than didactic, is remarkable for its accuracy, and its devotion to a high religious standard. His language is vigorous and correct, his style concise, simple, and polished. His work, conscious of artistic effort, is a classic of the time.

3. **The Virgin**; HERMAN DE VALENCIENNES; GAUTIER DE COINCI, 1177–1236. — The traditions concerning the Virgin derive mainly from the Scriptures and spurious gospels. — WACE versified the *Conception*. — HERMAN DE VALENCIENNES (a. 1150) wrote the *Joies Nostre Dame* and the *Assomption*. — Numerous were the tales of her intercession. These were translated frequently from the Latin — by an Anglo-Norman, ADGAR (XII c.); by JEAN LE MARCHANT (a. 1240), of Chartres; and by GAUTIER DE COINCI (1177–1236), prior of Vic-sur-Aisne. His *Miracles de Nostre Dame* (1214–), of some thirty thousand lines, illustrate the divorce between religion and piety. Crimes and sins are pardoned by the mere invocation of the Virgin, or are committed purposely by her devoted followers. The style of GAUTIER is poor. Rich rime and

plays on words and sounds are sought after. — The gem of the stories relating to the Virgin is the *Tombeur de Nostre Dame*, a clown turned monk, who performs before her image his most difficult tricks, while Mary wipes the sweat from his brow. Its artlessness is typical of the time.

4. **Devout Tales**; JACQUES DE VITRI, † 1240. — The primitive form of the stories of the saints and the Virgin is probably seen in the tales of piety. These come generally from the Latin, as from the *Liber exemplorum* of JACQUES DE VITRI († 1240), itself compiled from Eastern stories. — Among them are the *Ange et l'Ermite*, on the ways of Providence, versions of which are found in the *Gesta Romanorum* (no. 80), in PARNELL'S *Hermit* and in *Zadig* (c. XX.), by VOLTAIRE. — The popular *Enfant juif* is the escape of a boy from a furnace into which he was thrown by his fanatical father.

5. **Moral Narratives; Vogue of** OVID; **Satire**; ÉTIENNE DE FOUGÈRES, † 1178; GUIOT DE PROVINS, a. 1170–a. 1220; **Politics**. — Moral teachings are found in translations from the Latin, as the *Distichs*, attributed to CATO, or the *De consolatione* of BOËTHIUS. Eastern proverbs were also put into verse. — Notable is the influence of OVID. His *Ars amoris*, taken seriously and subjected to scholastic analysis, was translated by CHRÉTIEN DE TROIES, by ÉLIE, and by the author of the *Clef d'amour*. — JACQUES D'AMIENS (XIII c.), a lyric poet, gave also a free rendering, which borrowed much from the *De arte honeste amandi* (a. 1200), of ANDRÉ LE CHAPELAIN — the love code of the Breton cycle. These

translations had great effect on allegorical poetry. — Universal **satire** was expressed in poems, called *États du monde*. — Especially severe is the *Livre des manières*, of ÉTIENNE DE FOUGÈRES († 1178), bishop of Rennes, in octosyllabic monorime quatrains. — The *Bible* (a usual term for satires), of GUIOT DE PROVINS (a. 1170–a. 1220), minstrel and monk, attacks the nobles and upper classes. — Satires against women, clerks, and peasants, as the fableaux, are numerous, and show Oriental influence. Against women is the *Évangile des femmes*, which was worked over many times, beginning with the twelfth century. — Political satire starts early, as the *Roman des Français*, by ANDRÉ DE COUTANCES (XIII c.), against the French. — Satires against papal avarice abound. The *Complainte de Jérusalem* (a. 1214) accuses Rome of appropriating Crusade money.

6. **Dogmatic and Hortatory Works; Sermons;** RECLUS DE MOLLIENS, a. **1150–a. 1230**; HÉLINAND, a. **1229**; *Poème moral; Dits; Débats;* HENRI D'ANDELI, **XIII** c.; GUILLAUME LE CLERC, **XIII** c. — Sermons in verse, on the vanity of life, precede those in prose. The earliest is the *Grant mal fist Adam* (a. 1110), in verses of five syllables. — BARTHÉLEMI (a. 1150–a. 1230), a monk, calling himself the Recluse of Molliens, wrote the *Roman de Charité* (1180–1190) and, five years later, the *Miserere*. Both, on the evil of life, are distinguished by rhetorical figures and a striving for rich rime. Twenty-five and thirty manuscripts, respectively, attest their popularity, as does also the frequent imitation of their strophic structure — twelve octosyllabic verses riming *aab aab bba bba*. — In this form was written the *Vers de la mort*, by HÉLI-

NAND († a. 1229), monk of Froidmont, the most successful poem of the kind, and often revised. — The *Poème moral* (1190–1210), in monorime alexandrine quatrains, is important from a literary and sociological standpoint. It incorporates the *Vie de Sainte Thaïs*, a tale of Eastern asceticism. — *Débats* and *dits* — poems of argument and description — become popular in the thirteenth century. French versions of the *Débat du corps et de l'âme*, in which body and soul accuse each other of their eternal loss, date from the beginning of the twelfth century. — The *bataille*, a kind of *débat*, is a combat between allegorical personages, after the *Psychomachia* of PRUDENTIUS. Parodies occur, as the *Débat du vin et de l'eau* and the *Bataille de carême et de charnage*. — The most famous *dit* is the *Trois morts et trois vifs*, the meditation of three young men over three corpses. Many versions of this exist. — Closely connected with the *dits* are various didactic poems, like the *Quinze signes du jugement dernier*, based on the prophecies of a sybil and often cited. — Among didactic poets of note is HENRI D'ANDELI, (XIII c.), of Paris, who imitates the *débats* in his *Bataille des vins*, a list of the white wines in vogue, and in the *Bataille des Sept Arts* (a. 1240), the conflict between the literary studies (the Latin poets) and the rising dialectic. He also wrote *dits*. — GUILLAUME LE CLERC (XIII c.), of Normandy, is the author of a *Bestiaire* (1204–1210), a life of the Magdalen, an imitation of the book of *Tobit*, a *Joies Nostre Dame*, a satirical poem, the *Trois mots*, and of the *Besant de Dieu*, a much-cited allegorical development of the parable of the Talents, containing observations on society.

7. **Allegorical Poetry**; RAOUL DE HOUDAN; HUON DE MÉRI; GUILLAUME DE LORRIS. — Personification of abstract ideas is due to religious teachings. — The first French writer of allegory known is RAOUL DE HOUDAN. In the allegorical journeys, the *Songe d'Enfer* and the *Voie de Paradis*, he employs the form of a dream, seen in the *Débat du corps et de l'âme*, which is probably due to the *Somnium Scipionis*, of MACROBIUS. In his *Roman des ailes de courtoisie* a rule of generosity or courtesy is written on the separate feathers. — HUON DE MÉRI imitates RAOUL and GUILLAUME LE CLERC, as well as PRUDENTIUS, in the *Tournoiement d'Antéchrist* (1235), a combat in Paradise between the Saviour, at the head of the Virtues, and the Antichrist, leading the Vices. — Resuming previous didactic literature, GUILLAUME DE LORRIS (a. 1212-) began the *Roman de la Rose* (a. 1237). A love romance, in the form of a dream (*Somnium Scipionis*), the plot is the same as in the *Dit de la rose*. The mistress is a rose growing in the paradise of love (a frequent conception), and the actors, save the lover, are personifications of specific attributes, which aid or resist the plucking of the rose. Evident is the influence of OVID and of ANDRÉ LE CHAPELAIN. The poem of GUILLAUME stops abruptly, after having attained over four thousand verses. Its style and the carrying out of the plot make it one of the best poems of the age, the elegance and superficiality of which it so well reflects.

8. **Translations of Scripture and Religious Writings**. — HERMAN DE VALENCIENNES versified *Genesis*, as did EVERAT, for Mary of Champagne. — SAMSON DE NANTEUIL (XIII c.) rimed the *Proverbs*, adding alle-

gorical explanations. — Apocryphal books were favorite subjects for French versions, among which were those by GAUTIER DE COINCI and ANDRÉ DE COUTANCES (*Nicodème*).

9. **Scientific Works.** — Lapidaries and Bestiaries in prose and verse are frequent, as the *Bestiaire* of GERVAISE and the prose *Bestiaire d'amour*, of RICHARD DE FOURNIVAL († b. 1260), a lyric poet and disciple of OVID. In this the lovers are likened to animals. — Various scientific treatises were translated from the Latin. GAUTIER DE METZ wrote the *Image du Monde* (1245), based on the *Imago Mundi* (a. 1120), of HONORIUS, and other Latin works. A kind of encyclopædia, it treats of Man, his birth, education, and free will; of Physical Geography and of Astronomy, citing various legends, among them that of VERGIL, the astrologer. The success of this book, preserved in some sixty manuscripts, is seen in the writings of BRUNETTO LATINO, JEAN DE MEUN, DU BARTAS, and DELILLE, in Provençal and Italian works and in CAXTON's translation of a prose version.

10. **Lyric Poetry of French Origin; AUDEFROI LE BÂTARD, XIII c.; New Kinds.** — *Romances* continued in favor until the thirteenth century, and were then artistically imitated by AUDEFROI LE BÂTARD (a. 1200), of Arras, who substituted a varied rime for assonance and lengthened the strophe. — *Pastourelles* flourished still later, but were changed by Provençal influence. — New kinds, purely French in origin, are : *motets*, from the Latin, and generally coarse in theme; lyric *laïs*, probably from Latin sequences, the essential feature being entire difference of the various strophes, and thus later

confused with the Provençal *descort;* and *rotrouenges,* (*romances* with refrain), the proper term for all songs not subject to Provençal influence. Those more serious were called *serventois.* — The *chansons de croisade* become affected by Provençal models. — Arras was the great lyric center of France.

11. Lyric Poetry of Provençal Origin; Structure; Points of Contact; Kinds. — The lyric of Provence, based on a metaphysical and courtly conception of love, had attained exact laws of verse and strophe. — The lyric unit, the *chanson,* was divided by the rime into three strophic parts. Within the strophe the verses form also three parts, the first two always *abba* or *abab,* and the third variable. New strophic forms and a complicated system of rimes, following rigorously the order of the first strophe, are other innovations. — This studied form of verse met the simple French measures by the middle of the twelfth century, but its propagation in the North is due to the courts of Eleanor of Poitou, of Alice of Flanders, queen of France, and especially of Mary of Champagne. Its chosen field became Northeastern France. Its first known imitator was CHRÉTIEN DE TROIES. — Besides the *chanson,* it introduced the *salut d'amour,* a love letter of varying form; the *tençon,* a dispute in alternate strophes, rare, but akin to the *jeu parti,* where the poet opening the debate proposes the subject. — Only *chansons* and *jeux partis* are frequent.

12. Poets of the Provençal School. — This modified lyric owing to its form and content remained mainly within court circles. — CONON DE BÉTHUNE († 1224), of the Sully family, sings at the court of Alice (1180) and of Mary (a. 1182), to whom he addresses several poems. His works, about ten in all, are full of grace and energy. — GACE BRULÉ (a. 1200), of Champagne, wrote some seventy *chansons* for one mistress. They excel in harmonious verse. — BLONDEL DE NESLE (a. 1200), of Picardy, known by his legendary connection with Richard I. (himself a poet), left some thirty light but polished *chansons*. — The CHÂTELAIN DE COUCI, probably GUI († 1201), wrote a score of *chansons*, tender and even sad in sentiment. He appears later in fiction. — THIBAUT OF NAVARRE (1201-1253) is the most famous of all. He left about seventy *chansons* and *jeux partis*, of pleasing form and sprightly thought. He continued the work of Mary, in making Champagne a literary center, by protecting numerous poets. — Religious lyric scarcely exists. GAUTIER DE COINCI parodies, in honor of the Virgin, secular songs.

13. **The Drama; Mysteries and Miracles; the Puis.** — But two specimens of the many liturgical dramas of this period remain. — *Adam* (XII c.), written in England, is developed from the sermon of the Prophets. It shows a stage outside of the church and in variety of verse and rendering of certain scenes manifests considerable literary merit. — A fragment of the *Résurrection* (XII c.) shows a great scenic development. — A *miracle* is the *Jeu de Saint Nicolas* by JEAN BODEL, after the Latin of HILARY. The religious subject is but a pretext for secular scenes of the Crusades and tavern life, which show that the clergy were no longer the actors. — The *Puis*, fraternities at first in honor of the Virgin, and later literary guilds, now furnished both pieces and

players. To the *Pui*, at Arras as early as 1192, BODEL addressed his *Congé* (a. 1206), much imitated later.

14. **Translations in Prose; the Bible, 1235; Ancient History; Chronicles;** GEOFFREI DE VILLEHARDOUIN, a. 1160–a. 1213; **Laws; Sermons.** — The most important prose of the period is found in the Breton romances. — Biblical translations are also numerous, as the *Quatre Livres des Rois* (XII c.), in pure style, and the complete version of the Bible (a. 1235), probably by members of the University. This rendering has affected all subsequent translations. The movement of translation around Metz Innocent III. was obliged to check (1199). — The chronicle *Turpin* was frequently translated. The earliest versions, as that (b. 1198) of NICOLAS DE SENLIS, for Yolande of Flanders, claim to be novelties, and may have been the models for the Breton romances and for VILLEHARDOUIN. The translation of NICOLAS was enlarged into the *Chronique saintongeaise* (1230). — Ancient history first appears in the *Faits des Romains*, selections taken from Latin historians, and the *Livre des histoires* (a. 1225), a compilation made at Lille. — *Jules César* (a. 1240), by JEAN DE THUIN, is based on a glossed LUCAN, and contains romantic developments in the Breton manner. It was versified later by JACOT DE FOREST, and was translated into Italian, as was also the *Faits des Romains*. — The first original **chronicler** in French is GEOFFREI DE VILLEHARDOUIN (a. 1160–a. 1213), marshal of Champagne, who relates the events of the fourth crusade (1198–1207) in a straightforward style and in terms drawn often from epic poetry. He was poorly continued by HENRI DE VALENCIENNES. — ROBERT DE

CLARI, a Picard knight, represents the lesser nobility in his account of the same crusade. — Chronicles were written in Palestine, as that (1228) of ERNOUL. — Normandy abounded in prose chronicles in the thirteenth century. — Interesting is the *Description de Jerusalem* (b. 1187), by a pilgrim. — Compilations of **laws**, as those of William the Conqueror and the *Assises de Jérusalem*, charters and *coutumiers* are numerous. — The **sermons** of SAINT BERNARD, translated (a. 1200), and those of MAURICE DE SULLY († 1195), bishop of Paris, given in French, though perhaps written in Latin, with a few others in the vernacular, show a familiar style and present the manners of the time. They are laden down with stories and parables.

Mediæval Literature. To 1327.

CHAPTER VI.

THIRD PERIOD. 1250-1327.

1. **Epic Poetry.** National epic; ADENET LE ROI, a. 1240-a. 1298; GIRARD D'AMIENS, a. 1300. Crusade epic; *Baudouin de Sebourg*, a. 1310. Epic of antiquity; *Vœux du Paon*, 1312. Breton epic; *Claris et Laris*, 1268.
2. **Narrative Poetry.** Romans d'aventure; *Richard le Beau*, XIII c.; *Châtelain de Couci*, XIII c.; PHILIPPE DE BEAUMANOIR, a. 1246-1296. Popular stories and fableaux; RUSTEBEUF, †a. 1280; JEAN DE CONDÉ, a. 1280-a. 1345. Sequels to the *Roman de Renard*. Historical; GUILLAUME GUIART, 1306; GEOFFREI, 1300-1316.
3. **Didactic Poetry.** Devout tales; *Vrai anneau*, XIII c.; *Roman de Mahomet*, 1258. Moral; CHRÉTIEN LE GOUAIS, a. 1300; WILLIAM DE WADINGTON, XIII c. Satirical; RUSTEBEUF; *Paix aux Anglais*, 1264. Hortatory; ROBERT DE BLOIS, a. 1250; BAUDOUIN DE CONDÉ, a. 1230-a. 1290; WATRIQUET DE COUVIN, 1319-1329. Allegorical; JACQUES DE BAISIEU, XIII c.; JEAN DE MEUN, a. 1250-b. 1305. Translations; MACÉ DE LA CHARITÉ, a. 1300. Scientific; The *Chasse*, b. 1284.
4. **Lyric Poetry.** GUILEBERT DE BERNEVILLE, a. 1260; ADAM DE LA HALLE, a. 1235-b. 1288.
5. **Drama.** *Miracles.* Comedy; ADAM DE LA HALLE; *Farce*, a. 1277.
6. **Prose.** Translations; GUIART DES MOULINS, 1251-a. 1320;

Régime du corps, a. 1256; JEAN DE MEUN; *Institutes; Chroniques de St. Denis*, 1260. Chronicles; *Histoires de Baudouin; Récits d'un ménestrel de Reims*, 1260; JEAN DE JOINVILLE, 1224–1317. Letters. Treatises; *Livre de Sidrac*, XIII c.; BRUNETTO LATINO, †1294; *Somme le Roi*, 1279; MARCO POLO, 1298. Laws; *Établissements de Saint Louis*, XIII c.; PHILIPPE DE BEAUMANOIR. Language; GAUTIER DE BIBELESWORTH, a. 1300. Fiction.

1. **Decline of Epic Poetry**; ADENET LE ROI, a. 1240–a. 1298. — The third period of mediæval literature is that of its decline, particularly in epic and lyric poetry. Yet allegory makes progress in didactic poetry, and the drama increases in favor. Prose becomes general. — In the national epic the tendency is towards cyclic and genealogical poems, based on material already used. An exception is the work of ADENET (a. 1240–a. 1298), king of the minstrels of Brabant. He works over the poem of RAIMBERT in the *Enfances d'Oger*. From a lost source is his *Berte aux grands pieds* (a. 1275), in alternating masculine and feminine tirades, the story of the persecuted mother of Charlemagne and of his birth on a cart (Charles' Wain). *Bovon de Comarcis* is imitated from a previous poem of the cycle of Garin de Monglane. The style of ADENET, though prolix, is pure and his verse polished. ' His influence was felt for a century. — GIRARD D'AMIENS has neither style nor invention. His *Charlemagne* (a. 1300) is a poetical history compiled from poems and chronicles. — Burlesques of the epic exist, as the fableau *Audigier*, and the *Siège de Neuville*, in Picard and Flemish, the knights being Flemish weavers.

2. **The Crusade Epic; the Epic of Antiquity;** the

Breton Epic. — The poems on the Crusades end in a parody. *Baudouin de Sebourg* (a. 1310), by a poet of Valenciennes or vicinity, is a series of amusing adventures, digressions, and satires against monks and women. The same author wrote a sequel, the *Bastard de Bouillon*, inferior and more extravagant. — Of the cycle of antiquity, *Alexandre* received a fanciful episode, the *Vœux du Paon* (1312), by JACQUES DE LONGUYON, in which the Nine Valiants, so frequent a subject for art, first appear. — The Breton poems were artificially revived in *Claris et Laris* (1268), a summary of the series in over thirty thousand verses.

3. **Romans d'Aventure**; PHILIPPE DE BEAUMANOIR, a. 1246–1296. — *Richard le Beau* unites the story of the son who fights unwittingly with his father (found in lais) with that of the grateful dead man, whose body is redeemed from his creditors (of Eastern origin). — *Escanor* (b. 1290), by GIRARD D'AMIENS, is taken from the Breton epic. — The *Châtelain de Couci* (a. 1300), by JAKEMON SAKESEP, is the story of *Ignaure*, applied to the lyric poet. It received many French imitations in the eighteenth century, and is the source of UHLAND's poem. — *Cléomadès*, by ADENET LE ROI, is the Eastern tale of the flying wooden horse. — It was worked over in *Méliacin* by GIRARD D'AMIENS, who inserted lyrics into the narrative. — PHILIPPE DE BEAUMANOIR (a. 1246–1296), a magistrate, and writer of lyrics and *fatrasies* (nonsense verses), is the author of *Jean de Dammartin et Blonde d'Oxford*, the abduction of a young girl by her lover, who is pursued by her father and her betrothed; and of the *Manekine*, an Eastern tale of the persecuted woman.

4. **Popular Stories; Fableaux;** RUSTEBEUF, †a. 1280; JEAN DE CONDÉ, a. 1280–a. 1345; **Sequels to the** *Roman de Renard.* — Popular stories and fableaux become more artistic. — RUSTEBEUF (†a. 1280), of Paris, satirized the clergy, women, and a rival poet in several witty fableaux. — JEAN DE CONDÉ (a. 1280–a. 1345), of Hainault, left five fableaux, and some poetical narratives, though the greater part of his seventy poems, mainly *dits*, belong to didactic poetry. — The *Roman de Renard* recedes from popular sympathy in the *Couronnement de Renard* (a. 1251), full of covert allusions to contemporary events, — in *Renard le Nouvel* (1288), by JACQUEMART GELEÉ, of Lille, a work of merit, yet rather didactic than narrative in its satire and allegory, — and in *Renard le Contrefait* (1319–1342), a recast of the whole by a clerk of Troies, which preserves episodes otherwise unknown, and is valuable for sociology. Scholasticism, moralizing, and allegory are its principal features.

5. **Historical Poetry** had generally given way to prose. The *Branche des royaux lignages* (1306), by GUILLAUME GUIART, of Orleans, relates the Flemish wars of Philip IV. and ridicules the epic traditions. — A chronicle of Paris (1300–1316) was written by a citizen, GEOFFREI. — Other short chronicles in verse are found.

6. **Didactic Poetry; Legends and Tales;** CHRÉTIEN LE GOUAIS, a. 1300; WILHAM DE WADINGTON, XIII c. — Though allegory and satire prevail in didactic poetry, lives of saints, legends of the Virgin, and devout tales are still numerous. — Of the latter, the *Vrai anneau*, a parable against religious persecutions, due to a Jew, is later the theme of the *Decameron* (I. 3) and of LESSING's

Nathan der Weise. — Many similar tales were compiled by the Englishman, NICOLE BOZON (XIII c.), for pulpit use. — The *Roman de Mahomet* (1258), by ALEXANDRE DU PONT, represents the prophet as a trickster. — CHRÉTIEN LE GOUAIS translates the *Metamorphoses* (a. 1300), adding allegorical explanations. Many manuscripts attest the success of this long composition (over 72,000 verses). — More dogmatic is the *Manuel des Péchés* (XIII c.), by WILHAM DE WADINGTON, a collection of stories from the Scriptures, the *Vitae Patrum* and other sources. It was popular in spite of its degenerate French, and was translated into English (1303) by ROBERT DE BRUNNE.

7. **Satirical Poetry**; RUSTEBEUF; **Political**. — The note of personal feeling is struck by RUSTEBEUF, the needy hack-writer of Paris, the ancestor of VILLON. — A forerunner had been the lyric poet, COLIN MUSET (b. 1230). — RUSTEBEUF avenges his poverty on the peasants and citizens in his fableaux, and on the Beggar Friars by pamphlets in favor of the University. The poems on his own life, as the *Mariage Rustebeuf*, though full of plays on words and of grammatical and leonine rimes, are the most real of the century. Among others true to life, are the *Dit des ribauds de Grève*, in the spirit of VILLON, the *Dispute de Charlot et du barbier*, and the *Dit de l'herberie*, the parody of a quack. Lives of saints written to order, allegories, as the *Voie de Paradis*, after RAOUL DE HOUDAN, and poems on events, satirical in bent, as the *Débat du Croisé et du Non-Croisé*, make RUSTEBEUF the most varied as well as the most interesting author of the age. — Political satires against the English are found, as the *Paix aux Anglais* (1264) and

the *Charte aux Anglais* (1299), which ridicule by the forms and sounds of the words the English ignorance of French.

8. **Moral Poetry**; ROBERT DE BLOIS; BAUDOUIN DE CONDÉ, **a. 1230–a. 1290**; WATRIQUET DE COUVIN, **1319–1329**. — ROBERT DE BLOIS inserted in a narrative poem, *Beaudous* (a. 1250) — the son of Gawain, — didactic poems, sermons in verse, and the *Chastiement des dames*, a manual of etiquette for women. —BAUDOUIN DE CONDÉ (a. 1230–a. 1290), the father of JEAN, wrote stories, allegories, as the *Prison d'amour;* dits, as the *Trois morts et trois vifs;* and verses on death, striving after equivocal and artistic rimes. — WATRIQUET DE COUVIN (1319–1329) wrote allegories and parables, as the *Miroir aux dames* and the *Miroir aux princes* (1327), the *dits* of the *Quatre Sièges* (guarded in Paradise by Arthur, Alexander, Naimon, and Girard de Fratte), and of the *Fontaine d'amour*, historical poems and fableaux, all burdened with plays on words, and rich and leonine rimes. Poetry was in full decadence.

9. **Allegorical Poetry**; JEAN DE MEUN, **a. 1250–b. 1305**. — Modelled on RAOUL DE HOUDAN, or the *Roman de la Rose*, JACQUES DE BAISIEU wrote, besides the fableau, *Vessie au prêtre*, and the narrative, *Trois chevaliers au chainse*, three symbolic poems, as the *Dit de l'épée*. — The great allegorical poet of France is JEAN DE MEUN (a. 1250–b. 1305). A student at Paris, he continued the *Roman de la Rose* (a. 1277) in an entirely different spirit from that of GUILLAUME DE LORRIS. The action ceases, reason displaces love, and the tender and graceful allegory becomes a pretext to embody all

the ideas and learning of the author—a satirical encyclopædia, which puts before the people the wisdom and strifes of the schoolmen. It is notable for the beginnings of modern thought, as the knowledge of antiquity, and philosophic meditation. On account of its attacks on women, it was violently censured by succeeding writers. United to the poem of GUILLAUME, it had unexampled success, attested by a hundred manuscripts (a. 22,000 verses), and gave literature for two centuries an allegorical dress and a positive, prosaic character.

10. **Translations of Scripture ; Science.** — Few poetical translations of Scripture or treatises on science are found. — MACÉ, curate of La Charité, versified (a. 1300) several books of the Bible. — The *Chasse du cerf* (b. 1284), on hunting, and the *Ordre de chevalerie*, on knighting and knightly virtues, are the most interesting practical treatises.

11. **Lyric Poetry;** ADAM DE LA HALLE, **a. 1235-b. 1288; Popular Forms.** — The learned Provençal lyric vanished with feudalism, on which it was based. — GUILEBERT DE BERNEVILLE, attached to Henry III. of Brabant (1248–1261), left thirty-two poems, superior for their delicacy of sentiment and finished form. — ADAM DE LA HALLE (a. 1235–b. 1288), of Arras and Naples, wrote *chansons, jeux partis, motets, rondeaux* (short, undivided songs of dance music, of which a part is repeated); a *Congé*, imitated from BODEL, but here a satire on Arras; an epic poem for Charles d'Anjou ; and two comedies. He excelled as a musician, and considerable portions of his notation are preserved. — Poetesses are known, as a duchess of Lorraine. — Popular poetry was cultivated,

especially by the Puis, which held poetical tournaments. The *ballette*, in consecutive rimes, was developed; the *estampie*, a dance song with time beaten by the foot; the *vireli*, a long *rondeau;* and parodies on the learned lyric, as *sottes chansons* and *fatrasies*. — The united body of mediæval lyric amounts to some eight hundred poems, many anonymous, but the greater part signed by over one hundred and sixty authors.

12. **The Drama.** — But one play of the sacred drama belongs to this period, the *Miracle de Théophile*, written by RUSTEBEUF for a Pui probably, and showing a variety of verse. — Genuine comedy appears in the plays of ADAM DE LA HALLE. In the *Jeu de la Feuillée* (a. 1262), at Arras, the author appears on the stage and ridicules his family and neighbors. A variety of scenes follow, including a fair and an inn. It is a short comedy of manners. — *Robin et Marion*, at Naples, is a kind of operetta, made up from *pastourelles*. Marion is carried off by a knight, but escapes to Robin. A lively dialogue advances the action, popular songs and refrains are introduced, and a village festival closes the play. The style is clear, and the verse flowing. A prologue, the *Jeu du Pèlerin* (a. 1288), was composed for it at Arras. Art borrows from it its types of pastoral scenes, as in tapestries. — A *farce, Du garçon et de l'aveugle* (a. 1277), at Tournai, consists of a series of tricks played on a blind man by his guide, as in *Lazarillo de Tormes*.

13. **Prose Translations.** — In prose, GUIART DES MOULINS translates (1291-1294) an abridgment of the historical part of the Bible and adds various books. — The

Régime du corps (a. 1256), by ALDEBRAND, an Italian, concerns hygiene. — In law, the *Code* and *Institutes* were translated; and in history, the *Chroniques de Saint-Denis* (1260). — The most noted translator is JEAN DE MEUN. To him is due the prose version (1284) of the *De re militari*, of VEGETIUS (versified, 1290, by JEAN PRIORAT, of Besançon, as had been, 1280, the *Institutes* by RICHARD D'ANNEBAUT). Translations of the *De mirabilibus Irlandi* of GIRAUD DE BARRI, of the letters of Abelard and Héloïse, of a treatise by ÆLRED and of BOËTHIUS followed. The *Testament* (after 1291) of JEAN DE MEUN is a devout satire on the times, in monorime quatrains.

14. **Historical Works**; JEAN DE JOINVILLE, **1222-1317**; **Letters**. — The *Histoires de Baudouin* of Hainault († 1205) are a vast compilation of chronicles, continued by BAUDOUIN D'AVESNES († 1289). — The *Chronique de Reims* (1260) is a minstrel's narrative, of slight historical worth, but full of popular stories and traditions. The style is lively and simple. — JEAN DE JOINVILLE (1224-1317), seneschal of Champagne, is the great chronicler of the age. His *Histoire de Saint Louis* (1304-1309) is a biography mingled with reminiscences, relating the wars and moral teachings of Louis IX. It is made up from a diary, from a life of the king and from the *Chroniques de Saint-Denis*. The account is of much historical worth, and the style is easy and familiar. JOINVILLE is also the author of a popular *Credo* (1250), and of a letter in French to Louis X. — Other letters on public events are preserved, including a series on the war in Egypt, by JEAN SARRAZIN.

15. Scientific and Doctrinal Treatises; Laws; Language. — The *Livre des métiers* (1268), by ÉTIENNE BOILEAU, treats of the guilds and corporations of Paris. — The *Trésor* (a. 1265), of BRUNETTO LATINO († 1294), is an encyclopædia, combining observations on society with material taken from the *Image du monde* and from Latin sources. — The *Livre de Sidrac* is a series of erudite answers to questions. — More dogmatic is the *Somme du Roi* (1279), for Philip the Bold, by his confessor, LORENS. Moral advice, drawn from religious teachings to aid in adapting a devout mind to its worldly condition, is given in a simple and polished style, which made it one of the leading works of the age. — In law, the *Établissements de Saint Louis*, derived from the usages of Anjou, and the *Coutumier de Beauvaisis* (1283), by PHILIPPE DE BEAUMANOIR, are the most important. — Treatises on French for use in England begin, as that (b. 1300) of GAUTIER DE BIBELESWORTH. — Latin-French glossaries are found. Hebrew-French date from the eleventh century.

16. Travel; Fiction. — The first book of travel was dictated (1298) to RUSTICIANO, of Pisa, by MARCO POLO, in prison at Genoa. — For fiction there are prose versions of popular tales, as *Ami et Amile, Floire et Jeanne* — a variant of the theme of *Guillaume de Dole* — and *Constant l'empereur*, on overruling destiny. The last exists also in verse.

PART II.

PRE-RENAISSANCE LITERATURE.
1327–1515.

CHAPTER VII.

FIRST PERIOD. 1327-1422.

1. **Poetry.** Epic; *Combat des Trente*, 1351; CUVELIER, 1384; JEAN DES PRÉS, 1338–a. 1400; NICCOLÒ DA VERONA, a..1340; JEAN DE LE MOTE, a. 1340; *Brun de la Montagne.* Didactic; GUILLAUME DE DEGUILLEVILLE, † a. 1360; PHILIPPE DE VITRI, † 1361; JEAN LE FÈVRE, a. 1320–a. 1376; GACE DE LA BIGNE; GILLES LE MUISIT, 1271-1352. Lyric; JEAN DE LESCUREL; New school; GUILLAUME DE MACHAUT, † a. 1377; EUSTACHE DESCHAMPS, a. 1339–a. 1407; JEAN FROISSART, a. 1337–a. 1410; CHRISTINE DE PISAN, a. 1363–a. 1430; *Livre des Cent Ballades*, a. 1386–a. 1392.
2. **Drama.** *Miracles de Notre Dame.*
3. **Prose.** Translations; PIERRE BERÇUIRE, † b. 1362; RAOUL DE PRESLES, a. 1351–a. 1383; NICOLE ORESME, † 1382. Treatises; PHILIPPE DE MAIZIÈRES, a. 1327–a. 1405; HONORÉ BONET, a. 1370; JEAN GERSON, 1363–1429. Chronicles; JEAN LE BEL, a. 1290–1370; JEAN FROISSART; CHRISTINE DE PISAN. *Saint Voyage de Jérusalem*, 1396. *Manière de Langage*, 1396. Fiction; *Mélusine*, 1387; *Perceforest*, a. 1400.

1. **The Literature Preceding the Renaissance; Changes in Language and Spirit; Divisions.** — The period from the advent of the Valois (1327) to the reign of Francis I. (1515) sees the decay of mediævalism and the rise of modern society. Literature leaves the nobles and clergy to find a broader and more enduring support in the third estate, as was foreshadowed by JEAN DE MEUN. Poetry was dominated by the allegorical form and prosaic sentiment of the *Roman de la Rose*, though the national songs remained unfettered. Drama and prose were the favorite kinds of composition. — Language undergoes a change with society and thought. Most striking is the loss of the nominative case, which causes great confusion in the old poems and aids the use of prose. — Pre-Renaissance literature can be divided into two periods. The first ends with the reign of Charles VI. (1422), and represents the century of the Hundred Years' War, destructive to patriotism and thought. The second (1422-1515) begins with the national awakening, continues with the alliance of the third estate and the royalty, and ends with the Italian expeditions, which open the way for the new birth. — From the scanty material at hand, the first period resolves itself into a movement of translation, guided by PETRARCH and Charles V., a vogue of chronicles, culminating in FROISSART, and the recasting of the exotic Provençal lyric in the national school of GUILLAUME DE MACHAUT.

2. **Epic Poetry** is almost dead. An alexandrine version of *Girard de Roussillon* (1336-1348) is found. — The old poems, however, inspire imitations relating to the English war, as the *Combat des Trente Bretons contre*

Trente Anglais (1351), in monorime alexandrines. — The *Chronique de Du Guesclin* (1384), by CUVELIER, is supplemented by GUILLAUME DE SAINT-ANDRÉ. — JEAN DES PRÉS (a. 1338-1400) expands his *Geste de Liège*, of some forty thousand verses, into the prose chronicle, the *Miroir des Histoires* (1399). — The last of such imitations is the *Geste des ducs de Bourgogne* (a. 1400). — The Crusade epic, under the title of the *Chevalier au Cygne*, was worked over (1350-1355) by a Flemish poet. — The *Vœux du Paon* received a sequel by JEAN BRISEBARRE, the *Restor du Paon* (b. 1338), which was in turn continued in the *Parfait du Paon* (1340), by JEAN DE LE MOTE, known also by the *Regret de Guillaume* of Hainault († 1339), written for Queen Philippa. Both works are insipid and pedantic. — *Brun de la Montagne* (after 1350) is a *roman d'aventure* in alexandrines. Prolix and commonplace, it has a technical interest in its observance of the modern law concerning the feminine cæsura.

3. **The French National Epic Abroad**; NICOLÒ DA VERONA. — The French heroic epic, the influence of which, in Germany and England, has been noted, passed from the latter country into Norway, where, under King Haakon (1217-1263), it was rendered into a connected prose narrative, the *Karlamagnus Saga* and into separate translations, still popular. — Dutch translations are also numerous, and in Spain the ballads derive from it much material. — Its great success was, however, in Italy. Known from the beginning of the thirteenth century, it inspired poets of the fourteenth to sequels in French. Among them, NICCOLÒ DA VERONA, the author of the

Pharsale (1343), writes part of the long *Entrée d'Espagne*, in which the cycle takes on a new development. Changed and enlarged, the Carolingian epic passed from the Franco-Italian poems of the North to the Tuscan prose and *ottava rima*, until, fused by the court poets of the Renaissance with the refinement of the Breton romances, it evolved into the *Orlando Furioso* and the sensuous element in TASSO.

4. **Didactic Poetry**: GUILLAUME DE DEGUILLEVILLE, † a. 1360; PHILIPPE DE VITRI, † 1361; JEAN LE FÈVRE, a. 1320–a. 1376; GACE DE LA BIGNE; GILLES LE MUISIT, 1271–1352. — The few poems which are known previous to the revival under MACHAUT are mainly didactic. Allegory and the *Roman de la Rose*, which he violently opposed, inspired GUILLAUME DE DEGUILLEVILLE, between 1330 and 1335, to compose his *Pèlerinage de la vie humaine* and *Pèlerinage de l'âme*, to which he added the *Pèlerinage de Jésus-Christ* (b. 1360). His work had great success, was imitated by CHAUCER, and perhaps gave the impulse to *Pilgrim's Progress*. — Less popular is the *Dit des huit blasons* by JEAN DE BATERI, on eight lords killed at Crécy. — Possibly more lyric than didactic is the work of PHILIPPE DE VITRI († 1361), attached to John the Good, and friend of PETRARCH. His only poem extant, the *Dits du Franc-Gontier*, in decasyllabic verse, is on country life. It was imitated by DESCHAMPS and translated into Latin. He was also noted as a musician, and is said to have remodeled motets, ballades, lais, and rondeaux. — JEAN LE FÈVRE (a. 1320–a. 1376) translated *De Vetula* of RICHARD DE FOURNIVAL, a treatise on music, hunting and like subjects, the *Proverbes* of CATO,

and especially the *Matheolus*, a satire against woman, of the last part of the thirteenth century. — GACE DE LA BIGNE, attached to John the Good and Charles V., wrote the *Déduits de la chasse*. — GILLES LE MUISIT (1271-1352) is the author of numerous Latin works and French poems of a historical character, and not without merit.

5. Lyric Poetry, Old School: JEAN DE LESCUREL, b. 1350? **New School**; GUILLAUME DE MACHAUT; EUSTACHE DESCHAMPS; FROISSART; CHRISTINE DE PISAN; *Cent Ballades*. — A poet, probably of the first half of the century, JEAN DE LESCUREL, wrote ballades and rondeaux, and shows thus the transition to the forms of GUILLAUME DE MACHAUT († a. 1377). — The latter, attached to John of Bohemia, and later to John the Good, is no less celebrated as a musician than as a poet, having composed a mass, the music for his poetry, and introduced a new style of musical notation. In light poetry he is assigned some two hundred ballades, eighty motets and rondeaux, many lais and virelais, and various *complaintes* and *chants royaux*. His earliest works comprise several *dits*. Two long poems, the *Livre du Voir-Dit* (1363-4), a love story of short lyrics, divided by prose letters, pretending to be autobiographical; and the *Prise d'Alexandrie* (1369-), a chronicle of Peter of Lusignan, are best known. His literary merit is mainly in the form of his verse, whence his authority. The content shows the artificial character of the amorous poetry of the time. — The chief pupil and follower of MACHAUT is EUSTACHE DESCHAMPS (a. 1339-a. 1407), attached to Charles V. and VI., a constant enemy of decaying feudalism, a pessimist. He wrote one thousand and seventy-five ballades, one hundred and seventy-one rondeaux; also virelais, lais, *chants royaux, dits,* and the *Miroir de mariage,* a satire against woman, imitated from JEAN DE MEUN — all without literary value though interesting for the history of the time. Prolix, without taste, full of digressions, his language is proverbial and popular. Many of his poems resemble those of FROISSART and CHAUCER, as the *Marguerite.* His *Art de dicter* (1392), in prose, is important for the study of the versification of the age.— JEAN FROISSART (a. 1337–a. 1410), the chronicler, is the author of some twenty-five thousand lines of lyric and didactic poetry. He delights in allegory and in biographical works, as the *Espinette amoureuse.* He excels in pastourelles. His verse is delicate, fresh, graceful. His rimes are artificial, and in the taste of the time. — CHRISTINE DE PISAN (a. 1363–a. 1430), daughter of the Italian astrologer of Charles V., wrote light lyrics from 1389, as the *Cent ballades,* virelais, rondeaux, *jeux à vendre* (a social pastime in the form of an epigram), lais, and separate ballades. These poems have both grace and sentiment. Her more serious works, later in date, include *Proverbes moraux,* addressed to her son; the *Livre du chemin de longue étude* (1403), inspired by BOËTHIUS; the dit of the *Pastoure* (1403), directed against the *Roman de la Rose;* and many other works of occasion, both prose and poetry. Her last known composition is a national song on Joan of Arc (1429). — A collection of poems is the *Livre des Cent Ballades* (1386–1392), of which the first fifty are virile counsels given to a young knight on loyalty and love, while the remainder represent a poetical tournament on the question: "Whether loyalty or deceit avail more in love." In pure style and polished verse this book became the favorite reading of the time.

6. **New Kinds of Lyric**: *Ballade; Chant royal; Rondeau, Lai;* **Decay of Rime.** — The French lyric of Provençal origin, affected by the principles of native versification during the first part of the fourteenth century, was fixed by GUILLAUME DE MACHAUT in forms which lasted, with slight changes, until the Renaissance. — The *ballade*, which seems to derive from French models, is composed of three strophes, similar in verse and rime, the last line of every strophe being the same. It has an *envoi*, a half-verse, often omitted, which contains the address, generally to the prince of a Pui. — The *chant royal* is a double *ballade*, having five strophes of eleven decasyllabic verses and an *envoi* of five. — The *rondeau*, originally a strophe of eight verses, in which the first was repeated at the fourth, and the first and the second at the seventh and eighth (called later *triolet*), became a poem of three strophes, in which the last verse of the second and third strophes is the same as the first of the first, or their last two verses are the same as the first two (4 + 3 + 5, or 4 + 4 + 6). — The lyric *lai* was developed into a long poem of twelve strophes, each divided into two parts of eight, nine, ten, or twelve verses. The rimes of every strophe were different, excepting those of the last, which agree with those of the first. — Corresponding to the difficulties of versification the rime was subjected to artificial handlings, which ended by destroying poetry. Not content with *rich* rime (agreement of the tonic vowel and preceding consonant) and *leonine* (rime of two syllables), the poets of the decadence strove for

equivocal rimes (the same form of word but different in meaning), *annexed* rimes (where the last syllable of one verse becomes the first of the verse following), and other juggleries, which reached their limit at the end of the fifteenth century.

7. **The Drama**: *Miracles de Nostre Dame;* Eustache Deschamps. — The dramatic works preserved are almost all *Miracles*. Forty such pieces, composed for some Pui, are found in one manuscript. In octosyllabic verse, cut at the end of each speech by a verse of four syllables riming with the first verse of the following speech, they all develop common subjects derived from church traditions, narrative poetry, as *Ami et Amile, Robert le Diable*, or from history. The Virgin appears only at the end to save the sinner. They are consequently devoid of interest, and, owing to their poetical structure, of literary merit. Many of them contain rondeaux, and are followed by serventois, having an envoi. The larger part are accompanied by a short prose sermon. — Of the three other *Miracles* known, two are of the same order, and the third, the *Histoire de Griselidis* (1395), resembles rather a morality, having in it nothing of the marvelous. — Fragments of a mystery belonging to this century supplement the frequent allusions to their representation. — Of comedy, only two dialogued pieces of Eustache Deschamps are preserved, and they were probably not intended for the stage; one a morality, the other a farce (dishonest lawyer and deceitful plaintiff).

8. **Prose: Translations; Indications of the Renaissance;** Petrarch; **Charles V.**; Pierre Berçuire, † b. 1362; Jean d'Arkel, a. 1314–1378; Raoul de Presles, a. 1315–

1383; Nicole Oresme, † 1382. — The rise of prose is first seen in a series of translations from classical works by which neologisms were introduced into the language. The impulse came from the papal court at Avignon, and is manifested particularly in the clerical friends of Petrarch. Later, Charles V. (1364–1380), the patron of art and learning, urged on in the same direction, and made the royal court, for the first time, the literary center of France. — It was perhaps due to Petrarch's influence that one of his friends, Pierre Berçuire († b. 1362), a Benedictine, translated Livy (1352–) for John the Good. — Jean d'Arkel (a. 1314–1378), bishop of Liège, dedicated to Jean Le Bel the *Art d'amour, de vertu et de bonheurté*, selections translated from Seneca, Persius, classical authors and Church Fathers, in a prose which differs but slightly from that of the later fifteenth century. — Raoul de Presles (a. 1315–1383), magistrate, wrote Latin works, and, in French, translated for Charles V. the *De civitate Dei* of Saint Augustin, and various other works, including the Bible (1377). — The most active of all in this early Renaissance movement is Nicole Oresme († 1382), bishop of Lisieux, a writer of Latin treatises and a translator for Charles V. He turned into French prose a good share of Aristotle, including the *Ethics* (1370), and the *Economics* (1371); besides writing learned treatises, as the *Traité de la sphère*. To express the new ideas he was obliged to add many Latinisms to the vernacular. — In the propagation of learned derivatives the numerous translations of the Bible in this period are important.

9. **Didactic Treatises**: Philippe de Maizières, a. 1327–

1405; JEAN DE BRIE; HONORÉ BONET; JEAN GERSON, 1363-1429. — In the same spirit are most of the didactic works of the age, mainly ordered by Charles V. — PHILIPPE DE MAIZIÈRES (a. 1327-1405), partisan of a new crusade, attached to the house of Lusignan, a friend of PETRARCH and counselor under Charles V., wrote Latin letters and works. In French he is the author of the *Songe du vieux pèlerin* (1382), with admonitions for Charles VI.; the *Poirier fleuri;* the *Pèlerinage du pauvre pèlerin* (1392); and, most noted of all, the *Songe du verger* (1376-1378), translated from his *Somnium viridarii* (1374-1376), which is a compilation, in dialogue form, of arguments relating to the spiritual and temporal power of the pope. A clerk presents the papal arguments, a knight the royal claims. — Of a different style is the *Bon Berger* (1379), by JEAN DE BRIE, a kind of Georgic written for shepherds, at the order of the king. — HONORÉ BONET, a Provençal, dedicated to Charles VI. the *Arbre des batailles* (a. 1390), on the art of war; and also, at the illness of the king, wrote the *Apparition de Jean de Meun* (1398), a dialogue, in which the latter speaks in verse, the author in prose. — JEAN GERSON (1363-1429) has a place in French literature as the author of many sermons, which, though pedantic, scholastic and allegorical, have movement and pathos. He was a bitter enemy of the *Roman de la Rose*, while undergoing its influence and praising its style. — CHRISTINE DE PISAN wrote *Épîtres sur le Roman de la Rose* (1407), and various treatises on the affairs of the time.

10. Chronicles: JEAN LE BEL, a. 1290-1370; JEAN FROISSART; CHRISTINE DE PISAN. — The second movement in prose is in chronicles, which became the pastime of the learned. — The *Chroniques de Saint-Denis* were continued, as by PIERRE D'ORGEMONT († 1389). — Notable are the *Récits d'un bourgeois de Valenciennes* (1366), and the *Livre des faits du maréchal de Boucicaut* (b. 1421). — Besides JEAN DES PRÉS, another chronicler was JEAN LE BEL (a. 1290–1370), of Liège, also a writer of lyrics. His chronicle (1326–1361), in two parts, is the source of the first book (1325–1377) of the *Chronique* of FROISSART, whose remaining three books (1377–1400) rest on personal observation. — FROISSART is the great writer of the age. He sees the brilliant side of court life, and reflects it in his narrative. Though fickle in sentiment, contenting himself with a mere succession of deeds and events, his style is vivid, picturesque, familiar, and original. — CHRISTINE DE PISAN wrote a historical eulogy, the *Livre des faits et bonnes mœurs du roi Charles V.* (1404).

11. **Travels; Language; Fiction.** — Succeeding MARCO POLO is the record (1357–1371) of the travels of SIR JOHN MANDEVILLE, and the anonymous *Saint Voyage de Jérusalem* (1396). — In linguistics, the *Manière de langage* (1396), and a reading-book for children (1399), are both by Englishmen. — Fiction is seen in short tales, as *Troilus* from the Italian, and *Mélusine* (1387) compiled by JEAN D'ARRAS from a lai and legends localized at Lusignan. — The long *Perceforest* (a. 1400), an imitation of the Breton prose romances and a precursor of the romances of chivalry, mixes legends of Alexander with the history of England.

PRE-RENAISSANCE LITERATURE.
1327–1515.

CHAPTER VIII.

SECOND PERIOD. 1422–1515.

1. **Poetry.** Didactic; *Danse Macabré*, 1424; PIERRE MICHAUT, -1437-1466-; JEAN MESCHINOT, † 1509; MARTIN LE FRANC, a. 1410-1461; GEORGES CHASTELLAIN, a. 1415-1475; GUILLAUME COQUILLART, a. 1422-1510; JEAN MOLINET, † 1507; GUILLAUME CRETIN, † 1525. Lyric; ALAIN CHARTIER, a. 1392-b. 1440; CHARLES D'ORLÉANS, 1391-1465; RENÉ D'ANJOU, 1409-1480; MARTIAL D'AUVERGNE, a. 1433-1508; JEAN REGNIER, a. 1385-b. 1465; FRANÇOIS VILLON, 1431-1462-; OCTAVIEN DE SAINT-GELAIS, 1466-1502; JEAN MAROT, † a. 1527; *Vaux de Vire*.
2. **Drama.** Mysteries and miracles; EUSTACHE MERCADÉ, -1414-1441-; JACQUES MILLET, a. 1425-1466; ARNOUL GREBAN, -1440-1474-; JEAN MICHEL, † 1501; *Vieux Testament*, b. 1458; *Confrérie de la Passion*, 1402. Comedy; *Farce; Monologue; Moralité; Sermon joyeux; Sottie; Basoche; Enfants sans souci; Sots;* HENRI BAUDE, a. 1430-1486-; PIERRE BLANCHET, 1459-1519; PIERRE GRINGORE, † after 1527; *Pathelin*, a. 1470.
3. **Prose.** Chronicles; *Mont Saint-Michel*, 1343-1468; *Journal d'un bourgeois de Paris*, 1405-1449; PIERRE COCHON, † a. 1451; GEORGES CHASTELLAIN; OLIVIER DE LA MARCHE, a. 1426-1502; JEAN LE MAIRE, a. 1473-1524. History; PHILIPPE DE COMINES, a. 1445-1511. Treatises; BAUDET HE-

RENC, 1432; *Débat des Hérauts*, 1453–1461; ROBERT DE BALSAC, † a. 1503; Sermons. Fiction; Epic prose; JEAN WAUQUELIN, † 1453; *Pierre de Provence; Jean de Paris;* ANTOINE DE LA SALLE, 1398–1462–.

1. **Characteristics of the Fifteenth Century Literature; Drama; Lyric Poetry; History.** — The literature of this period shows the political changes, the rise of the third estate. The epic poems were thrown into prose narratives, which reached ultimately the peasantry. Didactic and lyric poetry, still ruled by the *Roman de la Rose*, were broken in upon by the personal current of REGNIER and VILLON, but soon engulfed it. — It is pre-eminently the dramatic century. The great mysteries were written, and comedy reached its highest point under Louis XII. — Prose fiction shows a strong development, and becomes modern in spirit. History begins with COMINES. It is a period of realism.

2. **Moral and Religious Poetry**: *Danse de Macabré*, 1424; JEAN MESCHINOT, –1442–1509. — Besides the usual lives of saints, songs by the Puis in honor of the Virgin (generally *chants royaux*), *débats, dits*, and moral poems, the notion of the vanity of life, seen in the *Vers de la mort*, and in the *Trois morts et trois vifs*, found its last and highest expression in the *Dance of Death* (*Danse de Macabré*), painted on the cemetery of the Innocents at Paris in 1424. This curious fresco, in which skeletons are represented as dragging into a dance men of every condition and age, is accompanied by strophes of eight octosyllabic verses (*a b a b b c b c*), alternating between Death and his victim. Its success was especially great in art. — Imitations of the *Danse de Macabré*, as the *Danse des hommes*

and the *Danse des femmes* soon followed. — PIERRE MICHAUT (–1437–1466–), secretary of Charles the Bold, wrote various didactic poems, among them the *Danse aux aveugles*, an allegory beginning with a dream, where Love, Fortune and Death are the blind; and the *Doctrinal du temps présent*, an allegory in twelve chapters, where the poet, wandering in a forest, meets Virtue, who becomes his guide in moral instruction. — JEAN MESCHINOT († 1491 or 1509), of Nantes, in the *Lunettes des princes* is pessimistic. He also wrote a poem on the Passion, and ballades to twenty-five envoys sent him by CHASTELLAIN. He is notorious for his extravagant rimes.

3. **Allegorical and Satirical Poetry:** MARTIN LE FRANC, a. 1410–1461; GUILLAUME ALEXIS, † b. 1493; GUILLAUME COQUILLART, a. 1422–1510; JEAN MOLINET, † 1507; JEAN LE MAIRE, a. 1473–a. 1524. — The attacks on women in the *Roman de la Rose* called out one of the most important works of the century, the *Champion des dames* (1442), by MARTIN LE FRANC (a. 1410–1461), provost of Lausanne. It is an allegory in some twenty-four thousand octosyllabic verses, grouped in strophes of eight — a form borrowed from CHARTIER — and is dedicated to Philip the Good. Malebouche and Franc Vouloir are the respective champions. Besides the general defense of woman, the author displays a patriotic spirit, a knowledge of French literature and a classical learning, proven by frequent citations, which counteract to some extent the monotony of his action, all in narrative. A good poet, noble in sentiment, free in thought, but yet devout, he lacks in delineation of character and in vigor of expression. He dedicated later to Philip the *Estrif de la fortune et de la vertu*,

an erudite dialogue in prose and verse. Many minor poems followed the *Champion* in the defense of woman. — Among the writings which satirize woman are those of GUILLAUME ALEXIS († b. 1493), a monk of Lyre. He translated from the Latin of INNOCENT III. the *Passe-temps de tout homme et de toute femme* (1481), and composed various poems, as the *Blason des faux amours*, a coarse satire written in an irregular measure, much imitated later. — GUILLAUME COQUILLART (a. 1422–1510), of Reims, besides dramatic monologues, a translation of JOSEPHUS (1460–1463) and various lyrics, wrote the *Droits nouveaux*, a satire of the Code. His most important work, the *Plaidoyer d'entre la simple et la rusée* (1477), is a parody on a trial at court. A poet of the third estate, vigorous and coarse. — JEAN MOLINET († 1507), regarded with MESCHINOT and CRETIN as the model of fine language, was canon of Valenciennes and historiographer of Maximilian I. In prose he "moralized" the *Roman de la Rose*, explaining the allegory in a Christian sense. In poetry he wrote many pieces of occasion, as the *Temple de Mars*, on the horrors of war; the *Complainte de Constantinople;* and prayers to the Virgin, all rivaling one another in curious versification. — JEAN LE MAIRE (a. 1473–1524 or 1548), of Belges, nephew of MOLINET and historiographer of Margaret of Austria and Louis XII., exercised great influence on the sixteenth century in language and versification. Besides official poetry composed for the house of Burgundy, allegorical and steeped in classical lore, he shows originality in the *Épîtres de l'amant vert* (1510), addressed to Margaret. His sentiment of rhythm and his poetical phrase and images excel those of his predecessors.

4. **Didactic and Historical Poetry**: GEORGES CHASTEL-
LAIN, a. 1415-1475; GUILLAUME CRETIN, †1525; FRAN-
ÇOIS GUARIN, a. 1410-1460-. — GEORGES CHASTELLAIN
(a. 1415-1475), head of the rhetorical school in the last
half of the century, was historiographer of Burgundy,
and, like LE MAIRE, is best known by his prose. His
many poems were, however, highly valued at the time.
They are after the pedantic and Latinizing style of
CHARTIER. *Moralités, complaintes*, historical works, as
the *Miroir des nobles hommes de France* (1457), a satire,
the *Prince*, against Louis XI., chansons, ballades and
rondeaux are all pompous and bombastic. — GUILLAUME
CRETIN, or DUBOIS († 1525), of Nanterre, is a synonym
for fantastic and puerile versification. He composed a
dozen books of rimed chronicles, extending from the
Trojan origins of the Franks to the end of the Carolin-
gians, besides the customary amount of *chants royaux*,
ballades, rondeaux and epistles. An imitator of MOLI-
NET, he even attained greater renown at the time. —
FRANÇOIS GUARIN (a. 1410-1460-), of Lyons, is a poet
of doctrines, Protestant in spirit. A poem in strophes
of eight verses for his son, and another in couplets (1460),
attack the clergy and popular superstitions.

5. **End of the Old School in Lyric Poetry**: CHARLES
D'ORLÉANS, 1319-1465; **Rise of a New School**; ALAIN
CHARTIER, a. 1392-b. 1440; RENÉ D'ANJOU, 1409-1480;
MARTIAL DE PARIS, a. 1433-1508. — The last and best
representative of the purely mediæval lyric is the prince
CHARLES OF ORLÉANS. A prisoner in England (1415-
1440) and, on his return to France, a protector of letters
at Blois, he was regarded by his age as a poet of albums,

and remained unprinted, and almost unmentioned, until the nineteenth century. His poems, some four hundred rondeaux, over a hundred ballades, and a hundred and more chansons, were composed partly in captivity. They have little originality or variety; are influenced mainly by the *Roman de la Rose* and the *Cent Ballades*, but possess natural grace and delicacy, and are written in a clear and simple style. Invention, imagination tinged with melancholy, a mild patriotism, and employment of metaphors are his other qualities. His best poem, the gem of lyric poetry previous to the Pléiade, is a rondeau on the return of spring. — ALAIN CHARTIER (a. 1392-b. 1440), of Bayeux, secretary of Charles VII., was the great author of the age, whose fame eclipsed that of MACHAUT, and whose imitators comprise nearly all the poets of the century. Writing both in poetry and prose, he seems to have avoided the influence of the *Roman de la Rose* and to have drawn his inspiration, both patriotic and gallant, from the *Cent Ballades*. His most important works are the *Livre des quatre dames* (1415 or 1416), in which the loss of their lovers at Agincourt is deplored, the *Bréviaire des nobles* and particularly the *Belle dame sans merci* (1426), the sentiment and style of which dominated the poetry of the century. CHARTIER in this poem adapted the form of the ballade without refrain to long compositions. The poetry of CHARTIER, regular in versification, pure in language and easy in rhythm, is, in point of quality, inferior to his prose, which is both eloquent and noble. The *Quadrilogue invectif*, after the treaty of Troyes (1420), is a dialogue on the political outlook between the Three Estates and

France. The *Curial* is a lively description of court vices in the form of a letter. The language of CHARTIER is to be noticed for its Latinizing tendency. — RENÉ D'ANJOU (1409–1480), king of Naples, wrote prose and verse, as the *Livre des Tournois*, under the influence of the *Roman de la Rose*. — MARTIAL DE PARIS, or D'AUVERGNE (a. 1433–1508), procurator of the Parliament of Paris, is the most artistic poet of the century. Besides various didactic works, including a *Danse Macabré des femmes*, he wrote treatises on love, as the *Amant rendu cordelier à l'observance d'amour*, and the *Arrêts d'amour*, modeled on an imitation of CHARTIER (the *Échiquier d'amour*) and on ANDRÉ LE CHAPELAIN. The *Arrêts*, in prose, pretending to emanate from a parliament of love, are the most important.

6. **Personal Poetry**: JEAN REGNIER, a. 1385–b. 1465; FRANÇOIS VILLON, 1431–1462–. — In the midst of the formal and didactic poetry of the century a personal note is struck by two writers of merit. — JEAN REGNIER (a. 1385–b. 1465), of Auxerre, wrote in prison his *Testament* (1433) in quatrains, and later, ballades and other poems. — The great poet of the age, and perhaps the best before CHÉNIER, is FRANÇOIS DE MONCORBIER, called VILLON (1431–1462–). A student, living a lawless life in Paris, his works resemble those of his contemporaries in form alone. In spirit he is entirely original. His two chief poems, the *Lais*, or *Petit Testament* (1456), in strophes of eight verses, and the *Grand Testament* (1461), into which he inserts ballades and lais, are composed of a series of legacies, mainly satirical, made to his friends and acquaintances. They both rest on local allusions, jocose and

serious, on meditations on human vices and miseries, and on his own life. Besides these two compositions detached pieces are found, mainly ballades but also *dits, débats* and other poems in the manner of the time. Remarkable in style and spirit is the *Ballade des pendus* (1462?). The *Ballade des dames du temps jadis* is included in the *Grand Testament*. Almost without an exception the work of VILLON is distinguished by depth and sincerity of emotion, by vigor and precision of style. He looks back to RUSTEBEUF, and forward to ALFRED DE MUSSET, though perhaps he is more akin to HEINE.

7. **Last Lyrics of the Rhetorical School; Italian Influence;** OCTAVIEN DE SAINT-GELAIS, **1466–1502;** JEAN MAROT, †**1527; Popular Poetry; Versification and Rime of the Rhetorical School.** — All poets of the last part of the fifteenth century are both lyric and didactic. Two can be separated from the others as having undergone the influence of classical learning and of the Italian Renaissance. — OCTAVIEN DE SAINT-GELAIS (1466–1502), bishop of Angoulême, is of the rhetorical school in his *Chasse ou le départ d'amour*, a collection of ballades, rondeaux and *complaintes;* and in the *Séjour d'honneur*, a poem mixed with prose, giving in the form of an allegory the history of his life. But he shows the Renaissance movement in the translation of the *Eneid* (1500), and of a score of OVID's epistles. — JEAN DES MARES († a. 1527), called MAROT, under similar influences wrote epigrams, rondeaux, eclogues, epistles, the *Doctrinal des princesses et nobles dames* (a collection of twenty-four rondeaux), the *Voyage de Gênes* (1507) and the *Voyage de Venise* (1508). In these latter poems, written in various meas-

ures and styles, MAROT combines mythological allegory with history, and shows a talent for invention and description, but also great negligence in versification. — While this allegorical and pedantic poetry ran its course in the upper classes of society, the people still cherished its **popular songs**, of which some hundred and fifty have been preserved: pastourelles from the cycle of Robin and Marion, war and love songs, all natural and traditional. — To these can be added patriotic and drinking songs of the valley of the Vire in Normandy, which seem to have begun with the patriot, OLIVIER BASSELIN (a. 1450) and his friends, but remain only in the later imitations of JEAN LE HOUX. — On the whole, the poetry of the fifteenth century introduced no important change in **versification**, other than the adoption of the ballade form without refrain (*a b a b b c b c*) as a strophic basis for a long poem. This was already seen in the *Danse de Macabré*, and in the *Belle dame sans merci*. In rime it pushed the faults of the previous period to an extreme. From *equivocal*, often doubly so, and *annexed*, it proceeded to *empérière* (where the last part of the third word from the end of the verse is repeated twice successively), to *couronnée* (where the last word in the verse is the same as the last part of the word immediately preceding), or to *briseé* (where the first hemistichs rime throughout, as well as the several lines of the strophe). These, and various other kinds of rime, were supplemented by a strophic structure, which allowed often more than thirty different readings.

8. **Flowering of the Mediæval Drama: Mysteries and Miracles**; EUSTACHE MERCADÉ; ARNOUL GREBAN, b.

1452; JEAN MICHEL, 1486; SIMON GREBAN; JACQUES MILLET, 1452. — The fifteenth century saw the expansion and full bloom of the mediæval theater, both sacred and profane. Resting on popular favor it replaces epic poetry in the third estate. Representations of mysteries, whether in pantomime or orally, fill the chronicles of the time. The word *miracle* disappears, swallowed up by its more vigorous brother and by the tendency towards a cyclic development. — Among the subjects most in vogue that of the Passion fell into the hands of authors whose names are known, as EUSTACHE MERCADÉ (-1414-1441-), prior of the abbey of Ham. — The great dramatic author of the period is ARNOUL GREBAN (a. 1420-1473-), of Le Mans, who wrote for a Parisian society a *Passion* (a. 1450) of over thirty-four thousand verses, and later, together with his brother, SIMON (-1468-1472-) — also a lyric poet — the *Actes des Apôtres*, of nearly sixty-two thousand verses and five hundred characters, based partly on Scripture and partly on tradition. It is the greatest effort of the clerical drama. — JEAN MICHEL († 1501), of Angers, physician to the Dauphin, wrote a *Passion* (1486) and a *Résurrection* (b. 1499). — In 1507 the *Passion* of MICHEL was fused with that of GREBAN in a vast composition of sixty-five thousand verses. — The *Vieux Testament* (b. 1458 ?) is a compilation by various authors of over forty-nine thousand verses. — Besides these larger plays and many other anonymous ones founded on the Scriptures, the saints gave rise to some forty mysteries. — Profane subjects as well as profane material were used, as the *Siège d'Orléans* and the *Destruction de Troie* (1452), the latter by JACQUES

MILLET, or MILET (a. 1425-1466), of Paris, law student at Orléans, who translated the work of GUIDO COLONNA. — While the mystery was still essentially sacred, much that was profane, as comic and grotesque elements (especially the part of the devils), had been introduced. The verse remained, as a rule, the octosyllabic couplet, but other forms were frequent and lyric songs abound. The style is generally poor, but occasionally fine passages appear. — The actors were furnished by societies, the successors of the Puis, or by guilds. Best known is the *Confrérie de la Passion*, of Paris, which received a royal charter in 1402. — The total amount of extant mysteries exceeds one million verses.

9. **Kinds of Comedy**: *Moralité; Farce; Sottie; Sermon joyeux; Monologue; Pathelin*, a. 1470. — The positive, ironical character of the literature of the fifteenth century (that of Louis XI.) is seen best in the wholly popular comedy. Though resting on material accumulated during previous centuries, the known works of the comic poets belong almost wholly to the one hundred and fifty years preceding the Pléiade. They are divided into quite distinct categories. — The *moralité* forms the connecting link between the sacred and profane theater. It differed from the former in that its facts are imaginary and belong to domestic life. But it is essentially didactic and often allegorical. Historical moralities were also attempted, and at times a satirical tone brought them near the *farce*. Of the sixty-five preserved the greater part assail vice and preach virtue, as *Bien-avisé, mal-avisé, Charité, Enfants de maintenant* (spoiled by their indulgent parents) and the *Assomption de Notre-*

Dame. A more worldly moral is found in the *Condamnation des banquets* (1507), by NICOLAS DE LA CHESNAYE, full of comic details. A historical *moralité* which, like the miracles, could have been developed into true drama, is the *Empereur qui tua son neveu.* Among the authors are ANDRÉ DE LA VIGNE and PIERRE GRINGORE. — The *farce,* the oldest and the traditional form of comedy, is reinforced in this period by dramatizing the fableaux. Some one hundred and fifty are known, of which the *Cuvier* (where a hen-pecked husband takes his revenge) and the *Savetier Calbain* (an imitation of *Pathelin,* where husband and wife reply to each other in well-known songs) are comic, but devoid of the coarse elements which often disfigure the farce. — The masterpiece of the kind, and of French comedy previous to MOLIÈRE, is *Pathelin* (a. 1470). A genuine farce of the traditional polyglot type, the subject is that of a seedy lawyer who outwits a rascally tailor, but is himself beaten in cunning by a loutish shepherd, whom the tailor sues and who employs Pathelin as counsel. The success of this little play was so general that its title has passed into the language as a synonym for cajolery. — The *sottie* is a farce played by the *Sots,* sometimes a mere *fatrasie,* as the *Menus propos.* — The *sermon joyeux* began in the *Fête des fous* and is a parody on a sermon, retaining at its head the text in a turned sense, and imitating the scholastic divisions of the pulpit. Some twenty remain, wanton and irreverent to the highest degree, as *Bien boire.* — The *monologue* is a burlesque recital (a dramatized *dit*) of the vices and foibles of the speaker. About a score remain, the hero of which is invariably a lover, a braggart soldier, or a charlatan. The best known are the *Franc archer de Bagnolet* (a. 1470), a braggart frightened by a scare-crow, much imitated, and the *Grands et merveilleux faits de Nemo*, from a Latin sermon on Saint Nemo, due in turn to the jest of Ulysses in the *Odyssey*.

10. **Actors of Comedy**: *Basoche; Enfants sans souci; Sots*. **Authors**: HENRI BAUDE, a. 1430-1486-; PIERRE BLANCHET, 1459-1519; ANDRÉ DE LA VIGNE; PIERRE GRINGORE, a. 1475-1527. — The comic actors who succeed or perhaps rival the Puis formed in the fifteenth century regular corporations. Besides the various fraternities the *Basoche*, composed of clerks of the Parliament of Paris, and which claimed to date from 1303, and various other associations in Paris and other cities (called likewise *Basoches*), played farces and moralities, and later united with the *Confrérie de la Passion* in Trinity Hospital. — The *Enfants sans souci* were the successors probably of the church *Fous*, known also as *Sots*, who dressed in green and yellow. — Of the authors known, besides writers of monologues, like COQUILLART, or of moralities, like CHASTELLAIN, HENRI BAUDE (a. 1430-1486-), of Moulins, wrote for the Basoche of Paris, and PIERRE BLANCHET (1459-1519), of Poitiers, attained celebrity by his satires. — ANDRÉ DE LA VIGNE († 1527), secretary of Anne of Brittany, wrote the mystery of *Saint Martin* (1496), several *moralités*, and the *Complaintes et épitaphes du roi de la Basoche* (1504). — The most celebrated is PIERRE GRINGORE (a. 1475-1527-), a member of the *Enfants sans souci* and a didactic writer. Louis XII., who encouraged the drama and wished to make it a weapon against the pope, persuaded GRINGORE to write political

plays as well as to undertake festival pieces. Among moralities, farces, mysteries, *sotties* and poems of various kinds, is the trilogy of 1512, consisting of a *cri*, a *sottie* and a *moralité* (*Homme obstiné*), in favor of the king's warfare against the pope. The *Mystère de Saint-Louis* (a. 1514) is in pure and sober style. His last work is the *Notables enseignements* (1527).

11. **Prose Works: Chronicles, Diaries, and Memoirs;** PIERRE COCHON, † a. 1451; GEORGES CHASTELLAIN, a. 1415-1475; OLIVIER DE LA MARCHE, a. 1426-1502; JEAN LE MAIRE DE BELGES, a. 1473-1524?—After drama the great development of this period is in prose, through which many neologisms entered into the language. Chronicles were continued, as that of the *Mont Saint-Michel* (1343-1468), which dealt principally with the events of the Hundred Years' War. — PIERRE COCHON (1406-1451-), of Fontaine-le-Dun, used as sources for his chronicle (beginning in 1108) the *Récits de Reims* and his own observations. — GEORGES CHASTELLAIN wrote various political pamphlets, a funeral oration on Philip the Good, and a treatise of consolation, the *Temple de Boccace*, addressed to Margaret of Anjou. He undertook, in minute detail, the history of Philip and Charles the Bold (1419-1474), found in over one hundred manuscripts. Its effect on the literature of the time was great. Impartial, energetic in style, striving to mingle with his narrative reflections and judgments, he enriched the vernacular by a study of the ancients and endeavored to give the language color and breadth by varying its turns and expressions. His great trait is observation. He shows already Italian influence and transmits it to JEAN LE MAIRE. —

The latter, in his *Illustrations des Gaules* (1509–1512), fused the *Roman de Troie* (translated in 1464 from GUIDO COLONNA by RAOUL LE FÈVRE, chaplain of Philip) with various other traditions and inventions, thus forming a mixture of chronicle and epic poem. It is an attempt to compromise between the old legends and the rising spirit of classicism. LE MAIRE, in his erudite and simple language, gave new words and a poetical prose to the writers who followed him, and was cited as authority by the Pléiade. — OLIVIER DE LA MARCHE (a. 1426–1502), steward of Charles the Bold, wrote *Mémoires* (1435–1489) imitating CHASTELLAIN. — Diaries full of interesting details on the life of the time are seen in the *Journal d'un bourgeois de Paris* (1405–1449) and the *Chronique scandaleuse* (1460–1483), by DENIS HESSELIN.

12. **History.** — PHILIPPE DE COMINES (a. 1445–1511), of Burgundy, and later a French diplomat, writes philosophical history (already foreshadowed in CHASTELLAIN) in his *Mémoires*. These include the reign of Louis XI. and the Italian expedition of Charles VIII. They are the observations of a man of experience, who seeks in events causes and results. Their tone is practical, positive, but somewhat sad.

13. **Treatises; Sermons.** — Interesting from a literary standpoint is the *Poétique* (1432) of BAUDET HERENC, based on an anonymous work of 1415. — The *Débat des hérauts de France et d'Angleterre* (1453–1461) is a comparison of the pleasure, prowess and fertility of the two countries; answered later by JOHN COKE. — ROBERT DE BALSAC († a. 1503), seneschal of Agenais, wrote the *Nef des batailles*, a military treatise, and the *Chemin de*

l'hôpital, a moral satire. — **Translators** are numerous. CLAUDE DE SEYSSEL (1450–1520), archbishop of Turin, translated Greek authors into French, perhaps from the Latin. He also wrote a *Histoire singulière* (1508) of Louis XII. — The **sermons** of the time, as those of OLIVIER MAILLART († 1502), JEAN RAULIN († 1514), and MICHEL MENOT († 1518), are original, lively, but coarse. They assail the higher clergy, the nobility and magistrates in the language of the populace.

14. **Fiction: Prose Versions of the Epic Poems;** JEAN WAUQUELIN, † **1453.** — Like historical writing, the prose fiction of the time centered around the Burgundian court. The chief movement was the rendering of the old epic into prose. *Roland* and the *Pèlerinage de Charlemagne* went into popular form under the title of *Galien le Rétoré* or *Guerin de Monglane,* the latter a sequel of the cycle. — JEAN WAUQUELIN († 1453) wrote, for Philip the Good, *Girard de Roussillon* (1447) and the *Histoire du roi Alexandre,* introducing into both foreign elements. — The prose version of *Huon de Bordeaux* dates from 1454. — The Crusade cycle was worked over between 1465 and 1475 for Mary of Cleves, and in 1499 for Louis XII. The other chap books founded on the epic date from this period, as, in 1475, *Fierabras* and *Doon de Mayence.* — Stories evidently taken from the *romans d'aventure* abound, as *Pierre de Provence,* which resembles, in the episode of a ring stolen by a hawk, the poem *Escoufle;* and *Jean de Paris,* who wins the heroine wooed by the king of England, resembling *Jean de Dammartin.*

15. ANTOINE DE LA SALLE (1398–1462–), of Burgundy, is the great writer of fiction before RABELAIS.

His *Salade* (1445), dedicated to Jean d'Anjou, is a treatise on morals and ceremonies. The *Quinze joies de mariage* (b. 1448) is a satire on matrimony. The *Petit Jean de Saintré* (1459), addressed to Jean d'Anjou, is a didactic narrative presenting the rules of chivalry and also satirizing them. Another moral treatise (1461) precedes the *Cent Nouvelles nouvelles*, a hundred anecdotes taken from the fableaux, from BOCCACCIO and from POGGIO. Grace and sentiment are rarely found amidst the coarseness, but the style, clear and concise, is the best of the age. From this compilation, typical of the time, descend the *gaulois* stories of French literature.

PART III.

RENAISSANCE LITERATURE. 1515–1601.

CHAPTER IX.

FIRST PERIOD. 1515–1549.

1. **Poetry.** ALIONE D'ASTI, a. 1450–a. 1525; JEAN BOUCHET, 1476–1555; CLÉMENT MAROT, a. 1497–1544; MARGARET OF NAVARRE, 1492–1549; MELLIN DE SAINT-GELAIS, 1487–1558.
2. **Drama.** JEAN DU PONTALAIS, –1512–1535–; JEAN LOUVET, –1536–1550–; *Sotties de Genève*, 1523–1524. *Théologastres*, 1523–1529; Italian comedy.
3. **Prose.** Translators: LEFÈVRE D'ÉTAPLES, 1455–1537; ÉTIENNE DOLET, 1509–1546. History and memoirs: *Loyal serviteur*, 1527; JEAN BOUCHET. Treatises: JEAN CALVIN, 1509–1564. Fiction: FRANÇOIS RABELAIS, a. 1495–a. 1553; JEAN BONAVENTURE DES PÉRIERS, a. 1500–a. 1544; NOËL DU FAIL, a. 1520–1591; MARGARET OF NAVARRE; *Amadis des Gaules*, 1540–1548. Language: LOUIS MEIGRET, 1545–1550.

1. **Characteristics of the Sixteenth Century in Language and Literature; Division into Periods.** — The distinctive features of French thought in the sixteenth century are due to the revival of classical learning and the reform in religion. By the middle of the fifteenth century Greek teachers were at Paris. They were fol-

lowed before 1470 by German printers. These influences favored and strengthened the tendencies seen in the translators under Charles V. and in the subjects of Philip the Good. But it was not until the Italian expedition of Charles VIII. (1494) and the wars which ensued, that the mass of the nation became aware of the new birth beyond the Alps. French art and architecture were affected before the literature. The reign of Francis I. (1515) first sees a change in spirit, and in 1549, with the manifesto of the Pléiade by Du Bellay, the poetical form is changed. — The prose of the time, didactic and controversial, is inspired rather by the Reformation. — The language of the sixteenth century writers shows the uncertain, revolutionary condition of the country. That of the first half of the century is markedly different from the second half. Until the second manner of Malherbe (1601) there was no literary standard. — The vocabulary, for the most part modern, still retained many words now rejected or known only in restricted meaning. The Latinizing bent already noted took on greater proportions. The residence of Italians at the court of Francis I. and the later alliance with the Medicis brought in many new terms of art, court, pleasure, or war. The wars with Spain and the Spanish support of the League likewise affected the language. The Pléiade sought after new compounds and derivatives, especially diminutives. — The orthography was subjected to the theories of both the etymological and the phonetic schools. The former, known already in the previous century, loaded the words down with letters that had been dropped, changed, or had never existed. Ultimately the pronunciation became affected by this increase of signs. The phonetic school, defeated on the whole, was still able to introduce the cedilla from the Spanish, to distinguish between *i* and *j* and *u* and *v*, as well as to bring about the use of accents. — The syntax shows the same state of transition. The analytical structure gradually prevails and inversion becomes less frequent. — Literature is sharply divided about the middle of the century into two periods. In the first (1515-1549) the mediæval elements slowly disappear under the combined pressure of the Renaissance and the Reform. In the second (1549-1601) the new spirit assumes new forms.

2. **Poetry from 1515 to 1549; Old School;** ALIONE D'ASTI; JEAN BOUCHET, **1476-1555**; ROGER DE COLLERYE, -1494-1538-. — The reign of Francis I. (1515-1547) sees the gradual extinction of mediæval poetry, though the traditions of the rhetorical school of CHASTELLAIN and CRETIN still survive. — GIANGIORGIO ALIONE (a. 1450-a. 1525), of Asti, adopted often in his French poems the Italian octave and terzarima. His political and religious works show imitation of MOLINET. His lighter verse and songs have a pleasing vein of satire and are delicate in expression. — JEAN BOUCHET (1476-1555), of Poitiers, writes in the rhetorical style of pedantic allegory and complicated verse. His *Renards traversant les périlleuses voies* (1500) received the honors of a Dutch translation, which penetrated later into Germany. He is also the author of various chronicles, after LE MAIRE, of which the *Annales d'Aquitaine* (1531) is the best. He is noted for his care in alternating mascu-

line and feminine rimes. — ROGER DE COLLERYE (–1494–1538–), of Auxerre, is a disciple of COQUILLART, but also shows the influence of GRINGORE and CLÉMENT MAROT. Besides various *monologues* he wrote satirical and gay poetry, belonged perhaps to the *Sots*, and personified the popular type of *Roger Bontemps*.

3. **The Transition**; CLÉMENT MAROT, a. 1497–1544. — The favorite poet of Francis I., CLÉMENT MAROT (a. 1497–1544), of Cahors, son of JEAN, shows in his work the successive changes of the age. A member of the *Basoche*, his first poems, collected in the *Adolescence Clémentine* (1532), are in the old style of MOLINET and CRETIN, though refined somewhat by the influence of the court. From 1526 to 1536, persecuted as a supposed heretic, in prison and in exile at Ferrara, his talent is developed and his taste elevated. To this decade belong his best works: *Enfer* (1526), a satire on the Châtelet prison in decasyllabic verse, epistles to Francis I., an eclogue on the death of Louise of Savoy (1531), epigrams, dizains, and ballades. He revived the *blason* (a descriptive octosyllabic strophe) and the *fatrasie*, which he termed *coq-à-l'âne* and made satirical. All these pieces are notable for their wit, grace, and simplicity. During the same time he edited the *Roman de la Rose* (1527), revising the language, and also the works of VILLON (1533). On his return from exile in 1536 he was assailed by a poet of the old school, SAGON, a devout Roman Catholic, and a literary war ensued. His last work of importance was the translation of the first fifty Psalms, condemned by the Sorbonne (1543), and adopted by the Protestants. The spirit of MAROT is essentially *gaulois*.

His predecessor was VILLON, a follower is LA FONTAINE. His light and fickle character was steadied by the revival of classical learning, as is seen in his translations. He is keen and gay, simple and urbane. His style is easy and his verse elegantly turned. A master of the epigram, he had not sufficient feeling for the elegy. His epistles are models and have consecrated the style known as Marotic. As a versifier he succeeds best with the decasyllable.

4. **Imitators of** MAROT: MARGARET OF NAVARRE, 1492–1549; MELLIN DE SAINT-GELAIS, 1487–1558; the **Sonnet.** — All of the poets of the second quarter of the sixteenth century, who had freed themselves from the mannerisms of the rhetorical school, were followers of MAROT. — Among them his protectress, MARGARET OF NAVARRE (1492–1549), wrote farces, mysteries, epistles, *complaintes,* religious lyrics and other poems, published in 1547 under the title of *Marguerites de la Marguerite.* They are not without force and poetical merit. — The most noted disciple of MAROT, and the poet in vogue from his death to the time of the Pléiade, is MELLIN DE SAINT-GELAIS (1487–1558), son of OCTAVIEN, and almoner at the court. He had studied in Italy, and had come under the influence of its poets, especially of PETRARCH. He was the literary purveyor of the court amusements in his rondeaux, quatrains, and poetical masquerades, but is best known for his connection with Italian literature. He translated TRISSINO's *Sophonisba* (1554) into prose, and imitated BOCCACCIO and ARIOSTO. — SAINT-GELAIS is reputed also to have introduced the **sonnet** into France. ANDRÉ DE LA VIGNE († 1527) left

among his poems a sonnet which attempts the dialect of Lombardy, and CLÉMENT MAROT wrote sonnets in pure French (1529).

5. **Last Works of the Mediæval Drama**: JEAN LOUVET, -1536-1550-; JEAN DU PONTALAIS, -1512-1535-; Sotties; Foreign and Classical Productions. — The reign of Francis I. no longer tolerated the free dramatic movement of Louis XII. To the despotic character of the king was soon added the reaction against the representation of sacred subjects, which grew out of the attacks of the Protestants. — Yet **mysteries** were written, as those of MARGARET and the twelve mysteries of *Notre Dame de Liesse* (1536-1550), by JEAN LOUVET, which are miracles of the Virgin composed in a wholly devout spirit. — The old plays remained popular. The *Actes des Apôtres* were given seven months (1540-1541), and Parliament (1548) was obliged to forbid the *Confrérie de la Passion*, at the Hôtel de Bourgogne, to further represent sacred subjects. This was the official end of the old dramas, though they were still played in the provinces. — The **comedy** of the time was centered in an actor of renown, JEAN DU PONTALAIS (DE L'ESPINE), an *Enfant sans souci*. He played in various pieces from 1512, became director of public shows at Paris (1530), and is mentioned by the authors of the next decade. A work in prose and verse attributed to him, the *Contredits de Songe-creux* (1531), is a review of society, with sarcastic observations. — Certain *sotties* of this time are noteworthy, as those played at Geneva in 1523 and 1524, of a political character, and in the second of which occurs the word *huguenot*, applied to the enemies of the duke

of Savoy. — The way in which religious partisans seized on the stage as a means of propaganda is illustrated by the farce, *Théologastres* (1523-1529), against the Romanists of the Sorbonne. — While the popular drama still held its own the works of classical antiquity began to come in favor among the educated. Latin plays, those of PLAUTUS and TERENCE especially, were given in the schools. LAZARE DE BAÏF translates the *Electra* (1537) of SOPHOCLES, and CHARLES ESTIENNE the *Andria* (1542) of TERENCE. Many others followed. — Italian plays were brought to France by refugees, as ALAMANNI, and Italian courtiers. The *Calandra* of BIBBIENA was performed at Lyons in 1548 to welcome Catherine de' Medici. — BUCHANAN writes Latin tragedies at Bordeaux (1540), as does also MURET.

6. **Prose Translations**: LEFÈVRE D'ÉTAPLES, **1455-1537**; ÉTIENNE DOLET, **1509-1546**. **Historical Works**; MARGARET OF NAVARRE. — Translations from classical literature increased greatly in this period. — JACQUES LEFÈVRE (a. 1455-1537), of Étaples, an ardent student of Greek authors, translated the Gospels (1523) and the entire Bible (1528-1530). His work aided the Reform. — ÉTIENNE DOLET (1509-1546), printer at Lyons, a celebrated humanist, renders into French various books of CICERO and PLATO. — The latter author is the object of many other versions, as are also ARISTOTLE and XENOPHON. — Greek poetry, as the *Iliad* (1545) and the dramatists, was also rendered into the vernacular. — **Historical works** and chronicles are of but slight value. Two biographies of Bayard — of which the anonymous *Loyal serviteur* (1527) is interesting on account of its simplic-

ity — and a few memoirs, particularly those by MARGARET OF NAVARRE (who also left many letters), are worthy of mention.

7. **Doctrinal Works**: JEAN CALVIN, 1509-1564. — The Reformation has absolute influence on the doctrinal works of the time. It not only changed their spirit, but, in appealing directly to the people, it also substituted the vernacular for the Latin. The first theological treatise in French, and the first classical French prose, is the *Institution de la religion chrétienne*, of JEAN CALVIN (CAUVIN), of Noyon. The persecutions of heretics by Francis I. in 1535 called out a letter from CALVIN to the king, and in 1536 he published, at Basel, the *Institutio religionis christianæ*, which he translated into French in 1541. This exposition of the doctrines of the Reformation, in four books, retained in the French the constructions of the Latin original, though the language is not Latinized. In style it is logical, sober, and precise; but also sad, bitter, and sometimes stiff. The self-contained eloquence of CALVIN is seen in his other dogmatic writings, in his sermons and satirical pamphlets, and is known as the *refugee* style.

8. **Fiction**: FRANÇOIS RABELAIS, a. 1495-a. 1553. — The other notable authors of the period show rather a mixture of classical antiquity and free-thinking. — These elements, combined with the *gaulois* vein of the *Cent Nouvelles nouvelles*, and with the epic romances, are seen in FRANÇOIS RABELAIS (a. 1495-a. 1553), of Chinon, a restless monk and physician. His first works seem to have been editions of GALEN and HIPPOCRATES. These were soon followed by a revised edition of a chap-book,

the *Chroniques gargantuines* (1532), and the first book of *Pantagruel* (1533) (the name of one of the devils in the *Actes des Apôtres*). In 1535 he published the *Gargantua*, suggested by the romance, in 1546 the second book of *Pantagruel*, in 1552 the third, while the fourth, posthumous (1564), is possibly from notes left by RABELAIS. The *Gargantua* served as introduction to *Pantagruel*. The whole is a satire on the beliefs and superstitions of the age, under the cover of a burlesque narrative. Exaggerated descriptions, macaronic language, incoherent composition, coarse buffoonery, now jovial, now sarcastic, allow nevertheless ample room for the display of philosophic thought, for the delineation of character, and even, at rare intervals, for the use of a rich, colored, and precise style. One of the most original features of *Pantagruel* is the part devoted to the education of Gargantua. A union of bodily and mental exercise, hitherto kept apart by the system of mediæval education, is enjoined. Strict observation of the laws of hygiene, daily practice in all kinds of athletics, out-door lessons in astronomy, instruction derived from the amusements themselves, are joined to the scholastic demands for the vast acquisition of book-knowledge. — Besides *Pantagruel*, RABELAIS is the author of a series of almanacs written in the same vein.

9. **Story Writers**: NICOLAS OF TROYES; JEAN BONAVENTURE DES PÉRIERS, a. 1500–a. 1544; MARGARET OF NAVARRE; NOËL DU FAIL, a. 1520–1591. — The *Pantagruel* had various imitations and parodies of little value, but its influence is seen on several prominent authors of the time, who, in the main, followed the *Cent Nouvelles nouvelles*. — An exception, however, is NICOLAS, a sadler

of Troyes, the author of the *Grand parangon des Nouvelles nouvelles* (1535), composed of stories taken from Boccaccio, from a French translation of the *Gesta Romanorum*, and from heresay. His style is popular, simple, and clear. — JEAN BONAVENTURE DES PÉRIERS (a. 1500–a. 1544), secretary of Margaret of Navarre, a humanist of note, who translated the *Lysis* of PLATO and aided DOLET and LEFÈVRE, published the *Cymbalum Mundi* (1537), imitated from LUCIAN, a violent attack on the Gospels, which scandalized both Catholics and Protestants. His *Nouvelles récréations et joyeux devis* (one hundred and twenty-nine tales) were published in 1558. They come rather from the French farces and fableaux, and show a remarkable style, half-literary, half-popular. — MARGARET OF NAVARRE is best known for her *Contes*, or *Heptameron* (1558), a collection of seventy-two tales (modeled on the *Decameron*), which introduce long conversations on morals and gallantry. — The greater part of the stories of NOËL DU FAIL (a. 1520–1591), a magistrate of Rennes, belong to this period. His *Propos rustiques et facétieux* (1547) is a realistic report of conversations among peasants. The *Baliverneries*, or *Contes nouveaux d'Eutrapel* (1548), describe likewise country life and Breton manners, in which the author (Eutrapel) appears. The third collection, the *Contes et discours d'Eutrapel* (1585), is a succession of satirical dialogues between three persons on the life of the time. The influence of RABELAIS is evident.

10. **Romances of Chivalry.** — The sixteenth century witnessed in France the beginnings of the modern novel. The romances of chivalry, which had slowly and obscure-

ly developed from the epic prose romances or the *romans d'aventure*, appeared in the *Amadis des Gaules* (1540–1548), translated from MONTALVO and his successors by HERBERAY DES ESSARTS († a. 1550), for Francis I. Its success attracted sequels until, by 1625, it had grown, in France, from eight to twenty-five books. Its characteristics are knightly adventures, courtly conversations, love and the supernatural. These entered into the later novels.

11. **Treatises on Language and Grammar.** — The study of the vernacular is seen in the *Champ-fleuri* (1529) of GEOFFREI TORY, the printer, who introduced the cedilla from the Spanish. — The work (1530) of PALSGRAVE was unknown to France. — JACQUES DUBOIS (SYLVIUS) published in Latin (1531) the first grammar of French. — ROBERT ESTIENNE edited (1539) a French-Latin lexicon. — LOUIS MEIGRET wrote a treatise on pronunciation (1545) and the first grammar (1550) in the vernacular. His reforms aroused much hostility. — THOMAS SIBILET (a. 1512–1589), a translator of Greek dramas, wrote an *Art poétique* (1548), based mainly on MAROT.

Renaissance Literature. 1515-1601.

CHAPTER X.

SECOND PERIOD. 1549-1601.

1. **Poetry.** The Pléiade: PIERRE DE RONSARD, 1524-1585; JOACHIM DU BELLAY, a. 1525-1560; REMY BELLEAU, 1528-1577; JEAN-ANTOINE DE BAÏF, 1532-1589. Disciples of the Pléiade: OLIVIER DE MAGNY, 1529-1561; LOUISE LABÉ, a. 1526-1566. Protestant followers: GUILLAUME DU BARTAS, a. 1544-1590; AGRIPPA D'AUBIGNÉ, 1552-1630. Later imitators: JEAN PASSERAT, 1534-1602; JEAN VAUQUELIN DE LA FRESNAYE, 1536-1606; PHILIPPE DESPORTES, 1546-1606; JEAN BERTAUT, 1552-1611. Popular songs: JEAN LE HOUX, a. 1545-1616.
2. **Drama.** Mysteries: THÉODORE DE BÈZE, 1519-1605. New School: ÉTIENNE JODELLE, 1532-1573; JACQUES GRÉVIN, a. 1540-1570; JEAN DE LA TAILLE, a. 1540-a. 1608; ROBERT GARNIER, 1545-1601. Italian comedy: PIERRE LARIVEY, a. 1540-1611.
3. **Prose.** Translations: JACQUES AMYOT, a. 1513-1593. History and memoirs: BLAISE DE MONLUC, a. 1502-1577; FRANÇOIS DE LA NOUE, 1531-1591; PIERRE DE BRANTÔME, a. 1540-1614; PIERRE DE L'ESTOILE, 1546-1611; LANCELOT DE LA POPELINIÈRE, a. 1540-1608; JACQUES-AUGUSTE DE THOU, 1553-1617. Political writings: JEAN BODIN, 1529-1596; ÉTIENNE DE LA BOÉTIE, 1530-1563; GUILLAUME DU VAIR, 1556-1621; *Satire Ménippée*, 1594. Treatises on arts and

sciences: BERNARD PALISSY, a. 1510-1589; AMBROISE PARÉ, a. 1510-1590; OLIVIER DE SERRES, 1539-1619. Essayists: MICHEL DE MONTAIGNE, 1533-1592; PIERRE CHARRON, 1541-1603. Language: HENRI ESTIENNE, 1531-1598; ÉTIENNE PASQUIER, 1529-1615; CLAUDE FAUCHET, 1530-1601.

1. Adoption of Classic Models in Poetry and Drama; Work of the Pléiade. — The second period of Renaissance literature, from the manifesto of DU BELLAY in 1549 to the second manner of MALHERBE in 1601, sees an almost complete rupture with the literature of the past centuries. Not only are the forms of expression changed by the imitation of classic models, but the authors of this period ignore disdainfully their predecessors. The prevailing spirit in both prose and poetry is classicism. The drama is wholly remodeled and, while mediæval comedy survives in the new dress, the mystery is rejected for the tragedy of SENECA. — The influence of the Reformation is also evident in the thought of many writers, both Catholic and Protestant. — The linguistic treatises are directed against the invasion of Italian words and constructions. — The center of the classical movement is in a company of scholars at the Coqueret college in Paris, called after their Greek prototypes of the court of the Ptolemies, the *Pléiade*. Under the guidance of the humanist, JEAN DAURAT or DINEMANDY (a. 1508-1588), himself a writer of Greek, Latin and French poetry, PIERRE DE RONSARD, JEAN-ANTOINE DE BAÏF and REMY BELLEAU gave themselves up, the first from 1541, to the study of antiquity. In 1548 JOACHIM DU BELLAY joined them, and later ÉTIENNE JODELLE and PONTUS DE THYARD. Comparing the literature of Greece and

Rome with that of France (with MAROT especially), they conceived the notion of improving poetry and drama in four principal ways: first, in creating a poetical language distinct from that of prose; second, in bringing into French literature the kinds of composition which it lacked, as tragedy, comedy, epic poetry, and the ode; third, in enriching the versification with sonorous and striking rimes; fourth, in introducing ancient mythology into poetry. DU BELLAY presented these views in a pamphlet of some six-score pages, the *Défense et illustration de la langue française* (1549), but two months after the edict of Parliament against the mysteries. The *Défense* has three chief ideas: love for the French language, contempt for previous French poetry, intense admiration for classical literature. The motto of the school as expressed by DU BELLAY is: Enrich the French with the spoils of the ancients.

2. **The Poets of the Pléiade**: PIERRE DE RONSARD, 1524–1585. — The lyric impulse was given to the Pléiade by its leader, PIERRE DE RONSARD (1524–1585), of Vendôme. He followed up the *Défense* with a volume of odes (1550), modeled on PINDAR and HORACE, which had immediate success, rallied to him the contemporary poets of the old school, and made him for forty years poetical dictator. The imitation of PINDAR was too severe for RONSARD, and the *Amours de Cassandre* (1552), sonnets after PETRARCH with a strong element of mythology, shows in its various editions a more popular style. RONSARD united his poems in an edition (1560) for Mary Stuart. From 1561 to 1574 he is court poet after the manner of MAROT and SAINT-GELAIS. At the

same time the troubles of the age inspire in him true poetry, as the *Discours des misères du temps* (1562), directed against the Protestants. Yielding to the demand for epic poetry, general at the time, he published four cantos of the *Franciade* (1572), in decasyllabic verse, based on the *Illustrations* of LE MAIRE. It proved a failure and was not continued. His last poems, in retirement, sing the praises of nature in melancholy strains. The merit of RONSARD lies in his style. In the Horatian ode, as his *Mignonne, allons voir si la rose*, in the elegy, into which he introduced songs and even dialogues, in the epigram and in certain of his six hundred sonnets, as the *Sonnets à Hélène*, he unites to graceful expression harmonious verse and original rhythm. He especially excels in the management of the alexandrine. But in the higher poetry inspiration fails him. There was no passion in the school.

3. **Companions of** RONSARD: JOACHIM DU BELLAY, a. **1525-1560**; REMY BELLEAU, **1528-1577**; JEAN-ANTOINE DE BAÏF, **1532-1589**; PONTUS DE THYARD, a. **1521-1603**. — The associates of RONSARD are his inferiors as poets. — JOACHIM DU BELLAY (a. 1525-1560) is best known for his *Défense*. In lyric poetry he gave the sonnet of PETRARCH its fashion. He began with odes and sonnets, *Olive* (1549). The collection contains the *Musagnœomachie*, a mythological allegory in the old style. These poems, correct, simple, but without originality, yield in merit to the *Antiquités de Rome* (1558), a collection of sonnets inspired by the sight of its ruins (translated by SPENSER in 1591), the first of the kind. The *Regrets* (1559), occasioned by disgust for the papacy

and longing for France, are also sonnets, many satirical, the liveliness, force, and ease of which render them his best series. Of a different type but of equal charm are his *Jeux rustiques* (1558), imitated from NAVAGERO, and the *Poète courtisan*, a genuine satire. To his dainty simplicity of style he joined in his later pieces true personal emotion and unstudied elegance.—REMI BELLEAU (1528–1577), of Nogent-le-Rotrou, turned his attention to nature and descriptive poetry. His *Petites inventions* (1557) are descriptions of objects, with moral allegory and mythological tales. He also translated ANACREON (1557). The *Bergeries* (1565, 1572) are a collection of odes, sonnets, hymns, and other verse set in prose dialogues after the style of the *Arcadia* of SANNAZARO. His best and most original work is the *Pierres précieuses* (1566), a description of thirty-one stones, based on Greek poetry of the decadence (*Orpheus*), and on MARBODIUS. Other productions are commentaries on RONSARD's *Amours de Marie* (1557), eclogues from *Solomon's Song* and *Job*, macaronic poetry on the Huguenots, and a posthumous comedy, the *Reconnue* (1562). The qualities of BELLEAU are those of a poetical painter. His two best poems are *Avril of the Bergeries* and the *Pierre aqueuse*.—JEAN-ANTOINE DE BAÏF (1532–1589), son of LAZARE, began with the translation in quatrains of Latin distichs (1551), written for the tomb of Margaret of Navarre. Various collections of sonnets and love songs followed. The *Brave* (1567) is translated freely from the *Miles Gloriosus* of PLAUTUS. He also rendered into French the *Antigone* and the *Eunuchus*. The *Météores* (1567) were suggested by the

Georgics. About this time BAÏF conceived the notion of uniting poetry and music, and founded an Academy (1571). He also wished to introduce into French poetry the quantitative meter of the ancients and to simplify French orthography after the phonetic system of RAMUS. His *Étrennes* (1574) are phonetically printed, as is also his posthumous metrical translation of the *Psalms*, in rivalry of that of MAROT. His best work, the *Mimes* (1581), is a collection of fables, apologues and maxims, imitated with originality and poetical facility from THEOGNIS and HESIOD. The reputation of BAÏF is that of an innovator in versification. His facility renders his lines weak and his language incorrect. — The remaining lyric poet of the Pléiade, PONTUS DE THYARD (a. 1521–1603), bishop of Chalons, is rather its forerunner. The first book of his *Erreurs amoureuses* (1549), before the *Défense*, was followed by others, influenced by RONSARD. His verse is cold and stiff, though pure.

4. **Followers of the Pléiade**: OLIVIER DE MAGNY, **1529–1561**; LOUISE LABÉ, **a. 1526–1566**; MARC-CLAUDE DE BUTTET, † **a. 1584**; AMADIS JAMYN, **a. 1540–1593**. — Many versifiers crowded around the Pléiade. OLIVIER DE MAGNY (1529–1561), secretary of Henry II., writes sonnets and odes (1553–1559). Imagination, artistic form, and rhythm do not compensate for the absence of force and inspiration. — LOUISE LABÉ or CHARLY (a. 1526–1566), of Lyons, after a military career, became the center of a literary society and was celebrated by many poets of the time. Her works (1556) comprise elegies and sonnets, incorrect but ardent, and a prose comedy, the *Débat de la folie et de l'amour*, an allegory after the

old school. — MARC-CLAUDE DE BUTTET († a. 1584), official poet of Margaret of Savoy, published (1561) odes, sonnets, and epithalmia, of which the Sapphic odes are noted for the first attempt to combine rime with metrical rhythm. — AMADIS JAMYN (a. 1540-1593), the favorite pupil of RONSARD, translated the twelve last cantos of the *Iliad* and the first three of the *Odyssey* into alexandrines (1574), wrote a *Poème de la chasse* (1574) for Charles IX., and various odes, sonnets, elegies, and religious poems. His verse has movement and ease, but his thought is often coarse.

5. **The Protestant Poets.** — While the Pléiade is rather Pagan in spirit, the Reform furnishes the content to two followers and rivals of RONSARD. — GUILLAUME DE SALLUSTE DU BARTAS (a. 1540-1590), the warrior and diplomat, addressed to Jeanne d'Albret the epic poem, *Judith* (1573), in which the Catholics saw an apology for regicide. The *Semaine* (1579), an epic in seven cantos on the Creation containing the scientific learning of DU BARTAS, derived mainly from PLINY, passed through thirty editions in six years. Translated, it influenced MILTON, MOORE and BYRON, and is the original of the *Sette Giornate* of TASSO. In the same vein are *Uranie*, a eulogy of poetry, the *Neuf Muses*, and the *Triomphe de la foi*, all poor. The merits of DU BARTAS are ardor, eloquence, and imagination. His defects are absence of art, of taste, and a rough and often barbarous style. He exaggerated beyond discretion the poetical reform of the Pléiade and compromised it by his derivatives and his word-building, especially in the formation of compounds.
— THÉODORE AGRIPPA D'AUBIGNÉ (1552-1630), attached

to Henry of Navarre, wrote masquerades, sonnets, stanzas on the death of JODELLE, and a tragedy, *Circé*. His early poetry, *Printemps* and *Hécatombe à Diane*, shows the disciple of RONSARD, but lacks good taste. The *Création* is a poor imitation of DU BARTAS. His best work is the *Tragiques, a poem in seven cantos* (1577–1594). The first three refer to the wars of the League, the last four to the persecutions. Their titles, *Misères, Princes, Chambre dorée, Feux, Fers, Vengeance, Jugement*, reveal their spirit. Force, imagination, abundance of images, fine verse, are side by side with obscurity of phrase, superfluity of details, repetition and painful effort. The influence of the *Tragiques* on VICTOR HUGO, notably on the *Châtiments*, is seen in the likeness of his style to that of D'AUBIGNÉ. The same merits and defects appear in the latter's religious pamphlets, in his *Mémoires* (1557–1618), *Histoire universelle* (1550–1601), and in a species of fiction, *Les aventures du baron de Fœneste* (1517–1520), a satirical dialogue on dogmatic questions with attacks on the vices of the time.

6. **Later Poets of the School:** JEAN PASSERAT, **1534–1602**; JEAN VAUQUELIN DE LA FRESNAYE, **1536–1606**; PHILIPPE DESPORTES, **1546–1606**; JEAN BERTAUT, **1552–1611.** — Less forcible and more graceful are the later followers of the Pléiade. — JEAN PASSERAT (1534–1602) is a poet of the *gaulois* tendency of VILLON and MAROT. His works (1606), consisting of sonnets, elegies, epigrams, songs, eclogues, and light verse, are gay, witty, and in good taste. The eclogue *Catin* and the villanelle, *J'ai perdu ma tourterelle*, have given him a lasting reputation. — JEAN VAUQUELIN DE LA FRESNAYE (1536–

1606), magistrate at Caen, a pupil of RONSARD and TAHUREAU, published the *Foresteries* (1555), idylls descriptive of Normandy. These were followed later by *Satires*, after HORACE, the first appearance in French of the type as a species of literature. Patriotic sonnets and epigrams followed, and an *Art poétique* (a. 1575), based on HORACE and ARISTOTLE, and enlarged by personal experience and literary knowledge. It formulates the doctrines of the Pléiade in a diffuse and incorrect style. — The last of the school, with both merits and defects less striking, is PHILIPPE DESPORTES (1546–1606), canon of the Sainte-Chapelle and a protector of letters. An imitator, often a translator of the ancients and Italians, he shows in his graceful and elegant verse the conceits of the latter. Besides amorous poetry, he wrote religious lyrics and translated the *Psalms*. His language is classical. — JEAN BERTAUT (1552–1611), bishop of Séez, wrote gallant and religious lyrics, in imitation of DESPORTES. Harmonious verse coupled often with true emotion are his qualities. — Another version of the *Psalms* (1613), by JEAN-BAPTISTE CHASSIGNET (a. 1568–a. 1620), of Besançon, a purely religious poet, is superior to either that of BERTAUT or DESPORTES. — With the reform of MALHERBE the school of the Pléiade falls into oblivion to revive with the Romantic movement. But the seventeenth-century nevertheless owed to it a poetical language and a pure and exact expression.

7. **Popular Poetry**: JEAN LE HOUX, a. 1545–1616; **Moral Quatrains**. — Apart from the literary school, the popular poetry continued in love songs, and especially in political songs, excited by the civil wars. — In Normandy

the traditions of OLIVIER BASSELIN resulted in the *Vaux de Vire* (a. 1570) of JEAN LE HOUX (a. 1545-1616), a lawyer of Vire, followed later by some Noëls and other *Vaux de Vire* (1611). — More artistic are the *Quatrains moraux*, collected for the education of youth. Their authors were GUY DU FAUR DE PIBRAC (1529-1584), a magistrate of Toulouse and a poet of merit; ANTOINE FAURE (1557-1624) of Savoy, father of VAUGELAS; and PIERRE MATHIEU (1563-1621), historiographer of Henry IV. Both of the latter followed PIBRAC.

8. **The Dramatic Movement; Survival of Mysteries and Mediæval Comedy;** THÉODORE DE BÈZE, **1519-1605; Theater of the Pléiade;** ÉTIENNE JODELLE, **1532-1573.** — The plan of the Pléiade included a reform of the theater through the imitation of classical models, either directly, or indirectly by means of Italian copies. — The edict of Parliament against the mysteries in 1548 applied only to Paris. In the provinces they continued to be played and even written, as *Abraham sacrifiant* (1551), by THÉODORE DE BÈZE (1519-1605), who is known also in French literature as the continuator of the *Psaumes* of MAROT, as the author of a *Vie de Calvin*, and of a *Histoire ecclésiastique des églises réformées* (1521-1563). — At Paris the *Confrérie de la Passion*, at the Hôtel de Bourgogne, acted profane mysteries and moralities until, weary of the struggle with rival companies, mainly Italian, which were favored by the king, they leased the theater (1588) to an Italian troupe. — To ÉTIENNE JODELLE (1532-1573), of Paris, was assigned the **dramatic work of the Pléiade.** RONSARD himself had translated and played the *Plutus* of ARIS-

TOPHANES, but original French tragedy and comedy, in regular form, date from the _Cléopâtre_ and the _Eugène_ of JODELLE, played (1552) at the Boncourt college, by the author and his friends. _Cléopâtre_, from PLUTARCH, is modeled on SENECA's Latin imitations of the Greek dramatists. Divided into five acts with choruses, unity of time and unity of action are observed. Rather lyric than dramatic, abounding in conversations and monologues, nothing of interest takes place on the stage. All is narrated or announced. But the parts are few in number, and a noble style is striven for. Instead of the irregular measures of the mysteries, decasyllabic verse or alexandrine is employed. The choruses in strophes show the alternation of masculine and feminine rimes. — While _Cléopâtre_ is an absolute break with preceding drama, _Eugène_ is only a farce in octosyllabic verse, but divided into acts and having a more polished versification. It shows the influence of the Italian comedies. The success of both plays was immediate and set the style for subsequent dramatic productions. A later tragedy of JODELLE, _Didon_, taken from the _Eneid_, is inferior to _Cléopâtre_, save in style and verse. The lines are all alexandrine, and masculine and feminine rimes alternate. JODELLE also wrote Latin and French poetry and court masquerades, as the _Argonautes_ (1558).

9. **Followers of** JODELLE **in Tragedy; Influence of** SENECA; JEAN DE LA PÉRUSE, a. 1530–1555; JACQUES GRÉVIN, a. 1540–1570; PIERRE MATHIEU, 1563–1621. — Imitators of JODELLE were not lacking among the educated, who in tragedy turned to his model, SENECA. The plays of the latter, in vogue in the schools from the

beginning of the fifteenth century, recommended themselves by their tragic crises, by their moral maxims, and by their lack of invention, of study of character, and of analysis of passion. The dramatic system of SENECA was formulated into law by the *Poetices libri* (1561) of JULES-CÉSAR SCALIGER, and was predominant for a century. — In this track followed JEAN DE LA PÉRUSE (a. 1530-1555), a lyric poet of mark, with *Médée* (1553), from SENECA. — JACQUES GRÉVIN (a. 1540-1570) wrote the *Trésorière* (1558), a comedy imitated from *Eugène*, and the *Esbahis* (1560), from a French version of an Italian original. His *Mort de César* (1560) is from the Latin of MURET, and shows an advance in dramatic interest. Among the poems of GRÉVIN is a hymn on the marriage of Mary Stuart. — Religious plays were written by PIERRE MATHIEU against the court, as *Esther* (1585) and *Aman*, He also produced the political dramas, *Clytemnestre* and the *Guisiade* (1589). — JEAN DE LA TAILLE (a. 1540-a. 1608), the author of the poem, the *Courtisan retiré*, and of the *blason*, the *Marguerite*, wrote religious tragedies, *Saül furieux* (1562) and the *Gabaonites* (1573), which contain fine scenes. He also tried Italian comedy in the *Negromante*, translated from ARIOSTO, and the *Corrivaux* (1562), both in prose, the latter of considerable merit.

10. ROBERT GARNIER, **1545-1601**. — The best dramatist of the sixteenth century is ROBERT GARNIER (1545-1601), a magistrate of Le Mans, and a poet of the *Jeux floraux*. His tragedies are: *Porcie* (1568), *Cornélie* (1574), from LUCAN and PLUTARCH; *Marc Antoine* (1578), the same subject as *Cléopâtre*, and three transla-

tions made freely from SENECA and from the Greek: *Hippolyte* (1573), the *Troade* (1578), and *Antigone* (1579). In all these imitations of antiquity GARNIER excels his predecessors in nobleness of diction and elegance of versification. He is a lyric poet rather than a dramatic. — His master-piece, *Sédécie* or the *Juives* (1583), a sacred tragedy on the taking of Jerusalem by Nebuchadnezzar, has genuine dramatic movement, tragic inspiration, and delineation of character, combined with a vigorous and graceful style. The last work of GARNIER, *Bradamante* (1580), a tragi-comedy from the *Orlando furioso*, shows less of SENECA's influence, and is the best of all in composition. The dialogue rids itself of moral reflections and directly advances the action. In *Bradamante* the *confidante* appears for the first time. GARNIER surpasses the poets of his time in style and details.

11. **Comedy after JODELLE; Farces; Italian Comedy; PIERRE LARIVEY, a. 1540–1611.** — While tragedy flourishes and expands in the last half of the sixteenth century, regular comedy has few adherents. Nearly all the poets of note translated comedies from the ancients or from the Italians, who themselves had adapted the outlines of PLAUTUS and TERENCE to modern life. Below the literary class, and possessing the public stage, was the old French farce, which eventually gave way to the comedy of masks, introduced by troupes of Italian comedians, and itself an outgrowth of the farce. — The Pléiade wrote its comedies in the old farce verse, as those by GRÉVIN, BAÏF, and BELLEAU. Prose came in under Italian influence, and the principal writer is of Italian descent. — PIERRE LARIVEY (a. 1540–a. 1611), canon at Troyes, devoted him-

self to translations of both literary plays and those of the comedy of masks, changing his originals freely to suit French taste (as in the suppression of the female parts), and introducing his own wit and gayety. Of his twelve plays in prose, nine are preserved. The best is the *Esprits* (1579), from the *Aridosio* of LORENZINO DE' MEDICI. The *Fidelle* (1611) had imitators. Possibly MOLIÈRE and REGNARD made use of LARIVEY. None of the latter's plays were acted. The farce in verse resisted successfully its prose rival.

12. **Prose; Translations;** JACQUES AMYOT, **1513-1593.**— The prose of the second half of the sixteenth century, apart from comedy, is the organ of translations, and of historical, scientific, and didactic writings as before. It also enters a new field in essays and linguistic treatises. — JACQUES AMYOT (1513-1593), bishop of Auxerre, began his career as a translator with *Théagène et Chariclée* (1546), from HELIODORUS. In 1554 he continued with seven books of DIODORUS of Sicily. In 1559 appeared *Daphnis et Chloé*, translated from LONGUS, and the *Vies des hommes illustres* of PLUTARCH, his best work. The *Œuvres morales* of PLUTARCH were published in 1574. Free in his rendering, the work of AMYOT has the freshness of an original production. His pure style, his full and flowing diction and his choice of words have made him a classical writer. The popularity which he gave to PLUTARCH, making it the favorite reading of youth, has had a strong and perhaps unfortunate influence on the political development of France.

13. **Memoirs:** BLAISE DE MONLUC, a. **1502-1577;** FRANÇOIS DE LA NOUE, **1531-1591;** PIERRE DE BRAN-

TÔME, a. 1540–1614; PIERRE DE L'ESTOILE, 1546–1611. Letters: HENRY IV., 1553–1610; DUPLESSIS-MORNAY, 1549–1623. — Beginning with the reign of Henry II. (1548), memoirs and biographies abound. — The warrior, BLAISE DE MONLUC (a. 1502–1577), writes his *Commentaires* (after 1570), memoirs with moral observations for young soldiers. Sincere, original, fiery, his style is simple and vigorous. — The Huguenot, FRANÇOIS DE LA NOUE (1531–1591), combines history, politics, and religion in his *Discours politiques et militaires*. Moderate and impartial, his style is lively and energetic. — PIERRE DE BOURDEILLES (a. 1540–1614), abbot of BRANTÔME, soldier and diplomat, writes (after 1584) his impressions of the people he had met. His *Vies des hommes illustres*, both foreigners and Frenchmen, *Vies des dames illustres*, *Vies des dames galantes*, and other works, are valuable, though not strictly true to history, nor marked by regard for morality. His colored and lively but incorrect style resembles his opinions. — To BRANTÔME are dedicated the *Mémoires* of MARGARET OF VALOIS (1553–1615) on the youth of Henry IV. — PIERRE DE L'ESTOILE (1546–1611), of Paris, wrote *Registres-journaux* (1574–1611) of everything which came to his notice, invaluable for the doings of the time. His style is easy and bright. — HENRY IV. (1553–1610) shows good style in his voluminous correspondence. — The same is true of DUPLESSIS-MORNAY (1549–1623), who also wrote didactic treatises, as *Discours sur la vie et la mort* (1575) and *Traité de la vérité de la religion chrétienne* (1581).

14. **History**: LANCELOT DE LA POPELINIÈRE, a. 1540–1608; AGRIPPA D'AUBIGNÉ; JACQUES-AUGUSTE DE THOU,

1553-1617. — Historians are less numerous. LANCELOT DE LA POPELINIÈRE (a. 1540-1608), a Calvinist, writes a *Histoire de France* (1581) from 1550 to 1577, and attempts to interweave also the history of Europe. Poor in style, he has a high historic ideal, and his painstaking and impartiality render his work of documentary value. — The *Histoire universelle* of D'AUBIGNÉ is factional in spirit and full of digressions. — DE THOU wrote in Latin the *Historia mei temporis* (1544-1607), a universal history, impartial and valuable. — Other authors of little merit attempt a complete history of France from its origins.

15. Political Treatises: JEAN BODIN, **1529-1596**; ÉTIENNE DE LA BOÉTIE, **1530-1563**; GUILLAUME DU VAIR, **1556-1621**; *Satire Ménippée,* **1594.** — Political science finds a representative in JEAN BODIN (1529-1596), procurator at Laon, who wrote the *République* (1578), in which an absolute monarchy is advocated. Clear and concise style, extensive learning, and exact views made his work celebrated. — The mass of the political treatises of the time are polemics. ÉTIENNE DE LA BOÉTIE (1530-1563), the friend of MONTAIGNE, besides various French and Latin poetry and translations from the Greek, wrote, under the influence of antiquity, the *Discours de la servitude volontaire,* or *Contre un* (1546-1548), an ardent pamphlet against tyranny. — GUILLAUME DU VAIR (1556-1621), magistrate and orator, is one of the best prose writers of the period. To his oration in defense of the Salic law (1593) he joined various essays of moral philosophy, as the *Sainte philosophie* and the *Philosophie morale des stoïques,* both remarkable for thought and expression. — The *Satire Ménippée* (1594) is the last effort of the civil wars and at the same time one of the masterpieces of the time. It is a political pamphlet in two parts. The first, a prologue, by PIERRE LEROY, canon of Rouen, introduces two charlatans, cardinals, who vaunt the "catholicon" of Spain. The second part is a parody on the States General of 1593, partly ironical, but mainly serious. NICOLAS RAPIN (1535–1608), a French and Latin poet, contributed to it harangues and epigrams; JEAN PASSERAT French and Latin epigrams; FLORENT CHRÉTIEN (1540–1596) a speech in macaronic Latin; PIERRE PITHOU (1539–1596) the *Harangue de M. d'Aubray*, the essential part of the *Ménippée;* and GILLES DURANT (1555–1615) certain verses. The *Ménippée* demands order, toleration, the lawful king. Its spirit is wholly of the third estate, against the ambitious nobility and the credulous populace. Its success killed the League. — MICHEL DE L'HOSPITAL (1504–1573) advocates toleration in several works, as the *But de la guerre et de la paix*, addressed to Charles IX. — FRANÇOIS HOTMAN in the *Franco-Gallia* (1573, translated 1574) argues, from Frankish history, for an elective monarchy and a States General where laborers and artisans replace the clergy. — The **sermons** of CALVIN and DE BÈZE are dogmatic. Those of JEAN BOUCHER (1548–1644) are virulent against the monarchy and in favor of a theocracy.

16. **Scientific Works and Treatises:** BERNARD PALISSY, a. 1510–1589; AMBROISE PARÉ, a. 1510–1590; OLIVIER DE SERRES, 1539–1619. — The rise of art and science is also represented in the literature of the time. — BERNARD

PALISSY (a. 1510-1589), the potter, in his *Recette véritable* (1563), a compilation of views on landscape gardening, chemistry and geology, with moral digressions and genial fancies; and in the *Discours admirables* (1580), a series of treatises in dialogue form on theory and practice, shows himself a writer of imagination and of noble thought, clear in style and pure in expression. — AMBROISE PARÉ (a. 1510-1590), the surgeon, is a writer of varying merit. His best work is an autobiography, *Apologie et voyages*. — OLIVIER DE SERRES (1539-1619), the agriculturist, gives his experience in the *Théâtre d'agriculture* (1600), a manual for farming, of which the order, technical exposition, and style, relieved by poetic fancy, have perpetuated the success.

17. **Treatises on Language; Grammars**: JACQUES PELLETIER; ROBERT ESTIENNE; RAMUS; HENRI ESTIENNE, **1531-1598**; ÉTIENNE PASQUIER, **1529-1615**; CLAUDE FAUCHET, **1530-1601**. — The grammars of JACQUES PELLETIER, the *Dialogue de l'orthographe et de la prononciation française* (1554), of ROBERT ESTIENNE, the *Traité de la grammaire française* (a. 1557), and of RAMUS (1572), distinguished by its system of phonetics, are best known. — Treatises on rhetoric were written for Henry III.; one by AMYOT, and one anonymous. The *Poetices libri* of SCALIGER is, however, the standard adopted by the University. — Resistance to the Italianizing of the language prompted the linguistic works of HENRI ESTIENNE (1531-1598), the great humanist and printer, who edited no less than a hundred and seventy editions of the classics, mainly Greek, and published, to his own financial ruin, the *Thesaurus graecae linguae* (1572). His writings in the

vernacular open with an attack on the Catholics, the *Apologie pour Hérodote* (1566), under the pretense of establishing the veracity of the Greek historian by comparing his tales with the events of the civil wars. Its licentious character displeased the Calvinists as well. The remaining treatises relate to the origin and worth of the French language. The *Traité de la conformité du français avec le grec* (1565?) assumes the latter to be the parent of the former. The *Deux dialogues du nouveau langage français italianisé* (1578) is an excessive satire against the Italianizing influence of the court. The *Projet: De la précellence de la langue française* (1579) affirms the inferiority of Italian. The style of ESTIENNE, vigorous and argumentative, availed in preserving French against foreign contamination. — ÉTIENNE PASQUIER (1529-1615), the advocate and author of letters, religious pamphlets, and French and Latin poetry, published the *Recherches de la France* (1560), a series of studies on the political, administrative, and literary history of the country. His observations on the language, literature, and versification of the sixteenth century are most important. The only oration of PASQUIER preserved, is the one against the Jesuits in favor of the University (1565). — CLAUDE FAUCHET (1530-1601), president of the chamber of moneys, and historiographer of Henry IV., created historical and literary criticism in France. The *Antiquités gauloises et françaises* (1579-1601), in two books, treat of the history of the Gauls and Franks down to 840. The *Recueil de l'origine de la langue et poésie française* (1581) establishes the derivation of French from the Latin (though he considers it mixed with Celtic), and gives literary notices and extracts from manuscripts of one hundred and twenty-seven French poets previous to 1300. FAUCHET had, unfortunately, no successors in the history of literature.

18. **The Essayists:** MICHEL DE MONTAIGNE, **1533-1592**; PIERRE CHARRON, **1541-1603**. — The philosophical movement of the sixteenth century is best seen in the essayists. — PIERRE DE LA RAMÉE, or RAMUS (1515-1572), the follower of PLATO, published a treatise on logic (1555), the first philosophical work in the vernacular. — A skeptic is MICHEL DE MONTAIGNE (1533-1592), counselor to the Parliament of Bordeaux, a writer imbued with classical learning and polished by travel. After a translation (1569) of the *Theologia naturalis* of SEBONDE, followed (1571) by an edition of the French and Latin poetry of LA BOÉTIE, MONTAIGNE published his *Essais* (1580-1588). These are a collection of observations and moral reflections, which form the history of MONTAIGNE's thoughts and opinions. Supported by copious quotations from classic writers, they show a deep knowledge of human nature, and a wide experience. Frank, familiar, attractive, written in an easy style which is rich, varied, personal, though somewhat provincial, the views propounded err on the side of over-uncertainty. His philosophy is wholly destructive. The nucleus of the *Essais* is a defense of the *Theologia naturalis*, an apology of Christianity from the standpoint of reason. The rule of conduct evolved is that of convenience. An interesting chapter of the *Essais* is that on education. Exercise should fortify the body, travel discipline the mind. Books enter in for little; observation and attention fur-

nish the greater part. The leading principle should be a sense of honor, and not duty. Accomplishments are desired rather than learning; a well-bred man rather than a scholar, as with RABELAIS. MONTAIGNE is also the author of a journal of travel in Germany, Switzerland, and Italy (1580–1581). — A disciple and imitator of MONTAIGNE is PIERRE CHARRON (1541–1603), a theologian, who wrote various dogmatic treatises, and also the *Traité de la sagesse* (1600), a manual of skepticism in fact, which borrows much from MONTAIGNE and DU VAIR. A portraiture of the weakness of man and of his incapacity for self-elevation, it logically develops the views of MONTAIGNE and poses a system of doubt.

19. **Fiction; Translations of Greek, Spanish, and Italian Novels.** — The style of the *Cent Nouvelles nouvelles* was continued in the *Contes du monde aventureux* (1555), from Italian and French sources, and by translations (1560, 1572, the latter by LARIVEY), of the *Piacevoli notti* of STRAPAROLA. — Many versions of Italian and Spanish novels supplemented the *Amadis* and the translations of Greek novels begun by AMYOT. The *Arcadia* of SANNAZARO, in 1544, the picaresco *Lazarillo de Tormes*, in 1561, the *Diana* of MONTEMAYOR, in 1578, and *Guzman de Alfarache*, in 1600, introduced both the ideal pastoral and the realistic novel into France. — Their many renderings, together with those of TASSO's *Aminta*, were closely imitated in the *Bergeries de Juliette* (1585–1598), a pastoral by NICOLAS DE MONTREUX, the author also of the sixteenth book of the *Amadis*.

PART IV.

The Seventeenth Century. 1601-1718.

CHAPTER XI.

FIRST PERIOD. 1601-1659.

1. **Poetry.** François de Malherbe, 1555-1628; Mathurin Régnier, 1573-1613; François de Maynard, 1582-1646; Honorat de Racan, 1589-1670; Théophile de Viau, 1590-1626; Saint-Amant, 1594-1661; Adam Billaut, † 1662; Jean Chapelain, 1595-1674; Vincent Voiture, 1598-1648; Guillaume Colletet, 1598-1659; Paul Scarron, 1610-1660.
2. **Drama.** Antoine de Monchrestien, 1575-1621; Alexandre Hardy, a. 1560-a. 1630; Jean de Schelandre, a. 1585-1635; Jean de Mairet, 1604-1683; Pierre Du Ryer, a. 1600-1658; Tristan l'Hermite, 1601-1655; Pierre Corneille, 1606-1684; Jean Rotrou, 1609-1650. Comedies.
3. **Prose.** Didactic works: Saint François de Sales, 1567-1622. Essays and letters: Jean-Louis Guez de Balzac, 1594-1654; Voiture; Gui Patin, 1601-1672. Philosophy: René Descartes, 1596-1650; Blaise Pascal, 1623-1662. History: François Eudes de Mézerai, 1610-1683. Language: Claude Favre de Vaugelas, 1585-1650. Fiction: *Moyen de parvenir*, 1612. Novels: Honoré D'Urfé, 1568-1625; Jean Barclay, 1582-1621; Jean-Pierre Camus, 1582-1652; Charles Sorel, 1599-1674; Gomberville, 1600-1674; La Calprenède, a. 1609-1663; Madeleine de Scudéry, 1608-1701; Cyrano de Bergerac, 1619-1655.

THE SEVENTEENTH CENTURY. 123

1. **The Century of Classical Literature; Characteristics; Division into Periods.** — The seventeenth century is considered by the French to be the period of classical literature. From the *Cid* of CORNEILLE, in 1636, to the *Athalie* of RACINE, in 1691, there followed a succession of masterpieces in prose and drama. Poetry, apart from plays in verse, did not share in this prosperity. Exhausted by the sudden bloom of the Pléiade, subjection to arbitrary rules hindered its revival. — The general characteristics of the literary productions from the second manner of MALHERBE (1601) to the *Œdipe* (1718) of VOLTAIRE are: order, or common sense, and logic, both due to the spirit of criticism, which succeeded the lawlessness of the preceding age. In literature, as well as in administration, the same principle prevailed, that of discipline and submission to authority. — For some time the conflict between measure and excess went on. The finical tendency of the first quarter of the century, reinforced by a strong Spanish influence on dress and manners, as well as on the drama and language, Gongorism, — brought directly or indirectly through the Italian conceits of MARINO — successfully resisted the reforms of MALHERBE, until Richelieu, victorious over political factions, gave his aid to absolutism in literature also. For a while the Fronde disturbed again the even flow of art, but the broad judgment and the good taste of Louis XIV. stimulated it again. — His errors in government, beginning with 1685, mark another era, that of decline and transition. — The three subdivisions of this century express both political and literary relations. — The first extends from 1601 to the second manner of MOLIÈRE in

1659. — The second, the Age of Louis XIV., from 1659 to the war against the Grand Alliance in 1689. — The third from 1689 to 1718.

2. **First Period: the Work of** MALHERBE, **1555-1628.**
— The literary movement from 1601 to 1659 is divided unequally in time, but not in production, by the representation of the *Cid* (1636). The years previous are years of conflict between the advocates of literary liberty and those of literary discipline. They also experienced the influence of the Hôtel de Rambouillet and saw the founding of the French Academy. — The center of the reform is FRANÇOIS DE MALHERBE (1555-1628), of Caen, court poet from 1605 to 1628, and also a translator and letter-writer. His first works, as the *Larmes de Saint Pierre* (1587), imitated from the Italian poet TANSILLO, have all the defects of the old school. With the *Stances à Du Perrier sur la mort de sa fille* (1601-1605) MALHERBE began his true career as a poet and a critic. His work applied both to language and versification. He reduced the first to order by establishing as standard the French of Paris, by rejecting all foreign infiltrations, and by demanding a sober and simple style. The ideal poem to him was the exact and forcible expression of a few orderly general ideas in the ordinary language, but with unusual harmony. In versification he forbade hiatus, overflow, demanded that the line be complete in itself, and that the cæsura follow the sense (in the alexandrine, after the sixth syllable). Easy and weak rimes he condemned. — Clear construction and good taste in expression, joined to a highly polished versification, proceeded from the criticisms of MALHERBE, but at the

same time vigor, fancy, and variety were seriously endangered. The work of the Pléiade was thus systematized and perpetuated. MALHERBE himself is at times a poet of high rank. In the harmony and finish of his verse French literature offers few equals. Yet the greater part of his work is monotonous and too abundant in mythological allusions. His followers without his talent observed his rules. Lyric poetry lingers painfully until the time of ANDRÉ CHÉNIER. It was prose which profited most by the critical spirit of MALHERBE.

3. **Opponents of** MALHERBE: MATHURIN RÉGNIER, 1573-1613; THÉOPHILE DE VIAU, 1590-1626. — The two best poets, contemporaries of MALHERBE, are hostile to his reform. — MATHURIN RÉGNIER (1573-1613), of Chartres, nephew of DESPORTES, belongs in spirit to the sixteenth century, and rather to the school of VILLON and MAROT than to that of RONSARD. In his sixteen *Satires* (1608-1613), imitated and transformed from HORACE, PLINY, JUVENAL, or the Italians, as BERNI and DELLA CASA, he attacks the courtiers, parasites, hypocrites, and braggarts. One is directed against MALHERBE in defense of the Pléiade. The best is *Macette*, the portrait of a pious hypocrite. RÉGNIER is also the author of epistles, elegies, and religious stanzas. In all he is both good and bad. His language is popular and natural, his words exact, his phrases, at times obscure and incorrect, are often so many proverbs. He is a poet of talent, but undisciplined. — THÉOPHILE DE VIAU (1590-1626), from the Agenais, was the favorite poet of the time. A writer of pastoral dramas, as the *Amours tragiques de Pyrame et Thisbé* (1617), which had great success, though tainted

with Gongorism, and of an unfinished novel, the *Histoire comique* (b. 1620), THÉOPHILE is an adept in rhythm and versification. His attention is given to the form rather than the thought. In his criticism he holds a middle ground between MALHERBE and the Pléiade.

4. **Followers** of MALHERBE: FRANÇOIS DE MAYNARD, 1582-1646; HONORAT DE RACAN, 1589-1670; JEAN OGIER DE GOMBAULD, 1570-1666; FRANÇOIS LE MÉTEL DE BOISROBERT, 1592-1662. — The remaining poets of distinction are disciples of MALHERBE. Two, though inferior to their master, excel in merit. — FRANÇOIS DE MAYNARD (1582-1646), of Toulouse, was a writer of epigrams and sonnets and the author of a pastoral poem, *Philandre*, based on the *Astrée*. He is known as having definitely established a break in the six-line strophe after the third verse and in the ten-line after the seventh. He is vivacious and witty, essentially modern. — HONORAT DE BUEIL (1589-1670), marquis of RACAN, an intimate of MALHERBE, wrote amorous lyrics, paraphrases of the *Psalms* (1651), containing local allusions, and a pastoral drama, the *Bergeries* (1619), which set the fashion for the kind. Without dramatic interest, the verses are full of sentiment, simple and natural. A love of nature, unusual in the literature of the seventeenth century, is revealed. RACAN combines naturalness, simplicity, and emotion to a degree infrequent in French poetry. — Among the other writers of odes, sonnets, and epigrams, are two of the first Academicians. JEAN OGIER DE GOMBAULD (1570-1666), of Saintonge, passed as a master of the sonnet. He wrote also pastorals and epigrams. — Less important is FRANÇOIS LE MÉTEL DE

BOISROBERT (1592–1662), of Caen, abbot and favorite of Richelieu. A voluminous writer of epistles, unplayed tragi-comedies, and farces, his vogue died with his protector.

5. **The Hôtel de Rambouillet**: VINCENT VOITURE, 1598–1648; The *Guirlande de Julie*, 1641. — A great influence, second only to that of MALHERBE, was exercised by the literary circle, the Hôtel de Rambouillet. The daughter of the French ambassador to Rome and of a Roman lady, Catherine de Vivonne (1588–1665), marchioness of Rambouillet (1600), withdrew from the unpolished court of Henry IV. and opened to men of letters and sympathizing nobles the first literary **salon**. In manners, they there learned courtesy and refinement; in literature, good taste and moderation. The rendezvous of MALHERBE, BALZAC, CORNEILLE, or VAUGELAS, delicacy of sentiment and decency of language were enjoined by the Hôtel de Rambouillet, together with respect for literary men. — Besides BALZAC, the great exponent of the company was VINCENT VOITURE (1598–1648), of Amiens, whose period of production corresponds (1620–1645) with its prosperity. He wrote light, brilliant letters, wholly in the taste of the time but devoid of thought, elegies, epigrams, quatrains, and other poems of occasion, the success of which was unbounded. His sonnet *Uranie* (1638) and the rival sonnet *Job*, of ISAAC DE BENSERADE (1612–1691), a poet and dramatist, divided the literary world into opposing factions. — The typical production of the Hôtel de Rambouillet is the collection of madrigals, illustrating flowers painted in miniature, known as the *Guirlande de Julie*

(1641), the daughter of the marchioness, and offered to her on her birthday. Nineteen poets signed the pieces, among them CHAPELAIN, COLLETET, and CORNEILLE. It was the acme of the gallantry set in motion by the *Astrée*.

6. **The French Academy, 1635**: JEAN CHAPELAIN, 1595-1674; GUILLAUME COLLETET, 1589-1659. — Side by side with the Hôtel de Rambouillet grew up a much more enduring, though at the time less influential institution. A few literary men, who for some years had met privately at the house of VALENTIN CONRART (1603-1675), were persuaded by BÓISROBERT, acting in behalf of Richelieu, to take on a public character. The model was already at hand in the numerous academies of Italy. Accordingly, in 1634 (the royal approval dates from 1635), the French Academy was constituted. Its statutes, drawn up by CONRART, its first perpetual secretary, directed that its members, residents of Paris, should maintain the purity of the French language and should create a Dictionary, a Grammar, a Rhetoric, and an Art of Poetry. — Instrumental in accepting the overtures of Richelieu was JEAN CHAPELAIN (1595-1674), of Paris, the literary autocrat of his day. He wrote, among other poems, an epic on Joan of Arc, the *Pucelle*. The first twelve cantos (1656) had great success. But the emptiness and the prosaic character of the work prevented, by a change in taste, the publication of the remaining twelve. — Another Academician is GUILLAUME COLLETET (1598-1659), a lawyer of Paris, poet and critic. His essays on literature, collected in the *Art poétique* (1658), and his *Histoire des poètes français*, destroyed during the Commune, are his best works.

7. **Popular and Burlesque Poets**: ADAM BILLAUT, † 1662; SAINT-AMANT, 1594–1661; PAUL SCARRON, 1610–1660. — The popular vein was crowded out of literature by the prevalence of rules and coteries. Its only representative in this period is ADAM BILLAUT († 1662), a joiner of Nevers. Yet his productions, the *Chevilles* (1641), the *Vilebrequin* (1663), and the *Rabot*, are rather learned than popular, both in form and content. — The beginnings of burlesque poetry are found in MARC-ANTOINE DE GÉRARD, called SAINT-AMANT (1594–1661), a hanger-on of princes. Embracing both the *précieux* and the *gaulois* tendency, he writes descriptive and satirical poetry, an epic, *Moïse sauvé*, attacks on Rome and England, drinking-songs, and the like. A member of the Academy, his office was to collect grotesque terms for its dictionary. — The exponent of the **burlesque** in France is PAUL SCARRON (1610–1660). He wrote a realistic novel, the *Roman comique* (1651), stories, comedies, and tragicomedies, imitated from the Spanish and very successful, as *Jodelet, ou le maître valet* (1645) and *Dom Japhet d'Arménie* (1653). SCARRON began his poetic career with a burlesque epic, the *Typhon* (1644), followed by lyric poems (1645), a lampoon, the *Mazarinade* (1649), and the *Virgile travesti* (1648), a parody of the *Eneid*, which was considered the model of the kind. An outgrowth of Italian frivolity, burlesque poetry was foreign to French soil and never prospered there. — SCARRON had imitators, among whom is GUILLAUME DE BRÉBEUF (1618–1661), known by his translation of LUCAN's *Pharsalia* (1655).

8. **The Dramatic Movement: the Tragedies of** AN-

TOINE DE MONCHRESTIEN, 1575-1621. — The most noteworthy movement of the period is in drama. The learned productions, probably not played, of the followers of the Pléiade gave way to popular imitations of the Spanish theater, which, like the English, mingled both tragedy and comedy. These were in turn succeeded by the reaction of the classical drama and the renewed separation of tragedy and comedy. The latter gained, however, more than the former and became truly national, going back to the farces and the study of manners. Inspired by the vogue of the *Astrée* and modeled on the *Aminta* and the *Pastor Fido*, a series of pastoral plays began with THÉOPHILE and RACAN. — A disciple of GARNIER and a lyric rather than a dramatic poet is the Huguenot, ANTOINE DE MONCHRESTIEN (1575-1621), of Falaise. His tragedies, probably not given, began with *Sophonisbe* (1596), imitated from TRISSINO. It was followed by the *Lacènes*, or *Constance* (1599), after PLUTARCH; *David*, or *Adultère* (1600); *Aman*, or *Vanité* (1601), the original of the *Esther* of RACINE; *Hector* (1603); and the *Écossaise*, or *Marie Stuart* (1605), his masterpiece, offered to James I. All, in alexandrines, the regular verse since JODELLE's *Didon*, alternating masculine and feminine rimes, they differ from the previous tragedies by the sustained sentiment of heroism. The tendency of the French theater towards types appears in the double titles of the plays. Other works of MONCHRESTIEN are a poem, *Suzanne*, a *Bergerie* in prose and verse, and a *Traité d'économie politique* (1615), the first use of the term.

9. **The Popular Theater of** ALEXANDRE HARDY, a.

1560–a. 1630; his Sources; his Reforms. — In spite of the despotism exercised over the literary drama by the *Poetices libri* of SCALIGER, the popular theater was unconscious of the Three Unities in its adherence to *moralités*, profane mysteries, farces, and Italian masks. A man of genius imbued with national feeling might have saved the French stage. — It was a second-rate talent, however, which guided ALEXANDRE HARDY (a. 1560–a. 1630). Himself both actor and playwright, he began his Parisian career at the Marais theater in 1600, and in the next thirty years produced some six hundred plays, of which he printed forty-one tragedies, tragi-comedies, and pastorals. His subjects HARDY borrows from the Greeks, the Latins, the Italian pastorals, the Spanish stories and plays, and from obscure sources, but works them over and makes them his own. A professional actor, he frees the action from the long monologues and conversations. He banishes or reduces the chorus. He introduces dramatic situations and seeks sensational scenes. Forcible and natural, he has neither taste nor style. His verse is the worst in French literature. His plots were much imitated by subsequent authors.

10. **Minor Dramatists:** JEAN DE SCHELANDRE, a. 1585–1635; JEAN DE MAIRET, 1604–1683; TRISTAN L'HERMITE, 1601–1655; JEAN DESMARETS, 1595–1676; PIERRE DU RYER, a. 1600–1658. — A number of less important dramatists precede CORNEILLE or are influenced by his first triumphs. — The *Tyr et Sidon* (1628) of JEAN DE SCHELANDRE, the anagram of the poet, DANIEL D'ANCHÈRES (a. 1585–1635), a tragi-comedy in two days, of five acts each, is a protest against the laws of the classi-

cal drama and an attempt to restore to favor the freedom of the mysteries and of the Spanish stage. Certain traits are seen later in CORNEILLE. A preface to the edition, by FRANÇOIS OGIER, demands with modern critics that writings be judged by their environments. — JEAN DE MAIRET (1604–1683), of Besançon, begins his literary successes with the pastoral, *Sylvie* (1621), in which the characters approach nearer to real life. Its composition and style show also an advance on previous works. In his *Sylvanire* (1625), taken from the *Astrée*, an attempt is made to observe the three unities. Following up this notion through the tragi-comedy *Virginie* (1628), MAIRET produces the first classical tragedy, *Sophonisbe* (1629), which held for a long time popular favor. The essential traits of the classical French tragedy, as seen in *Sophonisbe*, are: "Nobility of style, exclusion of the comic element, refinement in analysis and expression of sentiments, oratorical tendency in the language, logical simplification of plot, abstract and powerful conception of characters" (PETIT DE JULLEVILLE). The remaining plays of MAIRET passed unnoticed. — TRISTAN L'HERMITE (1601–1655), of Souliers, a lyric poet of note and the author of the realistic novel, the *Page disgracié* (1643), began a series of successful plays at the Marais theater with *Marianne* (1635), after HARDY, one of the favorite tragedies of the century. Its delineation of character is noteworthy. — JEAN DESMARETS (1595–1676), of Paris, a lyric poet, member of the Academy, and favorite of Richelieu, wrote plays on plots suggested by his protector. A comedy, the *Visionnaires*, is directed against the finical society of the time.

His tragedies, of no value, were written in part by Richelieu. His favorite work was an epic poem, *Clovis* (1657), inspired by CHAPELAIN. In the quarrel between the ancients and moderns, DESMARETS sides with the latter. — PIERRE DU RYER (a. 1600-1658), of Paris, wrote pastorals, two of which were taken (1630-1631) from BARCLAY's *Argenis*. Influenced by CORNEILLE, he continued with local comedies and tragedies, as *Alcionée* (1640) and *Scevole* (1647). — Another unimportant favorite of Richelieu was CLAUDE DE L'ESTOILE (1602-1652), son of PIERRE, who wrote with BOISROBERT, COLLETET, CORNEILLE, and ROTROU, the *Comédie des Tuileries* (1635).

11. **Comedy before** CORNEILLE: **Farces; Italian Masks;** GAUTIER-GARGUILLE, † **1634**; TABARIN, † a. **1634.** — The pure comedy of the first three decades of the seventeenth century calls for little comment. At the Hôtel de Bourgogne, from 1588, reigned the comedy of masks, played by Italian companies, and farces performed by GAUTIER-GARGUILLE (HUGUES GUÉRU, † 1634), GROS-GUILLAUME (ROBERT GUÉRIN, † 1634), and TURLUPIN. On the Pont-Neuf TABARIN († 1634) and the Italian MONDOR gave their coarse dialogues and scenes of buffoonery. The influence of these low productions is seen at times in the literary plays, as in the *Galanteries du duc d'Ossonne* (1627) of MAIRET. — The **pastoral comedy** flourished but little longer than a decade. Its last important contribution is the *Amaranthe* (1625) of GOMBAULD.

12. PIERRE CORNEILLE, **1606-1684.** — The plays of PIERRE CORNEILLE (1606-1684), of Rouen, the greatest of French dramatists, fall naturally into three groups:

the first, composed mainly of comedies, begins in 1629 and ends in 1636; the second extends from 1636 to 1651; the third begins in 1652. — In the first group, *Mélite*, a comedy, is succeeded by the tragi-comedy, *Clitandre* (1632), lawless and bombastic, and four comedies, which bring before the spectators scenes of Parisian life: the *Veuve* (1633), the *Galerie du Palais* (1633), the *Suivante* (1634), where the nurse of comedy gives way to the *soubrette*, and the *Place Royale* (1634). In 1635 is produced *Médée*, taken from SENECA and EURIPIDES, the best tragedy up to that time, but which did not satisfy CORNEILLE. The *Illusion comique* (1636), a play in a play, representing theatrical life, an imitation of the Spanish drama, closes the first series. — The second group, mainly tragedies, begins with the *Cid* (1636), CORNEILLE's master-piece, imitated from the *Mocedades del Cid* of GUILLEN DE CASTRO, followed by four tragedies, almost equal in merit: *Horace* (1640), *Cinna* (1640), *Polyeucte* (1640), and *Pompée* (1641); the first from LIVY, the second from SENECA's *De Clementia*, the third from a Latin life of the saint, the last from LUCAN. Returning to Spanish sources, CORNEILLE produced the *Menteur* (1642), imitated from the *Verdad sospechosa* of ALARCON, the best comedy previous to MOLIÈRE, and the *Suite du Menteur* (1643), after the *Amar sin saber á quien* of LOPE DE VEGA. The tragedy *Rodogune* (1644) CORNEILLE preferred to his best works. *Théodore* (1645), another sacred tragedy, was a failure, as was *Héraclius* (1647). With *Andromède* (1650), based on OVID, CORNEILLE imitates the operatic plays of the Italians. *Don Sanche* (1650), a tragi-comedy, is suggested by Spanish works and history. *Nicomède* (1651), of the same style as *Don Sanche*, is the last superior piece of the dramatist. — The failure of *Pertharite* (1652) turned CORNEILLE aside to works of a religious nature, poems, and a translation in verse of the *Imitation de Jésus-Christ*. *Œdipe* (1659) was received with favor and was followed by the *Toison d'or* (1660), a spectacular play. *Sertorius* (1662), *Sophonisbe* (1663), from LIVY, *Othon* (1664), *Agésilas* (1666), in which verses of six syllables are mingled with alexandrines, *Attila* (1667), *Tite et Bérénice* (1670), inferior to the rival play of RACINE, *Psyché* (1671), a tragedy-ballet in collaboration with MOLIÈRE and QUINAULT, with music by LULLI, *Pulchérie* (1672), and *Suréna* (1674), though occasionally successful, are works of decadence. Besides his theater CORNEILLE wrote poems of occasion, translations of hymns and Psalms; and in prose, letters, criticisms and analyses of his plays and essays, as the three *Discours* (1660) on the scenic poem, on tragedy, and on the three unities. — The services of CORNEILLE towards the dramatic literature of France are inestimable. He found comedy in the hands of the populace. *Mélite* is a long step in advance both in composition and in language. In the plays on Parisian life, increasing clearness and observance of propriety are shown, until in the *Menteur* the process of reformation was complete. Excepting the *ingénue*, MOLIÈRE receives his leading types from CORNEILLE. — In tragedy the way was much smoother. The dramatic unities had been established by MAIRET. After a short hesitation between the Spanish imitations of HARDY and the lifeless tragedies of SENECA, COR-

NEILLE found his manner in the *Cid*. The criticisms of the purists of the Academy on this play, deficient in unity of place, affected, unfortunately, the genius of its author. His succeeding tragedies observe the rules of SCALIGER. — Though characters are well delineated by CORNEILLE in his serious pieces, the tendency towards types is already strong in them, and in the comedies, as in the *Menteur*, it is overwhelming. The qualities of CORNEILLE are imagination, invention, originality. The heroic plane of his thought and the sonorous eloquence of his phrase render him the greatest master of the alexandrine. His defects are the reverse of his merits: hollow rhetoric, prosaic verse.

13. **Followers and Rivals of** CORNEILLE: JEAN ROTROU, **1609-1650**; GEORGES DE SCUDÉRY, **1601-1667**. — The most eminent dramatist, contemporary with CORNEILLE, is JEAN ROTROU (1609-1650), of Dreux. Of his many plays, thirty-six in all, the *Sosies* (1636), imitated from PLAUTUS, begins the best series; in which are *Laure persécutée* (1637), a tragi-comedy of unusual force, and *Saint Genest* (1646), a tragedy due to the *Polyeucte* of CORNEILLE. *Venceslas* (1647), still played, presents a struggle between jealousy and honor on the part of a brother. *Don Bernard de Cabrère* (1647), a tragi-comedy, and *Cosroès* (1649), a tragedy, are also superior. Though a free imitator of the ancients and of the Spaniards, his poetic inspiration, his power of invention, and the force of his genius render ROTROU entirely original. His style, rough at times, abounds in sublime verse and eloquent tirades. Subsequent dramatists, and even CORNEILLE, owe much to ROTROU. — Followers of CORNEILLE,

as DU RYER, and rivals, as LA CALPRENÈDE, are numerous. — Of the latter GEORGES DE SCUDÉRY (1601-1667), brother of MADELEINE, distinguished himself as an especially bitter opponent of the *Cid*. A lyric poet, the author of the epic *Alaric* (1654), he wrote in his youth pastorals, taken from the *Astrée* but in the style of HARDY, tragedies notable for their observance of the unities, and comedies of which the *Comédie des comédiens* (1635), in prose, is interesting for theatrical history.

14. **Prose Writers: Sermons and Treatises by FRANÇOIS DE SALES, 1567-1622.** — The prose works of this period show a great advance on previous efforts. A spirit of analysis and subdivision separates more rigidly the kinds. Philosophy and moral treatises produce their best compositions in DESCARTES and PASCAL. It is also the great period of novel-writing so abundantly prepared in the last half of the sixteenth century. — In the florid style of fiction and in the spirit of the sixteenth century, SAINT FRANÇOIS DE SALES (1567-1622) composed his religious works. Beginning with the *Étendard de la croix* (1597), a controversial pamphlet against the Protestants, he continued with the *Introduction à la vie dévote* (1608), a treatise on piety for laymen, next to the *Imitation* in popularity. In reply to a criticism on the effeminacy of the book, SAINT FRANÇOIS published the *Traité de l'amour de Dieu* (1614), equally successful though less read to-day. His other writings comprise religious letters, dogmatic treatises, and sermons less declamatory and more spiritual than those of his predecessors. The style of SAINT FRANÇOIS, poetical, full of similes, flowery to the highest degree, gives grace and life to his severe and

solid thought, though at times his mysticism and subtlety, joined to over-delicacy of expression, detract from the effect.

15. **Letters and Essays**: JEAN-LOUIS GUEZ DE BALZAC, **1594–1654**; GUI PATIN, **1601–1672**. — While letters increased greatly with the increase of civilization, no epistolatory style had yet been set. — This became the ambition of JEAN-LOUIS GUEZ DE BALZAC (1594–1654), of Angoulême, historiographer of Louis XIII. His first collection of letters (1624) established a standard of prose composition. This was followed by a political essay, the *Prince* (1631), which sketched the ideal ruler, a despot. His remaining works are moral treatises, as the *Discours* (1544), which also discuss literary questions, the *Socrate chrétien* (1652), the *Entretiens* (1657), and *Aristippe* (1658), the ideal of a statesman. The style of BALZAC, his main merit, is sober, clear, measured, forming a harmonious, full, and well-balanced period. His principal defect is excessive use of the hyperbole. The first writer of academic prose, he influenced all the authors of the classical school. — His friend, VOITURE, imitates him. — The only author of the period whose correspondence is important is GUI PATIN (1601–1672), the physician, whose letters, written without regard for style, are valuable for the private life of the time.

16. **Philosophy**: RENÉ DESCARTES, **1596–1650**. — In this period pure philosophy first speaks in the vernacular. RENÉ DESCARTES (1596–1650), of La Haye, soldier, and, after 1629, resident in Holland, began in Latin, but published his first book in French in order to reach the greater number. His *Discours de la méthode* (1637), a

work of fourscore pages, founds the system of Cartesian philosophy and classical French prose at the same time. His other works, as the *Meditationes* (1641) and the *Principia* (1644), appeared in Latin, but were soon translated. The *Traité des passions de l'âme* (1649) was written in French. — The influence of DESCARTES on the ideas and the language of the seventeenth century was enormous. In ideas skepticism gave way to affirmation, morality pervaded literature, and reason ruled even poetry. The phrase of DESCARTES is periodic and Latin, ingeniously constructed, conformed to the thought, the accessories carefully subordinated to the principal idea by an unprecedented use of relative pronouns. Yet the style is clear and noble, the order and precision perfect. The logical simplicity of French literature and its psychological bent are the most enduring legacies of DESCARTES.

17. BLAISE PASCAL, **1623-1662**; **Moral Science.** — DESCARTES had taught his generation philosophical research; BLAISE PASCAL (1623-1662), of Clermont-Ferrand, the celebrated mathematician and physicist, concerned himself with moral truths of a practical bearing. Attracted by the Jansenist doctrines of the Port-Royal, PASCAL undertook the defense of his teacher ANTOINE ARNAULD (1612-1694) — a polemist, author of a *Grammaire générale* (1660) and an *Art de penser* — against the Jesuits. For this purpose he wrote the *Lettres provinciales* (1656-1657), the first theological discussions in the vernacular, in which the moral doctrines of the casuists and of the Jesuits are attacked. The success of the series, written in a logical, energetic, but witty and sarcastic style, was great. It was the best French prose

yet published. The *Pensées* of PASCAL, left incomplete at his death, are a series of notes and meditations which were to form a defense of the Christian religion, and to aid belief in religious truths. It was suggested by a conversation held by PASCAL and LE MAISTRE DE SACY (1613-1684) — translator of the Bible (1672) — on the views of EPICTETUS and MONTAIGNE. The true religion is the Christian, where the burden of sin, which the soul must feel, is taken away by the Messiah. The thought and the expression of PASCAL are unexcelled. His other works include a Latin treatise on conic sections (1639), and various moral writings.

18. **Memoirs; History; Journalism**: SULLY, **1560-1641**; FRANÇOIS EUDES DE MÉZERAI, **1610-1683**; the *Gazette de France*, **1631**. — The memoirs of the seventeenth century begin with a relic of the sixteenth, the *Œconomies royales* (1638, 1662), of MAXIMILIEN DE BÉTHUNE (1560-1641), duke of SULLY, a recital of the work of Henry IV. and of the author, but not historically reliable. — **Histories** of France were attempted, as that of SCIPION DUPLEIX, from 1621 to 1663. — The best historian of the period is FRANÇOIS EUDES DE MÉZERAI (1610-1683), of Ry. His *Histoire de France* (1643-1651) is better for the personal qualities of the author than for science. His *Abrégé chronologique* (1668) has availed to preserve the longer work. — This period saw also the beginning of **journalism**. The *Mercure français* (1605) is rather a chronological record. The first weekly newspaper, in the modern sense of the word, was the *Gazette de France*, which appeared on May 30th, 1631. Its founder was THÉOPHRASTE RENAUDOT (1584-1653), of Loudun, encouraged by Richelieu.

THE SEVENTEENTH CENTURY. 141

— JEAN LORET († 1665) addressed to Mme. de Longueville a weekly *Muse historique* (1650–1665) in which literary and social gossip was given in verse.

19. **Linguistics**: CLAUDE FAVRE DE VAUGELAS, **1585–1650**; GILLES MÉNAGE, **1603–1692**. — Besides the various essays on literature, especially on the drama, as the *Pratique du théâtre* (1657), by FRANÇOIS HÉDELIN (1604–1676), abbot D'AUBIGNAC, which is the code of the purists, this period saw the first standard treatise on grammar. — CLAUDE FAVRE DE VAUGELAS (1585–1650), of Savoy, had given himself to the study of the French language. Though entrusted with the Academy's dictionary, he published only the *Remarques sur la langue française* (1647), in which he established, as a rule of language, the usage of the court and of good writers. The choice of words by VAUGELAS was often arbitrary and mistaken, but he did good service in freeing French from foreign, provincial, and vulgar locutions. VAUGELAS became authority.
— GILLES MÉNAGE (1603–1692), of Angers, modeled on VAUGELAS many linguistic works, as the *Origines de la langue française* (1650) and *Observations* (1673), while RACINE and BOILEAU acknowledge his value.

20. **Fiction; Stories**: GUILLAUME BOUCHET; the *Moyen de parvenir*, **1612**; **Ideal Novels**; HONORÉ D'URFÉ, **1568–1625**. — The early part of the period abounds in stories. GUILLAUME BOUCHET, of Poitiers, gives in the *Serées* (1608) the gossip of that town. — The *Moyen de parvenir* (1612), of BÉROALDE DE VERVILLE, is a symposium of ancients and moderns, whose stories show a strong influence of RABELAIS. — The last noted work of the kind is the *Caquets de l'accouchée* (1623), a collection

of extremely coarse and bitterly satirical comments on people and the government. — The place left vacant by the *gaulois* stories was immediately filled, among the educated, by **novels**, mainly ideal. The elements of the *Amadis*, of the *Diana*, of the pastorals of Italy and the erotic novels of Greek literature were combined by HONORÉ D'URFÉ (1568–1625), of Forez, in the *Astrée* (1610–1627), a pastoral novel in five volumes comprising over five thousand pages. The story of the loves of noble shepherds and shepherdesses, interrupted by countless episodes, obstacles, and descriptions after the style of the Greek novels, is here made more vivid by personal observation of society and more attractive by the love for the birthplace of the author, where the scene is laid. The lyric parts are mainly imitated from PETRARCH. A well-ordered narrative, a fair delineation of character, and a good exposition of the subject united with the ideal spirit of the novel to make it the favorite reading of a time, which saw in it its own aspirations. The influence of the *Astrée* on the Hôtel de Rambouillet, and through this on the literature of the time, is seen most clearly in the many theatrical pieces dramatized from among its thirty-three episodes. In the *Astrée* and its imitations are found that romantic phraseology and erotic psychology which constantly crop out in the gravest writers. The *Astrée* aided much in making literature decent, but it also rendered it frequently insipid. Other works of D'URFÉ are *Épîtres morales;* a poem, *Sireine*, after the *Diana;* a dramatization of one of the episodes of the *Astrée*, in blank verse, *Silvanire;* religious poems; and an epic fragment, the *Savoysiade*.

21. **The Political Novel of** JEAN BARCLAY, **1582–1621;
the Allegorical Novel of** GOMBAULD; **the Religious
Novels of** JEAN-PIERRE CAMUS, **1582–1652.** — Following
the *Astrée*, JEAN BARCLAY (1582–1621), of Scottish
descent, wrote in Latin the *Argenis* (1621, translated into
French in 1623), a political novel representing the life
of prominent nobles. Unity of action, freedom from
retarding episodes, and a fair delineation of character are
among its merits. — The poet GOMBAULD attempts an
allegorical novel, the *Endymion* (1524), based on his
attachment to Marie de' Medici. It is complicated, dry,
and insipid. — A much more successful novelist is JEAN-
PIERRE CAMUS (1582–1652), bishop of Belley, and friend
of SAINT FRANÇOIS DE SALES. It is to the latter, who
advised also D'URFÉ, that the conception of CAMUS'
writings is doubtless due — to convert the world by fiction. The author of numerous historical, religious, and
moral narratives, his tales, *Darie* (1620) and *Aristandre*
(1624), have a sadness of tone which is essentially modern,
while his novels proper, *Palombe* (1624), on Spanish
life, and *Cléoreste* (1626), the story of Romeo and Juliet,
can be considered as anticipating the psychological novel.

22. **The Heroic-gallant Novel:** MARIN LEROY DE GOM-
BERVILLE, **1600–1674;** GAUTIER DE COSTES DE LA CAL-
PRENÈDE, **a. 1609–1663.** — A continuation of the romance
of chivalry, as the *Amadis*, in the form set by the *Astrée*,
and influenced greatly by the Greek novel of erotic
adventure, was the heroic-gallant novel. Its inventor
was MARIN LEROY DE GOMBERVILLE (1600–1674), of
Paris, a member of the Academy and a leader of the
précieux. Besides various treatises on history and phi-

losophy and poetry of occasion, GOMBERVILLE wrote the novel, *Carithée* (1621), of slight value, followed by *Polexandre* (1632–1637), in five volumes, in which love and knightly honor are the theme. *Cythérée* (1639), which borrows from the *Amadis* and HELIODORUS, and *Alcidiane* (1651), a continuation of *Polexandre*, are both inferior to the latter. — GAUTIER DE COSTES (a. 1609–1663), knight of LA CALPRENÈDE, likewise a follower of the Hôtel de Rambouillet, was also a dramatist of note. Among his plays the *Mort de Mithridate* (1635) and the *Comte d'Essex* (1639) had success. Thoroughly imbued with the *Amadis*, his novels are historical like his dramas. *Cassandre* (1642–1645), in ten books, upholds the lofty ideal of heroic virtues, dear to the time. *Cléopâtre* (1647), likewise of Eastern adventure, and *Faramond* (1661–1663), based on national tradition, continued his reputation. LA CALPRENÈDE is the first French novelist to adopt and follow a developed plan. He even observes unity of place. He refines love to gallantry under the influence of the *précieuses*, and the supernatural of the *Amadis* is here replaced by the dreams and forebodings of the Greek novel. The great success of LA CALPRENÈDE lasted to the time of ROUSSEAU in France, is seen in many German and Italian translations and in English borrowings.

23. MADELEINE DE SCUDÉRY, **1608–1701**. — A more voluminous but not more talented novelist was MADELEINE DE SCUDÉRY (1608–1701), of Le Havre, who became the center of the literary society of Paris, and wrote various stories and dialogues (*Conversations*) of much merit. Her first novel, *Ibrahim* (1641), received

with favor, was followed by *Artamène*, or the *Grand Cyrus* (1649-1653), an immense work of over sixty-six hundred pages. The great success of the latter was due to its representation of the society of the time, and its artifice of disguised characters and events. *Clélie* (1654-1660), which employs the same methods, contains the celebrated *Carte et description géographique du pays de Tendre*, the climax of the influence of the *précieuses*. More narrative and romantic are *Almahide* (1660), after the Spanish history of PEREZ DE HITA, and *Mathilde* (1667), on a Spanish theme. The change in taste soon destroyed the vogue of the heroic-gallant novel.

24. **The Realistic Novel**: CHARLES SOREL, 1599-1674. — The influence of the picaresco novels of Spain reveals itself in the first two decades of the seventeenth century in France in various unsuccessful attempts. Of such a nature are the *Euphormio* (1603), in Latin, of BARCLAY, a true picaresco sketch; the *Fragments d'une histoire comique* (a. 1620), of THÉOPHILE, a satire on the ideal novels; and the *Baron de Fœneste*, of D'AUBIGNÉ. — The first notable realistic novelist is CHARLES SOREL (1599-1674), of Paris. The author of various ideal stories and an ideal novel, the *Orphise de Chrysante* (1626), he began the novel of manners with *Francion* (1622-1641), which satirizes the higher society and the fashionable literature in the adventures of a young noble. The *Berger extravagant* (1627) is a direct parody of the *Astrée*, and contains valuable observations on French literature. Its model is *Don Quixote.* — Many imitations followed, as the *Gascon extravagant* (1639), of CLERVILLE. — The last novel of SOREL is the *Polyandre* (1648), a series of sketches of

Parisian life. SOREL is also the author of many satirical poems, allegories, controversial, historical, and scientific works, as the *Science universelle* (1641) and the *Bibliothèque française* (1664).

25. Minor Realistic Writers: JEAN DE LANNEL; ANDRÉ MARESCHAL; TRISTAN L'HERMITE; PAUL SCARRON. — Among the realistic novels of the time are the *Roman satirique* (1624), of JEAN DE LANNEL, a moral and political satire in the form of the *Amadis;* the *Chrysolite* (1627), of ANDRÉ MARESCHAL, which is of a genuine psychological character; the *Page disgracié* (1643), of TRISTAN L'HERMITE, an autobiography; and the *Roman comique* (1651), of SCARRON, the adventures of a troupe of wandering comedians, of interest to the history of the theater. Its model was the *Viage entretenido* of ROJAS; an imitation is the *Capitaine Fracasse*, of GAUTIER.

26. Fanciful Novels: CYRANO DE BERGERAC, **1619-1655**. — Opposition to idealism, love of nature, philosophical views and satire prompted the fantastic novels of travel of SAVINIEN CYRANO (1619-1655), of Paris, a resident of Bergerac. A writer of letters and of plays, as the *Pédant joué* (1645-1654), in prose, and the *Mort d'Agrippine* (1654), and of political and philosophical satires, CYRANO began his novels with the *Histoire comique ou Voyage dans la lune* (a. 1650). The sources, besides those found in antiquity and in scientific works, may have been the novels of JOHN WILKINS and FRANCIS GODWIN. The influence of RABELAIS and SOREL is also evident. Among the many imitators of CYRANO are SWIFT, POE, and VERNE. A sequel is the *Histoire comique des états et empires du soleil* (a. 1653), inferior in vividness of description, and abounding in philosophical speculations, hostile to Cartesianism. Both works satirize the manners and vices of the time. — Various other realistic novels of little value belong to this period, mainly anti-pastoral and anti-heroic.

THE SEVENTEENTH CENTURY. 1601-1718.

CHAPTER XII.

SECOND PERIOD. 1659-1689.

1. **Poetry.** Court poets. Fabulists: JEAN DE LA FONTAINE, 1621-1695. Critics: NICOLAS BOILEAU, 1636-1711. Librettists: PHILIPPE QUINAULT, 1635-1688.
2. **Drama.** Comedy: JEAN-BAPTISTE POQUELIN (MOLIÈRE), 1622-1673; EDME BOURSAULT, 1636-1701. Tragedy: THOMAS CORNEILLE, 1625-1709; NICOLAS PRADON, † 1698; JEAN RACINE, 1639-1699.
3. **Prose.** Memoirs and letters: PAUL DE GONDI (RETZ), 1614-1679; ROGER DE RABUTIN, 1618-1693; GÉDÉON TALLEMANT DES RÉAUX, 1619-1692; MARIE DE SÉVIGNÉ, 1626-1696. Moralists: FRANÇOIS DE LA ROCHEFOUCAULD, 1513-1680; PIERRE NICOLE, 1625-1695; JEAN DE LA BRUYÈRE, 1645-1696. Philosophy: NICOLAS DE MALEBRANCHE, 1638-1715. Critics: CHARLES DE SAINT-ÉVREMOND, 1613-1703. Language: OLIVIER PATRU, 1604-1681; ANTOINE FURETIÈRE, 1620-1688; DOMINIQUE BOUHOURS, 1628-1702. Sermons: JACQUES-BÉNIGNE BOSSUET, 1627-1704; LOUIS BOURDALOUE, 1632-1704; ESPRIT FLÉCHIER, 1632-1710. Novels: MARIE-MADELEINE DE LA FAYETTE, 1634-1693; FURETIÈRE.

1. Court Poetry: FRANÇOIS DE MAUCROIX, **1619-1708**; JEAN DE SEGRAIS, **1624-1701**; ANTOINETTE DESHOULIÈRES, **1637-1694.**—The period which covers the most fortunate part of the reign of Louis XIV. and from which many of the masterpieces of French literature date, is almost entirely deficient in lyric poetry. Emotion, naturalness, poetic thought, are scarcely found outside of drama and the works of LA FONTAINE. Poems of occasion, sonnets, madrigals, rondeaux, dealing with the most trivial subjects, succeeded the longer efforts and the epic strivings of the previous generation. — FRANÇOIS DE MAUCROIX (1619–1708), the friend of LA FONTAINE, besides translations of the Church Fathers, wrote madrigals and epigrams of a certain grace and wit. — JEAN DE SEGRAIS (1624–1701), of Caen, a literary aid of the Great Mademoiselle, and renowned in the circles of the *précieuses*, exercised his poetical talent in pleasing pastorals. — ANTOINETTE DESHOULIÈRES (1637–1694), a *précieuse* of taste, published poetry in the *Mercure* and imitated RACAN in idylls and madrigals. Odes, eclogues, epistles, and tragedies, as *Genséric* (1680), increased her reputation. She was called the Tenth Muse. Her correspondence with FLÉCHIER is of interest.

2. JEAN DE LA FONTAINE, **1621–1695.** — It was national literary tradition which established the fame of the most prominent versifier of the time, JEAN DE LA FONTAINE (1621–1695), of Château-Thierry. Of an idle and dreamy disposition, a lover of nature, indifferent to duty, independent and restless, he lived under the protection of the wealthy. His career as author began with an imitation of TERENCE's *Eunuchus* (1654). A poetical narrative, the *Adonis* (1658), addressed to Fouquet, was followed by various poems of occasion, as the *Élégie aux nymphes de Vaux* (1661), and by a play, *Clymène* (1660).

To amuse the duchess of Bouillon (Marie Mancini) he wrote the *Contes et nouvelles* (1665, 1666), in two volumes, a poetical version of stories from the Italian, as the *Decameron*, or from the French collections, as the *Cent Nouvelles nouvelles*. The *Fables*, which had already circulated in manuscript, he published (1668) for Margaret of Lorraine. They were already a favorite composition of the court poets of the century. A realistic novel in prose and verse, the *Amours de Psyché* (1669), modeled on APULEIUS, was followed, under the protection of Mme. de la Sablière, by new *Fables* (1678, 1679), by a libretto, *Daphné*, for Lulli, whose refusal of it called out the satirical play, the *Florentin* (1685). Various plays, as *Galatée* (1682), the libretto, *Astrée* (1691), and poems of occasion, as the *Quinquina* (1682), preceded new *Contes* (1685), translations of Psalms, and the twelfth book of the *Fables* (1694), dedicated to the duke of Burgundy. — The merit of LA FONTAINE is mainly in the *Fables*, which are either pictures from life without morals, or rules for life with morals. Having great powers of observation, he is simple, natural, and often gay. He began as a disciple of MALHERBE, but enlarged later his verse and vocabulary by the study of the classics, of the older French writers, as VILLON and RABELAIS, and of the Italians, as ARIOSTO and TASSO. He opposed Cartesianism through his sympathy for animals. To his friendship with MAUCROIX and BOILEAU he owes much in taste and style.

3. NICOLAS BOILEAU, **1636–1711.** — The work of MALHERBE was continued and established beyond controversy by the critic, NICOLAS BOILEAU-DESPRÉAUX (1636–1711), of Paris. Endowed with a critical spirit and a severe

literary taste, he began with various short lyrics which were followed by nine *Satires* (1660–1667), against the poor poets of the age, the burlesque and the *précieux*, or on moral themes. The nine *Épîtres* (1667–1677), after HORACE, on various subjects; the *Lutrin* (1672–1683), a mock heroic poem which contains his best verse; and the *Art poétique* (1669–1674), in four cantos, which shows BOILEAU's ignorance of previous French literature, while giving rules for drama and poetry (modeled on the ancients) and moral advice to poets, combined to make his authority absolute. Historiographer with RACINE (1677), the last years of his life saw three *Satires* (1693–1703) and three *Épîtres* (1695). In the quarrel of the ancients and moderns he took the side of the former. — The work of BOILEAU is that of a critic rather than poet. His verse is little else than rimed prose. His aim was to make literary composition simple and true to life. His mistake was to pay excessive attention to form, to erect into general principles a part of literary truth. His influence on his contemporaries is his greatest service. He corrected and guided RACINE and LA FONTAINE, upheld and defended MOLIÈRE, directed the natural good sense and judgment of Louis XIV., and discredited the bombastic and finical writers of the day. He established solid taste in style and language.

4. PHILIPPE QUINAULT (1635–1688), of Paris, is the most important of the poets condemned by BOILEAU. Among his seventeen plays, beginning with the *Rivales* (1653), a comedy, the tragedy, *Astrate* (1664), and the comedy, the *Mère coquette* (1665), under the influence of MOLIÈRE, were received with great favor. His style is

of the school of the *précieuses*, and a tragedy, the *Mort de Cyrus* (1656), is from the *Artamène* of MLLE. DE SCUDÉRY. But the reputation of QUINAULT rests on his fourteen librettos (1671–1686), written for Lulli. Besides his part in *Psyché* (1671), his *Proserpine* (1680), *Roland* (1685), from the *Orlando furioso*, and *Armide* (1686), after TASSO, are poems of much lyric merit. His verse is harmonious, his expression graceful. Many passages are even brilliant and forcible.

5. **Comedy**: MOLIÈRE, **1622–1673**. — The great creation of the period is the theater of JEAN-BAPTISTE POQUELIN, called MOLIÈRE (1622–1673), of Paris. Up to his time, with the exception of CORNEILLE's plays, French comedy had been an imitation of PLAUTUS and TERENCE, of Spanish tragi-comedy, and of the Italian comedy of masks and adaptations from antiquity. The interest centered in a complicated intrigue. The *Menteur* stood alone as a character play. — MOLIÈRE, after studying the classics and hearing the lectures of the sensualist philosopher, PIERRE GASSENDI (1592–1655), joined the *Illustre théâtre* (a. 1643) of Madeleine Béjart. For it he wrote many farces on Italian models, of which the *Jalousie du barbouillé* and the *Médecin volant* are preserved. More ambitious are the comedies of character, due perhaps to the *Menteur*, the *Étourdi* (a. 1655), at Lyons, a free imitation of the *Inavvertito* of BARBIERI, and the *Dépit amoureux* (1656), at Béziers, an improved and enlarged version of the *Interesse* of SECCHI. The set types of the old comedy remained, but observation and invention gave them life and interest. — Returning to Paris (1658), MOLIÈRE devoted himself to the study of manners.

With the *Précieuses ridicules* (1659) he begins his warfare against the affectations in language and conduct of the *précieuses*. *Sganarelle* (1660), a farce, was followed by the unsuccessful *Don Garcie de Navarre* (1661), a cape-and-sword comedy of the Spanish type, taken from the *Gelosie fortunate* of the Italian, CIGOGNINI. He returns to true comedy in the *École des maris* (1661), the plot of the *Adelphi* of TERENCE improved upon, and the *Fâcheux* (1661), written for Fouquet, a series of character sketches including that of the pedant. The *École des femmes* (1662) was severely attacked by the *précieuses*, to whom MOLIÈRE replied in the *Critique de l'École des femmes* (1663). A letter to the king from the envious actors of the Hôtel de Bourgogne was answered by the short *Impromptu de Versailles* (1663), defending, as did the *Critique*, his presentation of real life. — The third period of MOLIÈRE's career begins with a farce, the *Mariage forcé* (1664), followed by the *Princesse d'Élide* (1664), a poor imitation of the *Desden con el desden* of MORETO, written for the Versailles festivals. *Tartuffe*, begun (1664), was forbidden for a time. *Don Juan* (1665) was taken probably from the *Festin de pierre* (1659), of DE VILLIERS, itself a translation of GILIBERTIS' version of the *Burlador de Sevilla* of TIRSO DE MOLINA. A farce, the *Amour médecin* (1665), was followed by one of MOLIÈRE's best works, the *Misanthrope* (1666), in verse, a keen study of society. The merry farce, the *Médecin malgré lui* (1666), is the plot of the *Vilain mire*. A pastoral scene, *Mélicerte* (1666), for the king, and an act of comic opera, the *Sicilien* (1667), preceded the finished *Tartuffe* (1667), on devout hypocrisy.

— The last division of MOLIÈRE's plays sees again imitations from antiquity and studies of contemporary manners, satirical in spirit. *Amphitryon* (1668), from PLAUTUS, *Georges Dandin* (1668), a satire on ambitious marriages (the development of the *Jalousie du barbouillé*), and the *Avare* (1668), in prose, suggested by the *Aulularia* of PLAUTUS and the *Esprits* of LARIVEY, but entirely remodeled and one of the dramatist's best efforts, were followed by a farce, *Monsieur de Pourceaugnac* (1669), by the poor *Amants magnifiques* (1670), and by the comical satire against social ambitions, the *Bourgeois gentilhomme* (1670). The festival play, *Psyché* (1671), suggested by the novel of LA FONTAINE, was worked on also by CORNEILLE and QUINAULT, and set to music by Lulli. Two farces, the *Fourberies de Scapin* (1671), a valet of comedy, and the *Comtesse d'Escarbagnas* (1671), a satire on provincial nobility, may have had their origin in MOLIÈRE's lost works and show borrowings from other authors. The *Femmes savantes* (1672) is a new and more finished attack against the *précieuses* and the pedants. The last play of MOLIÈRE, the *Malade imaginaire* (1673), a farce, is a satire on the medical profession, assailed often in his previous plays, and a favorite theme of comedy. — After the death of MOLIÈRE, the Palais-Royal theater came into the possession of Lulli. The actors, transferred to another stage, were amalgamated with those of the Hôtel de Bourgogne, and the *Comédie française* was founded (1680). — The present admiration for MOLIÈRE, and his rating as the first writer of France, was not shared by his contemporaries. Producing little but comedy (as the poem, the *Gloire du Val-de-Grâce* (1665)), and actor as well as author, he suffered from the prejudice against the stage. His buffooneries were urged against him; his style, too poetical and rich for the taste of the purists, was blamed for its negligence and its strange expressions. His picturesque and original language, taken from the people, was considered incorrect and even barbarous. MOLIÈRE succeeded in presenting exactly and forcibly the society of his time, not as individuals with many-sided character, but as types, the general failure of the French theater. Where the types are universal, his work belongs to the world and is superior to that of any other dramatist. Where they are local and temporary, they have lost interest.

6. **Opponents and Imitators of** MOLIÈRE: SAMUEL CHAPUZEAU, **1625-1701**; EDME BOURSAULT, **1636-1701**; JEAN DONNEAU DE VIZÉ, **1638-1710**; MONTFLEURY, **1640-1685**. — MOLIÈRE stands alone in French literature. Among the many dramatists of the time who opposed and imitated him, none, save QUINAULT and THOMAS CORNEILLE, have remained in favor. — Of the minor writers, SAMUEL CHAPUZEAU (1625-1701), theater director at Hannover, the author of a treatise on comedy, the *Théâtre français* (1674), produced in prose the *Cercle des femmes* (1656), versified later in the *Académie des femmes*, which may have influenced the *Femmes savantes*. — EDME BOURSAULT (1636-1701), of Champagne, attacked the *Critique* in the *Portrait du peintre* (1663), and BOILEAU in the *Critique des satires* (1670). He is the author of various other plays, as the *Comédie sans titre* (1679), the *Fables d'Ésope* (1690), and *Ésope à la cour* (1701). He also wrote historical fiction. — JEAN DONNEAU DE VIZÉ (1638-

1710), founder of the literary journal, the *Mercure galant* (1672), collaborated with THOMAS CORNEILLE, as in the *Inconnu* (1675), opposed the *Critique* of MOLIÈRE with *Zélinde* (1663), and, among other plays, imitated MOLIÈRE in the *Gentilhomme Guépin*, a satire on the provincial nobility. He also devoted himself to memoirs of the times. — ANTOINE JACOB (1640–1685), called MONTFLEURY, the son of the actor, assailed MOLIÈRE and wrote many plays, all lacking in invention and observation. The best is the *Femme juge et partie* (1669). — Two actors of the Hôtel de Bourgogne, RAIMOND POISSON (1633–1690) and GUILLAUME MARCOUREAU DE BRÉCOURT († 1685), wrote many one-act comedies. — None of these writers, save BOURSAULT, aimed at literary form or solid content.

7. **Tragedy**: THOMAS CORNEILLE, **1625–1709**; NICOLAS PRADON, † **1698**. — Many minor dramatists followed in the track marked out by CORNEILLE, as QUINAULT and THOMAS CORNEILLE (1625–1709). — The latter exercised his talent in both comedy and tragedy. In his fifteen comedies, beginning in 1647, he follows the Spanish cape-and-sword plays, as *Don Bertrand de Cigarral* (1650), imitated from ROJAS; or sketches manners, as in the *Berger extravagant* (1653). They are all poor in thought and language. Of his seventeen tragedies, the first, *Timocrate* (1656), was played six months in succession, a unique instance in this century. In romantic style it shows the influence of the *Cid*. In the same manner is *Camma* (1661). The later tragedies of CORNEILLE imitate the style of RACINE. Of them, *Ariane* (1672) and the *Comte d'Essex* (1678), pathetic in sentiment, are still read. Various librettos are found among his plays. He

versified MOLIÈRE's *Don Juan*. Other works of COR-
NEILLE are *Observations* (1687) *sur Vaugelas*, and dic-
tionaries of popular science: *Des arts et des sciences* and
Géographique et historique (1708), an innovation in his
time. The chief defects of CORNEILLE arise from his
subserviency to fashion and his weak composition. —
NICOLAS PRADON († 1698), also of Rouen, is remembered
as a self-constituted rival of RACINE, whom he imitated.
His *Phèdre et Hippolyte* (1677) displaced the *Phèdre* of
RACINE through a literary cabal.

8. JEAN RACINE (1639–1699), of La Ferté-Milon, a
pupil at Port-Royal, began with Latin and French poems
on the beauties of nature. His ode, the *Nymphe de la
Seine* (1660), on the marriage of Louis XIV., brought
him into public notice. After some attempts he produced,
under the influence of MOLIÈRE and BOILEAU, the *Thé-
baïde* (1664), played at the Palais-Royal by the company
of MOLIÈRE. In it he follows the dramatic method of
CORNEILLE, while imitating EURIPIDES, SENECA and
ROTROU. Its slight success prompted *Alexandre le Grand*
(1665), an imitation of CORNEILLE and QUINAULT, a mixture of force and gallant tenderness, received with little
favor. — RACINE's true manner appears in *Andromaque*
(1667), imitated freely from EURIPIDES, his master-piece
in the delineation of womanly constancy and female
jealousy. A short comedy or farce, the *Plaideurs* (1668),
based on ARISTOPHANES, is a clever satire of legal pro-
cedure. *Britannicus* (1669), from TACITUS, and *Bérénice*
(1670), written for Henrietta of England, a poetical dialogue between lovers, almost an idyll, which triumphed
over the rival play of CORNEILLE, were followed by a

tragedy from Turkish history, *Bajazet* (1672), which shows the influence of Port-Royal. *Mithridate* (1673), more faithful to the spirit of antiquity, and *Iphigénie* (1674), after EURIPIDES, one of the best works of French poetry, which increased the enmity of his rivals, preceded his most dramatic piece, *Phèdre* (1677), after EURIPIDES, a vivid delineation of passion and remorse. — Beset by unjust critics and harassed by religious scruples, RACINE renounced the further imitation of the Greek stage, which he had planned. Made historiographer with BOILEAU (1677), he writes a libretto, translates the *Symposium*, and eulogizes CORNEILLE (1685). At the request of Mme. de Maintenon he writes for the school of Saint Cyr two religious plays, *Esther* (1689), on the model of the old plays, containing choruses of unusual beauty; and *Athalie* (1691), perhaps his best drama, joining to his lyric qualities, force, interest, and the study of character. — The other works of RACINE include many letters, a *Histoire de Port-Royal*, religious poems, odes, sonnets, epigrams, and a lost *Histoire de Louis XIV.* — In his tragedies RACINE is noted for refined sentiment, polished verse, and correct language. He aims, in the study of character, to be psychological, and excels in the portraits of women. His action is simple, freed from extraneous matter, and proceeds from the characters themselves. His dramatic ideal was evidently SOPHOCLES. In style he follows VERGIL. The great defect of RACINE lies in the contrast between his subject, often sanguinary, and his delicacy of expression. But he presents more individuals and fewer types. In him is seen again the great mistake of French tragedy — the lack of a national basis.

9. **Memoirs and Letters.** — Prose in this period developed essentially in the line of memoirs and letters. — JEAN-FRANÇOIS-PAUL DE GONDI (1614-1679), cardinal DE RETZ, is the most important of the **memoirists**. His *Mémoires* (1662-1679) concern the intrigues of the Fronde, and are in the nature of confessions. Of doubtful historical accuracy, they are valuable for the portraits they contain. Their style is vigorous and original. RETZ is also renowned as a pulpit orator, the *Discours* (1645), before Louis XIV., being of much merit. — Memoirs of the regency of Anne of Austria were written by MME. DE MOTTEVILLE (1621-1689). — The same period is also covered by the *Mémoires* (1646) of LA ROCHEFOUCAULD. — Of a different style are the *Mémoires* of ROGER DE RABUTIN (1618-1693), count of BUSSY, the author of the scandalous *Histoire amoureuse des Gaules* (1665), of letters and minor works. — A rival to BUSSY was found in GÉDÉON TALLEMANT (1619-1692), called DES RÉAUX. His *Historiettes* are a series of anecdotes, social scandals, and jests, prompted by love of gossip, and valuable for the private life of the time. — The greatest of French **letter-writers**, erecting the art into literature, as did BALZAC and VOITURE, is MARIE DE RABUTIN-CHANTAL (1626-1696), marchioness DE SÉVIGNÉ. Her daily correspondence with her daughter, Mme. de Grignan, of which over fifteen hundred letters remain, is the best document extant for the literary, social, and moral history of the epoch. In a most artistic style and in the purest language, she records (1669-1693) all the news of the court and country, and mingles her own observations, often brilliant and always interesting. Her cor-

respondence with others, notably with BUSSY, shows the same traits of style and mind. — A **historiographer** is PAUL PELLISSON (1624–1693), of Béziers. His *Mémoires* and *Discours au Roi*, in behalf of Fouquet, are models of argument and exposition. His most valuable work is the *Histoire de l'Académie française* (1653). He also wrote historical fragments and fables.

10. **The Moralists.** — The philosophical impulse, proceeding from DESCARTES and PASCAL, had incited the *précieuses* of the circle of Mme. de Sablé to the composition of maxims. — Following them, FRANÇOIS DE LA ROCHEFOUCAULD (1613–1680), embittered by his failures, published the *Réflexions ou sentences et maximes morales* (1665–1678), which are based on observation and personal experience. Their leading principle is that human actions arise from self-love and personal interest. Their form, epigrammatic, polished, and expressive, belongs to the best of French literature. — Different in spirit is the Port-Royalist, PIERRE NICOLE (1625–1695), the author of a long series of *Essais de morale* (1671–1695), much admired at the time, but now tiresome through their monotonous style and excessive analysis. He also shared in the educational works of Port-Royal and in the *Provinciales* of PASCAL. — A moralist is also JEAN DE LA BRUYÈRE (1645–1696), of Paris. Besides a translation of THEOPHRASTUS and dialogues on Quietism, LA BRUYÈRE wrote the *Caractères* (1688–1696), sketches of types of society with special animus against the nobles. They show the influence of MONTAIGNE, PASCAL, and LA ROCHEFOUCAULD. Good sense, lively description, independent observation in the restricted

field, are expressed in witty and delicate portraits, too often of the weak side of human character. His style shows that simple prose was passing from favor.

11. **Philosophy and Criticism.** — Among the followers of DESCARTES, the only **philosopher** who shows original thinking is NICOLAS DE MALEBRANCHE (1638–1715), a monk of Paris. His book, *De la recherche de la vérité* (1674), is a religious development of Cartesian metaphysics, in a pure and poetical style, which gave it great success. His other works are theological expansions of the first, as the *Traité de morale* (1684). — The most distinguished **critic** of the period, also a skeptical philosopher, was CHARLES DE SAINT-DENIS (a. 1613–1703), lord of SAINT-ÉVREMOND, exiled to England in 1661. Two comedies, the *Académiciens* (1643), on their quibbling and pedantry, and the *Comédie des opéras*, against the Italian novelties, preceded essays, *Sur la morale d'Épicure, Réflexions sur les divers génies du peuple romain*, which inspired MONTESQUIEU, and many criticisms on French literature, one-sided in view, but which had authority in France. His bent was satirical. — Of authority at the time were the *Entretiens sur les tragédies de ce temps* (1675), by the abbot DE VILLIERS, who advised Biblical subjects.

12. **Language.** — Of writers on linguistics, the orator, OLIVIER PATRU (1604–1681), rivaled the authority of VAUGELAS. He introduced orations at receptions into the Academy. — ANTOINE FURETIÈRE (1620–1688), of Paris, author of satirical essays and the *Roman bourgeois* (1666), compiled a *Dictionnaire* (1690) of the French language, for which he was unjustly expelled from the Academy

as a plagiarist. — DOMINIQUE BOUHOURS (1628–1702), Jesuit and grammarian, wrote various treatises, among them the *Entretiens d'Ariste et d'Eugène* (1671), and *Doutes et nouvelles remarques sur la langue française* (1674). The mixture of religion and grammar contributed to the success of these works.

13. **Sermons and Funeral Orations.** — Taste and simplicity entered into court and pulpit oratory during the reign of Louis XIV. In the former OLIVIER PATRU is the most eminent. — In the latter the chief is JACQUES-BÉNIGNE BOSSUET (1627–1704), perhaps the greatest writer of the century. His first sermon was improvised at the Hôtel de Rambouillet. The two hundred and more which followed, mainly before the court, are unsurpassed in logical development of dogma, in aptness of metaphor, in nobility of expression, and in simple, vigorous, and colored language. They all teach practical morality. — The same qualities are perfected in his **funeral orations**, a kind of sermon which BOSSUET made classical literature. His best are those on the Queen of England (1669), on Henrietta of England (1670), on Maria Theresa (1683), on Anne de Gonzague (1685), on Michel Le Tellier (1686), and on the Prince of Condé (1687). A mixture of eulogy and of moral instruction, they excel in recital of events and in portrayal of character. — Among the other works of BOSSUET are treatises for his pupil, the Dauphin, as the *Traité de la connaissance de Dieu et de soi-même*, a summary of Cartesian philosophy; the *Politique tirée de l'Écriture sainte*, a manual on royal duties; and the *Discours sur l'Histoire universelle* (1681), a sketch of sacred and profane history down to Charlemagne, from

THE SEVENTEENTH CENTURY. 163

the philosophical standpoint. It strongly influenced
MONTESQUIEU. Various polemical works against the
Protestants, in favor of the Gallican Church, against
the Quietism of FÉNELON, and against comedy, increased
the authority of BOSSUET. The leading element of his
style is grandeur. — LOUIS BOURDALOUE (1632–1704),
Jesuit, was ranked unjustly above BOSSUET as a preacher.
Some seventy-four sermons remain distinguished for rigorous dialectic, for moral analysis, and for the portrayal
of vices, in a sober and exact style. He pronounced
funeral orations, as on Condé (1687). — ESPRIT FLÉCHIER
(1632–1710), bishop of Nîmes, began his literary career
with Latin and French poems, defending the *précieuses*.
As an orator he gained his reputation in the funeral oration, those on Mme. de Montausier (1672) and on Turenne
(1676) being most noted. His style, modeled on BALZAC,
is highly artificial. — JULES MASCARON (1634–1703),
bishop of Agen, a preacher of great force and frankness,
is known to-day by his funeral oration on Turenne (1675).

14. **Psychological Novels; Realistic.** — Psychological
studies are found first in the novels of MARIE-MADELEINE, countess DE LA FAYETTE (1634–1693), the friend
of LA ROCHEFOUCAULD. Besides memoirs she wrote
two stories, *Mademoiselle de Montpensier* (1660) and the
Comtesse de Tende, the latter a pathetic narrative in the
defense of the *Princesse de Clèves*. — Her first novel, *Zayde*
(1670), was inspired by MLLE. DE SCUDÉRY, and rests on
the history of PEREZ DE HITA. Having the form of the
heroic-gallant novel, *Zayde* shows mental analysis, simplicity, and naturalness. The style is correct and graceful. — The *Princesse de Clèves* (1677) is the author's

master-piece. Short and simple in action (which is wholly mental), it represents faithfully true sentiments, and is the starting-point of the modern school. — To *Zayde* was prefixed the *Traité de l'origine des romans* by PIERRE-DANIEL HUET (1630–1721), bishop of Avranches. It seeks their source in the East and forms a landmark in literary history. — The writer of **realistic novels** in this period, besides the *Psyché* of LA FONTAINE, is ANTOINE FURETIÈRE. The *Nouvelle allégorique* (1658), a literary satire against the ideal novels, is followed by the *Roman bourgeois* (1666), in two books, the first a narrative of middle-class life in Paris, pessimistic and satirical, the second a satire against SOREL. — Various parodies of the ideal novels were written by minor authors.

The Seventeenth Century. 1601–1718.

CHAPTER XIII.

THIRD PERIOD. 1689-1718.

1. **Poetry.** GUILLAUME AMFRYE DE CHAULIEU, 1639-1720; JEAN-BAPTISTE ROUSSEAU, 1670-1741.
2. **Drama.** Comedy: CHARLES RIVIÈRE DUFRESNY, 1648-1724; JEAN-FRANÇOIS REGNARD, 1655-1709; FLORENT CARTON DANCOURT, 1661-1725; MARC-ANTOINE LEGRAND, 1673-1728. Tragedy: ANTOINE DE LA FOSSE, 1654-1708; JEAN GALBERT DE CAMPISTRON, 1656-1723; PROSPER JOLYOT DE CRÉBILLON, 1674-1762.
3. **Prose.** Memoirs and letters: FRANÇOISE D'AUBIGNÉ DE MAINTENON, 1635-1719; BERNARD DE FONTENELLE, 1657-1757. History: CLAUDE FLEURY, 1640-1723. Philosophy: PIERRE BAYLE, 1647-1706. Language: FRANÇOIS-SÉRAPHIN RÉGNIER-DESMARETS, 1632-1713. Essays: FRANÇOIS DE LA MOTHE FÉNELÓN, 1651-1715. Sermons: JEAN-BAPTISTE MASSILLON, 1663-1742. Fiction: CHARLES PERRAULT, 1628-1703; ANTHONY HAMILTON, 1646-1721; MARIE-CATHERINE D'AULNOY, 1650-1705; ALAIN-RENÉ LESAGE, 1668-1747.

1. Transition in Literature; Poetry. — The political decline of Louis XIV. and the impoverishment of the country were accompanied by a literary change. Already in LA BRUYÈRE simple prose is replaced by a somewhat affected style. In drama, comedy ridicules new vices, while tragedy is a weak imitation of the great masters. Poetry almost ceases. — GUILLAUME AMFRYE (1639–1720), abbot of CHAULIEU, wrote drinking and love songs for the circle of the princes of Vendôme, and *Épîtres*, full of skeptical sensualism. — His friend CHARLES-AUGUSTE (1644–1712), marquis of LA FARE, is the author of light poems and of the libretto, *Panthée*. — ANTOINE BAUDERON DE SÉNECÉ (1643–1737) is known by his satires, epigrams, and *nouvelles en vers*, all poor in style and language. — The only poet of lasting reputation is JEAN-BAPTISTE ROUSSEAU (1670–1741), of Paris. His best work is in his epigrams and *Épîtres*, after the manner of BOILEAU. He also wrote *Odes*, declamatory in style and moral in content, *Cantates* in harmonious verse, allegories, Psalms, and comedies, as the *Flatteur*. Highly valued in his day, he adds little to the forms of MALHERBE and is merely a skillful versifier.

2. **Comedy.** — CHARLES RIVIÈRE DUFRESNY (1648–1724), of Paris, wrote at first, with REGNARD, for the Italian comedians. Of his eighteen French plays (1692–), mainly in prose, the *Joueuse* (1698), a vivid portrayal of the passion for gambling, the *Esprit de contradiction* (1700), the *Double veuvage* (1702), his best, and the *Désir* (1719) show much wit, but little dramatic talent. — JEAN-FRANÇOIS REGNARD (1655–1709), of Paris, is the only follower of MOLIÈRE who recalls his qualities. After writing masks for the Italian comedians, which contain the germ of his later plays, as the *Divorce* (1688), he begins at the *Comédie française* with farces (1694–1696), followed by a comedy, the *Joueur* (1696), his master-piece, in the spirit of the eighteenth century, vigorous,

witty, and polished, but with little depth of observation. In it the valet begins his future importance. The *Distrait* (1697), after LA BRUYÈRE, is jocose. *Démocrite* (1700) violates unity of place. The *Ménechmes* (1705), after PLAUTUS, abounding in unexpected situations and containing much fine verse, and the *Légataire universel* (1708), a most amusing comedy of manners, in the style of MOLIÈRE, are still popular. Originality is wanting. Gayety and good poetry are his chief merits. REGNARD also wrote *Épîtres* and satires, a novel, the *Provençale* (a weak imitation of the *Princesse de Clèves*), and *Voyages*, both interesting and exact, as those on Lapland and Russia. REGNARD is the best poet of the period. — FLORENT CARTON DANCOURT (1661-1725), of Fontainebleau, was both actor and author. He succeeds MOLIÈRE in the farce. His forty-seven plays are mainly in one act, in prose. They represent the fashionable life of the day, with wit and aptness, and are valuable for sociology. His types, as valets and soubrettes, show the social changes. The *ingénue* of MOLIÈRE becomes accustomed to the world of self-seeking. His peasants are shrewd and calculating. His best pieces are the *Chevalier à la mode* (1687), the *Bourgeoises de qualité* (1700), and the *Comédie des comédiens* (1710). — MARC-ANTOINE LEGRAND (1673-1728), the actor, wrote comedies, as the *Roi de cocagne*. — The collaboration of DAVID-AUGUSTIN DE BRUEYS (1640-1723) and JEAN PALAPRAT (1650-1721) produced the *Grondeur* (1691) and the *Avocat Pathelin* (1706), the old farce adapted to the taste of the time. — **Opera** had now displaced comedy.

3. **Tragedy.** — Most of the writers of tragedy imitated

RACINE. — A follower of CORNEILLE is ANTOINE DE LA FOSSE D'AUBIGNY (1654-1708), an adherent of the *précieuses*. *Polyxene* (1696) preceded *Manlius Capitolinus* (1698), the best tragedy since *Athalie*, imitated from OTWAYS' play, who in turn took his plot from the *Histoire de la conjuration de Venise* (1674), of the abbot CÉSAR VICHARD DE SAINT-RÉAL (1639-1692). — JEAN GALBERT DE CAMPISTRON (1656-1723), of Toulouse, wrote both comedies and tragedies, the latter closely patterned on RACINE. *Andronic* (1685), the same theme as SCHILLER's *Don Carlos; Alcibiade* (1685); and *Tiridate* (1691), his most successful play, borrow both details and language from RACINE. — LA GRANGE-CHANCEL (1676-1758) gained a certain reputation with *Oreste et Pylade* (1697) and *Amadis* (1701). — The greatest writer of tragedy between RACINE and VOLTAIRE is PROSPER JOLYOT DE CRÉBILLON (1674-1762), of Dijon. He seeks to revive the drama by violent and bloody scenes and superhuman crimes. In *Atrée et Thyeste* (1707) and *Radamiste et Zénobie* (1711), his best work, terror and horror are the dramatic methods employed. His last plays, as *Catalina* (1742), were in rivalry of VOLTAIRE. Vigorous verse does not rid his plays of monotony of action or of a declamatory rather than a dramatic style.

4. **Memoirs and History**. — Prose already shows the trace of the restless, questioning spirit of the eighteenth century. — Memoirs continued a favorite diversion, as those of MME. DE MAINTENON (1635-1719), of Niort, mainly in letters regarding Saint-Cyr. Other works are, *Entretiens sur l'éducation des filles, Conseils aux demoiselles,*

and various essays written for the school. In a style simple and eloquent, she shows herself a moralist, an educator, and a keen observer of youth. — The memoirs of MME. LA DUCHESSE D'ORLÉANS (1653–1722) are letters on court life, valuable for the portraits of manners and men. — Approaching more the **historian** is BERNARD LE BOVIER DE FONTENELLE (1657–1757), the nephew of CORNEILLE. Beginning with unsuccessful tragedies and with librettos, he continued with the paradoxical *Dialogues des morts* (1683), followed by the *Pastorales*. His bent was revealed in the *Entretiens sur la pluralité des mondes* (1686), which brought science down to the vulgar comprehension. His more historical works are the *Histoire de l'Académie des sciences* and the *Éloges des académiciens* (1708, 1717), which made the scientists known to the public at large. In the barren quarrel between the ancients and moderns (1670–1720) FONTENELLE sided with the latter. He is also the author of a *Vie de Corneille*. — More claim to the title of historian has the abbot, CLAUDE FLEURY (1640–1723), of Paris. Essays, such as the *Mœurs des Israélites* (1681) and the treatise, *Du choix et de la méthode d'études* (1686), in which he proposes reforms in education, precede the *Histoire ecclésiastique* (1691–1720), a vast uncritical compilation of documents. — True critical research is seen in the Latin works of JEAN MABILLON (1632–1707).

5. **Philosophy; Language.** — The spirit of the eighteenth century is seen in the writings of PIERRE BAYLE (1647–1706), professor of philosophy at Rotterdam. Besides various essays on Cartesianism and polemics ir

favor of the Protestants he founded the literary review, *Nouvelles de la république des lettres* (1684), which became the literary authority. His great work, the *Dictionnaire historique et critique* (1697), conceived in a negative, impartial spirit, is a kind of encyclopædia, in which scientific criticism first appears. — In **linguistics** the publication of the *Dictionnaire* (1694) of the Academy was followed by the *Grammaire* (1705) of FRANÇOIS-SÉRAPHIN RÉGNIER-DESMARETS (1632-1713), its secretary.

6. FRANÇOIS DE LA MOTHE FÉNELON (1651–1715), archbishop of Cambrai, best illustrates the literary transition of the last years of Louis XIV. His first work was the *Traité de l'éducation des filles*, followed by the *Traité de la nature et de la grâce* (1680), against MALEBRANCHE. The three *Dialogues de l'éloquence*, in favor of simple, practical preaching, showed the tendency to improvise which has lost to posterity his sermons. — Having become preceptor (1689) of the duke of Burgundy, he wrote for his pupil *Fables*, in prose, to condemn his defects; the *Dialogues des morts*, between learned men of all epochs; and *Télémaque* (1699), the counsels of Mentor given to the son of Ulysses. Beauty of style, delicacy of expression, and skill of invention have made this imitation of antiquity the most popular narrative of France. — Embracing the mysticism of Quietism in his *Explication des maximes des saints* (1697), FÉNELON incurred the royal displeasure. His *Examen de la conscience d'un roi* (1711), for the duke of Burgundy, relates the ruin of the kingdom and advises local self-government. The *Lettre à M. Dacier sur les occupations de l'Académie*

THE SEVENTEENTH CENTURY. 171

française (1714) is the first literary criticism in French. The last chapter, on the quarrel of the ancients and moderns, shows FÉNELON ardent for the former. His posthumous *Lettres spirituelles* advocate a religion of entire self-renouncement. — In general, FÉNELON, though chimerical and reforming in character, is still a firm adherent of the theocratic monarchy of the seventeenth century.

7. **Sermons.** — JEAN - BAPTISTE MASSILLON (1663 – 1742), bishop of Clermont, was the last of the great pulpit orators. Court preacher after BOSSUET, he resembles more closely BOURDALOUE in his portrayal of vice and elegance of diction. His *Petit Carême* (1718), of ten sermons, is his most finished work. The *Avent* and the *Grand Carême* are more Christian and personal. In the funeral oration he acquired renown, as those on Conti (1709), on the Dauphin (1711), and on Louis XIV. (1715). The *Discours synodaux* (1723–1742) are less elaborate and more original. His defects are in preaching morals rather than dogma and in striving for too artistic a style.

8. **Fiction: Novels; Fairy Tales.** — The novelistic effort of the seventeenth century died away with MME. DE LA FAYETTE. Short stories and popular tales become the fashion. — Following the *Princesse de Clèves*, MARIE-CATHERINE D'AULNOY (1650–1705) wrote various novels, as the *Aventures d'Hippolyte, comte de Douglas* (1690). She is better known for her *Contes de Fées* (1698), the simplicity of which she ruined with contemporaneous allusions. She is also author of *Mémoires sur la cour d'Espagne* (1690). — MLLE. DE LA FORCE (1650–1724) wrote memoirs and the *Roman de Gustave Vasa*. —

ANTHONY, count of HAMILTON (1646–1721), imitates the *Contes* of LA FONTAINE in the *Contes de Féeries*, and writes the *Mémoires du comte de Grammont* (1713), valuable for the social life of the time. — The great writer of fairy tales is CHARLES PERRAULT (1628–1703), of Paris, who began with poor epic and lyric poetry. His *Siècle de Louis le Grand* (1687), a poem read before the Academy, renewed, by its comparisons with antiquity, the quarrel of the ancients and moderns. In answer to BOILEAU, PERRAULT published the *Parallèle des anciens et des modernes* (1688, 1693) in dialogue form, followed by the *Hommes illustres* (1696–1701), the biographies of the French leaders of the century. The fame of PERRAULT is due to the *Histoires ou Contes du temps passé* (1697) or the *Contes de ma mère l'Oie*, which he took from among the people and rendered in an attractive form. The *Contes en vers* (1694), similar tales, he had published in the *Recueil* of MOETJENS at The Hague. — Of interest are the *Mille et une nuits* (1704–1708), translated by ANTOINE GALLAND (1646–1715) from Arabian and Turkish manuscripts.

9. **Picaresco Novels.** — The great novelist of the epoch is ALAIN-RENÉ LESAGE (1668–1747), of Sarzeau. After many hack translations and literary failures, a prose comedy, *Crispin rival de son maître* (1707) established his reputation. A picaresco novel, the *Diable boiteux* (1707), freely imitated after the *Diablo cojuelo* of GUEVARA, revealed his talent in its realistic pictures of French life. Another comedy, *Turcaret* (1709), a bitter satire against the financiers, exact in view and lively in dialogue, was followed by farces for the fairs. His

master-piece is the picaresco novel, *Histoire de Gil Blas de Santillane* (1715–1735), a portrayal of the manners, weaknesses, and vices of all classes of society, due to the author's own observation. Its influence on English fiction was great. LESAGE translated many Spanish novels, the *Orlando innamorato* of BOJARDO, wrote the *Mille et un jours* (1710–1711), vaudevilles, and comic operas. His style is that of the seventeenth century, though his spirit is modern.

PART V.

The Eighteenth Century. 1718–1801.

CHAPTER XIV.

FIRST PERIOD. 1718–1750.

1. **Poetry.** François-Marie Arouet (Voltaire), 1694–1778; Louis Racine, 1692–1763; Jean-Baptiste-Louis Gresset, 1709–1777.
2. **Drama.** Tragedy: Voltaire; Antoine Houdart de La Motte, 1672–1731. Comedy: Pierre Carlet de Chamblain de Marivaux, 1688–1763; Philippe Néricault Destouches, 1680–1754; Alexis Piron, 1689–1773. Melodrama: Pierre-Claude Nivelle de La Chaussée, 1692–1754.
3. **Prose.** Voltaire. Memoirs and history: Louis de Rouvray de Saint-Simon, 1675–1755; Mme. de Staal-Delaunay, 1684–1750; Charles Rollin, 1661–1741. Essays: Charles de Secondat de Montesquieu, 1689–1755; Luc de Clapiers de Vauvenargues, 1715–1747. Philosophy: Julien Offray de La Mettrie, 1709–1751. Oratory: Henri-François d'Aguesseau, 1668–1751. Novels: Antoine-François Prévost d'Exiles, 1697–1763; Claude-Prosper Jolyot de Crébillon, 1707–1777.

1. **Characteristics of the Eighteenth Century; Divisions.** — The literature from *Œdipe* (1718) to *Atala* (1801) is, in general, typified by Voltaire. The spirit

THE EIGHTEENTH CENTURY. 175

is critical, scientific, inspired by English philosophy. NEWTON and LOCKE were the masters. Negation became the fashion. — The language is but slightly changed from that of the seventeenth century. Scientific terms were introduced, but the writers, striving after simplicity and purity, fell into monotony, poverty of expression, and a colorless style. — Poetry was still more enfeebled by these causes, working out the rules of BOILEAU and MALHERBE. — With poetry suffered also drama, though melodrama was invented, ideas were taken from the English stage, and various bright but superficial comedies appeared. The best of the century is in the prose and rather in the thought than in the style, which copied the authors of the classical period with decreasing vigor and richness. — Two periods are clearly marked. One of reaction against previous thought, from 1718 to the advent of ROUSSEAU in 1750 — a period satirical rather than revolutionary. — The second, from 1750 to 1801, is characterized by a virulent attack on the existing order of things, culminating in the Revolution.

2. **Poetry**; VOLTAIRE. — Poets of merit were few. FRANÇOIS-MARIE AROUET, called VOLTAIRE (1694–1778), of Paris, attempted pure poetry in an epic poem, the *Henriade*, published at London (1728). The subject is Henry IV. The episodes are imitated from the *Eneid*. Lack of inspiration, monotonous versification, and a rhetorical style did not hinder its success at the time. A second poem, the *Pucelle* (1730), is a coarse parody on Joan of Arc. — Besides fine passages in the *Henriade*, the best verse of VOLTAIRE is in his *Épîtres*, as those to BOILEAU and HORACE (1772), and his *Satires*, as the *Pauvre*

diable, against his opponents. His poetry of occasion and epigrams are also lively and elegant. Various didactic poems, as the *Discours sur l'homme*, after POPE, and the *Poème sur le désastre de Lisbonne*, present the ideas of the English deists and of NEWTON in a pure and poetical style. VOLTAIRE is best in the secondary kinds of verse. He lacks the talent and enthusiasm necessary to the higher poetry.

3. **Other Poets.** — LOUIS RACINE (1692–1763), son of JEAN, wrote odes, epistles, *Mémoires sur la vie de Jean Racine* (1747), and translated *Paradise Lost*. His best works are the didactic poems, *Grâce* and *Religion* (1742). His style is polished and clear. — JEAN-BAPTISTE-LOUIS GRESSET (1709–1777), of Amiens, is the author of a comedy, the *Méchant* (1747), witty and poetical. His best work is the humorous epic, *Vert-Vert* (1734), on a parrot's life. The *Carême impromptu* and the *Chartreuse* are narratives remarkable for style. GRESSET is saved by his wit.

4. **Tragedy.** — As in poetry so in drama VOLTAIRE is the best author of the period, though second-rate. He was inspired by the plays of the classical writers and of the English stage. *Œdipe* (1718), declamatory but vigorous, revived popular interest in tragedy. *Brutus* (1730), and *Zaïre* (1732), his master-piece, are inspired by notions of political liberty. *Mérope* (1743) is nearest his models in style and action. Several tragedies of CRÉBILLON were worked over by VOLTAIRE without success (1748–1752). *Tancrède* (1760) is his last good play. Of the dozen remaining, *Alzire*, or the *Américains* (1736) and *Mahomet* (1741) deserve mention. — The

theater of VOLTAIRE is brilliant but superficial. He established a larger choice of subject, improved the mechanism of the play and reformed costume and scenery in a practical way. His style, often animated and emotional, is more frequently declamatory and prosaic. His plots are generally arguments in favor of his views, and thus are wanting in the study of character and in passion. — ANTOINE HOUDART DE LA MOTTE (1672–1731) was an essayist, a writer of odes, and a leader of the moderns in their quarrel with the ancients. Though ignorant of Greek, he worked over the *Iliad* to prove HOMER a poor poet. His best work is the pathetic tragedy, *Inès de Castro* (1723).

5. **Comedy.** — The theater of the period is much more attractive on the side of comedy. — PIERRE CARLET DE CHAMBLAIN DE MARIVAUX (1688–1763), of Paris, invents his own plots and style. Superficial, avoiding dramatic scenes and character studies, he excels in grace, in wit, and in delicacy of sentiment. To his thought is fitted his language, termed *marivaudage* for its witty affectation. Several of his plays remain on the stage, as the *Jeu de l'amour et du hasard* (1730), the *Fausses confidences* (1736) and the *Legs* (1736). — PHILIPPE NÉRICAULT DESTOUCHES (1680–1754), of Tours, deeply imbued with English literature, shows its didactic and pathetic tendency in his many comedies, which are among the best of the century. The *Irrésolu* (1713), the *Philosophe marié* (1727), and especially the *Glorieux* (1732), a satire on the sudden fortunes of the Regency, are well written and skillfully wrought out, yet fail in gayety and observation. They were frequently translated into German.

—ALEXIS PIRON (1689-1773), of Dijon, noted for his brilliant epigrams and for his literary club, the *Caveau*, wrote vaudevilles, parodies, tragedies, and attained lasting dramatic success in the comedy, *Métromanie* (1738), a satire on poetasters, in fine style and polished verse.

6. **Melodrama.**—An attempt to revive comedy, suggested probably by English models, was made by PIERRE-CLAUDE NIVELLE DE LA CHAUSSÉE (1692-1754), of Paris. A union of the comic with the pathetic, called *Comédie larmoyante* or *Drame bourgeois*, the plays of LA CHAUSSÉE have a moral purpose and deal with social questions. Among them are the *Fausse antipathie* (1733), the *Préjugé à la mode* (1735), *Mélanide* (1741), the *École des mères* (1744), and the *Gouvernante* (1747). Poor in style, monotonous, abounding in maxims and didactic harangues, they still were popular, compelled VOLTAIRE to imitation in the *Enfant prodigue* (1736) and *Nanine* (1749), and opened the way for DIDEROT.

7. **Prose; Memoirs.** — Philosophic essays on people, customs, and institutions form the great body of prose in this period.—It saw, however, the greatest memoirist of France, LOUIS DE ROUVRAY (1675-1755), duke of SAINT-SIMON. From daily notes he compiled his *Mémoires* (a. 1740) of the decadence of Louis XIV. and of the Regency (1692-1723). A courtier, honest but prejudiced, he sketches his life and surroundings at the court, analyzing intrigues and delineating character. Vigorous and impassioned, neglecting style in his eagerness to narrate, his descriptive talent and his intimate knowledge of the times render his work most valuable.— MME. DE STAAL-DELAUNAY (1684-1750) owes her repu-

tation to her style. The *Mémoires* of her unimportant life, both witty and natural, often sad, are a model of clear and sprightly narration. — The *Souvenirs* of MME. DE CAYLUS (1673–1720), niece of Mme. de Maintenon, are life-like, graceful sketches of court scenes. — Interesting for the common life of the time is the *Journal* of MATHIEU MARAIS (1665–1737). — Many memoirs were written by magistrates and statesmen.

8. VOLTAIRE, eminent in this as in the other branches of literature, began with a study of the English people and laws in the *Lettres sur les Anglais* (1731), a eulogy of England, detractive of France, and inspired with a skeptical spirit. More historical is the *Histoire de Charles XII.* (1731), clear, concise, brilliant, but rather romantic. The *Siècle de Louis XIV.* (1752), finished at Berlin, had great influence in establishing the literary supremacy of that age. Making arbitrary use of his material, studying the events from the standpoint of civilization, he errs in the construction of his narrative and interrupts its continuity. Yet he is clear in exposition, easy in style, and sensible in opinion. It is his best historical work. The *Essai sur les mœurs et l'esprit des nations* (1756), developed from the *Abrégé d'histoire universelle*, though one-sided in its opposition to the views of BOSSUET, founded the history of national development. The *Histoire de Russie sous Pierre I.* (1759) resembles that of Charles XII. Other historical works, as the *Précis du siècle de Louis XV.* (1768), have the same merits of style and narration and the same critical defects. — Literary, political, moral, and religious subjects are discussed by VOLTAIRE in a multitude of essays pub-

lished separately, or in the Encyclopædia of DIDEROT, and collected in the *Dictionnaire philosophique*. They show his merits of style and good sense, but also his frivolity and superficiality. Hostility to Christianity pervades the greater part. His *Commentaire de Corneille* (1764) reveals good literary taste and judgment, but also his ignorance of the history of the French language and literature.— The best conception of VOLTAIRE's life and work is gained from his vast *Correspondance* of several thousand letters, models of the art, addressed to all ranks of society.

9. CHARLES DE SECONDAT (1689-1755), baron of MONTESQUIEU, rivaled VOLTAIRE in celebrity and excels him in lasting worth. The *Lettres persanes* (1721) are a satire on the manners and life of France under the Regency, keen and bold. It was followed by the *Temple de Gnide* (1725), a somewhat immoral narrative. After travels in Europe, where he came under the influence of Chesterfield, and a residence in England, MONTESQUIEU worked in retirement on the *Considérations sur les causes de la grandeur des Romains et de leur décadence* (1734), the first complete illustration of philosophical history. The style is concise, simple, sententious. A continuation is the *Dialogue de Sylla et d'Eucrate* (1745).— The *Considérations* were but an introduction to the great work of MONTESQUIEU, the *Esprit des lois* (1748), conceived in the same spirit and the product of the same method. It is a study of cause and effect in human affairs. Though divided into an excessive number of paragraphs the style is pure, vigorous, and precise. Its success is seen in its twenty-two editions in less than two years. Its influence

on subsequent legislation is incalculable. — Minor works of MONTESQUIEU are a story, *Lysimaque;* a novel, *Arsace et Isménie;* and a voluminous correspondence.

10. **Essays ; History; Oratory; Philosophy.** — Among the many writers of the time, few, by their thought and form, belong to literature. — CHARLES ROLLIN (1661–1741), of Paris, eminent in the history of **education**, began with the *Traité des études* (1726–1731), a system of public education, advocating instruction in French, the study of history, of the elements of science, and changes in discipline. As treatises for the youth he wrote the *Histoire ancienne* (1730–1738) and the *Histoire romaine* (1738–1741), both compilations from the historians of antiquity, uncritical, but well-ordered and attractive. The former remained the text-book for many decades and was much translated. — A **moralist** is LUC DE CLAPIERS (1715–1747), marquis of VAUVENARGUES. His unfinished work includes the *Introduction à la connaissance de l'esprit humain* (1746) and *Réflexions et maximes*, in which duty and virtue are enjoined in a pure and poetical style. The *Caractères* and *Dialogues* are short moral and critical treatises. An idealist, his writings attract by their emotion. — **Oratory** of the pulpit had declined. That of the bar was made eminent by HENRI-FRANÇOIS D'AGUESSEAU (1668–1751), of Limoges. His *Mercuriales* (before Parliament) and pleas are forcible, eloquent, but too ornate. In the *Instructions*, for his son, he imitates CHESTERFIELD. His correspondence is valuable for the knowledge of the times. — Materialistic **philosophy** is represented by JULIEN OFFRAY DE LA METTRIE (1709–1751), of St. Malo. Among his

numerous works are the *Histoire naturelle de l'âme* (1745) and the *Homme-machine* (1748). Man is merely body. There is no soul.

11. **Fiction.** — After LESAGE novels deteriorated. — MARIVAUX, who tried journalism in the *Spectateur français* (1722), after ADDISON, wrote the still readable *Vie de Marianne* (1731–1741), illustrating the triumph of virtue. Less successful is the unfinished *Paysan parvenu* (1735). Both influenced English fiction. — The *Histoire du Chevalier des Grieux et de Manon Lescaut* (1733), by the abbot ANTOINE-FRANÇOIS PRÉVOST D'EXILES (1697–1763), has alone survived of his two hundred volumes — mainly imitations and translations of the English school. Its accent of truth and fidelity to life give it lasting success. PRÉVOST also edited the *Pour et le Contre* (1733–1740), modeled on the *Spectator*. — Short stories were written by VOLTAIRE. *Zadig* (1747), *Candide* (1759), the *Ingénu* (1767), and the *Homme aux quarante écus* (1768) rival one another in irony, bitterness, and the satirical description of human faults and weaknesses. Though without plan or composition, they are in style the best of VOLTAIRE. The stories of CLAUDE-PROSPER JOLYOT DE CRÉBILLON (1707–1777), the Younger, are striking pictures of the social vices of the time, relieved by psychological keenness and a fine style. The *Lettres de la marquise* (1732), the *Égarements du cœur et de l'esprit* (1736) and the *Sopha* (1745) were imitated by a school of minor writers.

12. **Literary History.** — On the history of literature various important works appeared, as the *Histoire générale du théâtre français* (1745–1749) by CLAUDE (1701–

1777) and FRANÇOIS (1698–1755) PARFAICT; the *Histoire littéraire* (1733–), begun by the Benedictines and continued by the Institute; the *Bibliothèque française* (1741–1756) of CLAUDE-PIERRE GOUJET (1697–1767); and the *Usage des romans* (1734), by the abbot LENGLET DU FRESNOY. The *Histoire de l'Académie*, of PELLISSON, was continued by the abbot D'OLIVET (1682–1768), who also translated the classics and wrote treatises on grammar.

The Eighteenth Century. 1718–1801.

CHAPTER XV.

SECOND PERIOD. 1750-1801.

1. **Poetry.** Lyric: PONCE-DENIS ÉCHOUARD-LEBRUN, 1729-1807; CLAUDE-JOSEPH DORAT, 1734–1780; NICOLAS-JOSEPH-LAURENT GILBERT, 1751–1780; ÉVARISTE-DÉSIRÉ DESFORGES DE PARNY, 1753–1814; ANDRÉ-MARIE DE CHÉNIER, 1762–1794. Descriptive: CHARLES-FRANÇOIS DE SAINT-LAMBERT, 1716-1803; JACQUES DELILLE, 1738-1813.
2. **Drama.** Melodrama: DENIS DIDEROT, 1713–1784. Comedy: MICHEL-JEAN SEDAINE, 1719–1797; CHARLES PALISSOT DE MONTENOY, 1730–1814; PIERRE-AUGUSTIN CARON DE BEAUMARCHAIS, 1732–1799; JEAN-FRANÇOIS COLLIN D'HARLEVILLE, 1755–1806. Tragedy: JEAN-FRANÇOIS DUCIS, 1733–1816; MARIE-JOSEPH DE CHÉNIER, 1764–1811. Vaudevilles.
3. **Prose.** JEAN-JACQUES ROUSSEAU, 1712–1778. The Encyclopedists: DIDEROT; JEAN LE ROND D'ALEMBERT, 1717–1783. Treatises: FRANÇOIS QUESNAY, 1694–1774; TURGOT, 1727–1781; GABRIEL BONNOT DE MABLY, 1709–1785; GUILLAUME-THOMAS-FRANÇOIS RAYNAL, 1713–1796. Essays: CHARLES PINOT DUCLOS, 1704–1772; SÉBASTIEN-ROCH-NICOLAS CHAMFORT, 1741-1794; ANTOINE DE RIVAROL, 1753-1801. Science: JEAN-LOUIS LECLERC DE BUFFON, 1707–1788. Criticism: JEAN-FRANÇOIS MARMONTEL, 1723–1799; JEAN-FRANÇOIS DE LA HARPE, 1739–1803; FRIEDRICH MELCHIOR GRIMM, 1723-1807. Philosophy: CLAUDE-ADRIEN HELVÉTIUS, 1715–1771; ÉTIENNE BONNOT DE MABLY-CONDILLAC, 1715–1780. Ora-

tory: MIRABEAU, 1749-1791.. Fiction: DIDEROT; MARMONTEL; JEAN-JACQUES BARTHÉLEMY, 1716-1795; JACQUES-HENRI BERNARDIN DE SAINT-PIERRE, 1737-1814; JEAN-PIERRE CLARIS DE FLORIAN, 1755-1794.

1. Features of the Period; Poetry. — The second period of the eighteenth century includes two distinct features: the stage of revolutionary preparation in literature was followed by a revolutionary outbreak, beginning with BEAUMARCHAIS' *Mariage de Figaro* (1784). The spirit, however, was one of social reform. Elements of a literary transformation do not appear before CHATEAUBRIAND. — The drama and prose of the period testify to the national unrest, and consider, as a rule, social questions. In merit they differ but little from those of the preceding period. — Poetry, however, improves in the hands of more talented writers, and produces one of the best poets of France, ANDRÉ DE CHÉNIER. The descriptive kind is erected into a separate branch.

2. Lyric Poets of the Conventional Type. — A follower of J.-B. ROUSSEAU is LEFRANC DE POMPIGNAN (1709-1784), whose religious odes have often emotion and force. — Epic poetry was continued by MARIE-ANNE FIQUET DU BOCCAGE (1710-1802), in the *Paradis terrestre* (1748), after MILTON, and in the *Colombiade* (1756), both very poor. — PONCE-DENIS ÉCHOUARD-LEBRUN (1729-1807), of Paris, wrote good odes on public men and events, as the *Vengeur*. He excelled in the epigram and attempted didactic poetry. — CLAUDE-JOSEPH DORAT (1734-1780) imitated with skill the stories and fables of LA FONTAINE. He advocated, in the *Idée de la poésie allemande*, the study of German literature. — Much more talent and inspiration was shown by NICOLAS-JOSEPH-LAURENT GILBERT (1751-1780), of Lorraine. His *Dix-huitième siècle* (1775) is a forcible and bitter satire on the vices of the time, in the style of JUVENAL. The *Ode imitée de plusieurs psaumes* (1780) is the most poetical composition of the century previous to CHÉNIER. — ÉVARISTE-DÉSIRÉ DESFORGES (1753-1814), viscount PARNY, was the author of emotional elegies of much beauty, of gallant verse, the *Poèmes érotiques*, and of the anti-religious epic, the *Guerre des Dieux anciens et modernes* (1799). His influence on CHATEAUBRIAND and LAMARTINE is seen in their early works. — The patriotic poetry of JOSEPH ROUGET DE L'ISLE (1760-1836) is known through the *Marseillaise* (1792). He also wrote the *Chant de vengeance* and the *Chant de Roland.*

3. ANDRÉ-MARIE DE CHÉNIER (1762-1794), born at Constantinople, and guillotined under the Terror, stands apart from his age in talent and spirit. Son of a Greek mother, he began his poetic career with translations of ANACREON and SAPPHO. Traveling in Switzerland, he is the first French poet to celebrate the mountains (1783). On the approach of the Revolution, his poems show a desire for political freedom, and he becomes an editor of the Girondist *Journal de Paris*. His unfinished work comprises the *Bucoliques*, many imitated freely from the Greek; didactic poems, as *Hermes* (an encyclopædia of the world and man), *Invention*, and *Amérique*, all abounding in fine verse; *Élégies* and *Épîtres*, recounting his life and habits. After 1789 appear his *Odes*, as the *Jeu de Paume, À Charlotte Corday*, and *Versailles*, his best. In prison he wrote the *Iambes*, against the Jacobins, his master-pieces

being the poems, *Comme un dernier rayon* and the *Jeune captive*. He began also tragedies and comedies. — The inspiration of the pre-Revolutionary poetry of CHÉNIER is mainly that of antiquity. Yet he is still of the eighteenth century, skeptical, epicurean, calm. After the States General the hopes and passions of the time find in him their expression. In both periods he shows himself a master of form, of poetical language, and of harmonious rhythm. He freshens the alexandrine. His inspiration is inward, personal. Unknown for decades (1816), he had no followers.

4. **Descriptive Poetry.** — The last resource of art is description. The descriptive poetry of the period is in imitation of that of England. — CHARLES-FRANÇOIS DE SAINT-LAMBERT (1716-1803), of Nancy, imitated THOMSON in his *Saisons* (1769), which excited the admiration of the age. He also wrote the *Catéchisme universel* (1797-1800), a treatise on moral science. — JACQUES DELILLE (1738-1813) followed also the English school in translating the *Georgics* (1769), in writing the *Jardins* (1782), the *Homme des champs* (1800), and various other poems, all correct, but without emotion. He was the literary dictator of his time. — Many other poets copied them or their English models, as JEAN-ANTOINE ROUCHER (1745-1794), of Montpellier, author of the *Mois* (1779). — The French school was, in turn, imitated in Italy and Spain.

5. **Melodrama.** — The efforts of LA CHAUSSÉE to quicken comedy were systematically continued by DENIS DIDEROT (1713-1784), of Langres. The purpose of DIDEROT was to make the stage a mirror of real life, as

well as to inculcate moral lessons. He attacked the classical unities, the stiff tone of tragedy, and the separation of the comic and tragic. He chose the life of the middle class for his field, and substituted for poetry the prose of daily conversation. His plays, the *Fils naturel* (1757) and the *Père de famille* (1758), pathetic and didactic, had more influence abroad, as in Germany, than in France.

6. **Comedy.** — The notion of taking plots from the middle and lower classes prevailed likewise in comedy. — MICHEL-JEAN SEDAINE (1719-1797), after a volume, *Pièces fugitives* (1752), produced one of the best plays of the century in the *Philosophe sans le savoir* (1765), and took from a story of SCARRON the plot of the *Gageure imprévue* (1768). He also improved comic opera by his reforms and his librettos, as *Richard Cœur de Lion*. — LOUIS CARROGIS DE CARMONTELLE (1717-1806) introduced still further the popular element by dramatizing proverbs in his *Proverbes dramatiques* (1768-1781). — CHARLES PALISSOT DE MONTENOY (1730-1814) imitated VOLTAIRE in a satirical epic, the *Dunciade* (1764), against the Middle Ages, wrote unsuccessful tragedies, but called attention to his comedies by assailing ROUSSEAU and the Encyclopedists, as in the *Philosophes* (1760). He was also a fair literary critic. — JEAN-FRANÇOIS COLLIN D'HARLEVILLE (1755-1806) was lyric rather than dramatic in his *Inconstant* (1786), *Châteaux en Espagne* (1789), and *Vieux célibataire* (1792). — As director of the Opéra-Comique CHARLES-SIMON FAVART (1710-1792), a poet of the *Jeux floraux*, wrote vaudevilles, much in vogue, and light operas, as the *Trois Sultanes* (1761).

7. PIERRE-AUGUSTIN CARON DE BEAUMARCHAIS (1732-

1799), of Paris, was the most successful dramatist of the time. He began with sentimental dramas, in the style of DIDEROT, as *Eugénie* (1767) and the *Deux amis* (1770) which were well received. Democratic in spirit and hostile to the privileged classes is his comedy, the *Barbier de Séville* (1776), witty, abounding in dramatic situations and happy in invention. A sequel is the *Mariage de Figaro* (1784), in which the upper classes and their characteristics are keenly and forcibly held up to ridicule. Its great run foretold the coming Revolution. A continuation, the *Mère coupable* (1791), was lifeless and flat. BEAUMARCHAIS gained much fame from four *Mémoires* (1773) against bribery in law, which aroused public sentiment on the subject. — A follower of BEAUMARCHAIS is PHILIPPE-FRANÇOIS-NAZAIRE FABRE (1755–1794), called D'ÉGLANTINE from a prize won in the *Jeux floraux*. He satirizes the higher society in successful plays, as the *Philinte de Molière* and the *Précepteurs*. — **Vaudevilles** became very popular in this period and were cultivated by literary writers.

8. **Tragedy.** — The taste for classical tragedy had passed, though it was still written and played. — PIERRE-LOUIS DE BELLOY (1727–1775) wrote many national tragedies, of which the *Siège de Calais* (1765), deeply patriotic, had success. — English dramatic influence, introduced by VOLTAIRE, took shape in the *Théâtre de Shakespeare*, a poor prose translation by PIERRE LETOURNEUR (1736–1788), which aroused VOLTAIRE's jealousy. — On this translation JEAN-FRANÇOIS DUCIS (1733–1816), of Versailles, based his sentimental versions of *Hamlet* (1769), *Romeo et Juliette* (1772), *Macbeth* (1789), and

other plays which prepared the way for subsequent reforms. — A follower of VOLTAIRE is MARIE-JOSEPH DE CHÉNIER (1764–1811), brother of ANDRÉ, who brought into his plays political doctrines. *Charles IX.* (1789), *Henri VIII.* (1791), *Caïus Gracchus* (1792), *Timoléon* (1794), and his best drama, *Tibère* (1805), forbidden by Napoleon, are dissertations against tyranny and fanaticism. He is also the author of good *Épîtres.* — The period shows throughout a constant effort to put new ideas into the old forms.

9. **Prose: the Work of** ROUSSEAU. — The great writers of the period proclaimed the inferiority of poetry to prose. VOLTAIRE stood alone in his cultivation of the former. — JEAN-JACQUES ROUSSEAU (1712–1778), of Geneva, introduced into prose the language of poetry. An ardent musician and writer of comedies and operas, as the *Devin du village* (1752), he attracted universal notice in a prize essay (1750) for the Academy of Dijon on the benefits derived from civilization. The system of Rousseau is found already in this eloquent tirade against learning, society, and progress. The *Lettres sur la musique française* (1752) deny musical talent to France. The *Discours sur l'économie politique* (1753), in the Encyclopædia, advocates state control of property and manners. The *Discours sur l'origine et les fondements de l'inégalité parmi les hommes* (1755), for the Dijon Academy, assails society and property and affirms the ideal state to be that of nature, of the savage. The *Lettre à d'Alembert contre les spectacles* (1758) attacks the stage as glorifying vice. — To further advance his social views he chooses the form of a novel, *Julie, ou la Nouvelle Héloïse* (1760),

which excited great interest. Nominally in the interest of virtue, abounding in rhetorical figures, eloquent and often declamatory, this work in its description of landscapes introduces into literature the love of nature. — The *Contrat social* (1762) is an argument in favor of an absolute democracy which by majority vote may control the public and private life of the individual. The influence of PLUTARCH is evident. — The views of ROUSSEAU on education, derived partially from LOCKE, appear in *Émile* (1762). The child should be left to nature and learn by nature's laws, aided by a skillful instructor. In *Émile* ROUSSEAU takes occasion to affirm his belief in the immortality of an immaterial soul and in the existence of a personal God (the *Profession de foi du vicaire savoyard*). — The *Confessions* (1782) are a cynical autobiography, remarkable for style, for the sentiment of nature, the desire for a simple life, and for the enthusiasm for a new social fabric. Among his other works is a *Dictionnaire de musique*. — The influence of ROUSSEAU in politics is seen in the conduct of the French Revolution; in literature, by the sentimental spirit of subsequent fiction in France and Germany. On education, on religion, and on domestic life his views were studied and widely followed.

10. **The Encyclopedists.** — Opposed to ROUSSEAU in reality, though associated with him in work and reforms, were the disciples of VOLTAIRE. Their chief, DIDEROT, began his career with translations from the English, with philosophic essays, as *Sur le mérite et la vertu* (1745), after SHAFTESBURY, and with a defense of atheism, the *Lettre sur les aveugles* (1749). He undertook the *Encyclopédie* (1751-1777), in thirty-five volumes,

aided by D'ALEMBERT and the prominent writers of the time, with the object of bringing together all human knowledge and of presenting its principle. The part of DIDEROT, besides the editorial work, bore especially on the arts and trades. The spirit of the work was, in the main, materialistic. Its success was great, and translations spread abroad its doctrines. DIDEROT began art criticism in the *Salons* (1761–), but considered paintings rather from the standpoint of a moralist. His *Correspondance* is valuable for social and literary studies. His later essays, of which the most important are the *Lettre sur les sourds-muets* (1754) and the *Rêve de D'Alembert* (1769), show the same materialistic bent. — His style is unequal, sometimes precise, but often pretentious. It is always animated. — JEAN LE ROND D'ALEMBERT (1717–1783), of Paris, a scientist, wrote the *Discours préliminaire de l'Encyclopédie* (1751), after BACON, and the mathematical articles. Among his other works is a *Histoire des membres de l'Académie française morts depuis 1700 jusqu'en 1771* (1779–1787). His style is clear but lifeless.

11. Treatises. — Scientific, historical, and political writers abound, many of whom contributed to the Encyclopædia. — FRANÇOIS QUESNAY (1694–1774), physician to Louis XV., published various works on **political economy**, as the *Tableau économique* (1758), in which agriculture is given as the source of the national wealth. — ANNE-ROBERT-JACQUES TURGOT (1727–1781) wrote many essays on religion and economics, notably the *Recherches sur l'origine et la formation des richesses* (1774). — GABRIEL BONNOT DE MABLY (1709–1785) aided the revolutionary current in his *Observations sur les Grecs* (1749), *Sur l'histoire de France* (1765), *Sur les États-Unis* (1784), his *Entretiens de Phocion* (1763), and other works, poor in style, but filled with admiration for the constitutions of antiquity. — GUILLAUME-THOMAS-FRANÇOIS RAYNAL (1713–1796), the author of a *Correspondance littéraire* (1742–1754), attacks religion and state in the *Histoire philosophique et politique des établissements et du commerce des Européens dans les deux Indes* (1778), written under the influence of DIDEROT. — CHARLES DE BROSSES (1709–1777), president of the Parliament of Dijon, describes his **travels** in Italy in the *Lettres sur l'état de la ville de Herculanum* (1750), attempts scientific treatises, as the *Formation mécanique des langues* (1765), and history.

12. **Essays** are not less numerous. — CHARLES PINOT DUCLOS (1704–1772), a poor novelist and historian, succeeded in the witty *Considérations sur les mœurs de ce siècle* (1751), an agreeable and animated description of manners and men. — SÉBASTIEN-ROCH-NICOLAS CHAMFORT (1741–1794) wrote comedies, literary *Éloges*, but especially *Pensées, maximes, anecdotes*, bitter, keen, and embodying concisely the spirit of the age. — ANTOINE DE RIVAROL (1753–1801), a literary critic and translator of DANTE, satirizes contemporary writers in the *Petit almanach de nos grands hommes* (1788). A royalist, he contributes to their journals (1789–) many political articles. He possessed also the elements of a philologist. — More technical and less moral are essays on the **fine arts** by CHARLES BATTEUX (1713–1780). His *Principes de littérature* (1747–1755), based on ARISTOTLE, had much influence in Germany.

13. **Science** becomes literature in the hands of JEAN-LOUIS LECLERC (1707–1778), count of BUFFON. His investigations, conducted patiently and methodically, were embodied in the *Histoire naturelle* (1749–1804), of debatable technical worth, but remarkable for its noble and dignified style. The views of BUFFON on this point are given in his *Discours de réception à l'Académie française* (1753). Ideas are universal, style alone is peculiar to the individual: "Le style est l'homme même." BUFFON had a great aversion for poetry.

14. **Criticism** forms the lasting work of JEAN-FRANÇOIS MARMONTEL (1723–1799), of Limousin, who began with tragedies (1748–1753), after VOLTAIRE, and left *Mémoires* concerning particularly the literary *salons* of the century. His *Poétique française* (1763) was followed by the *Éléments de littérature* (1787), a collection of articles written for the Encyclopædia. He also wrote novels, an essay, *Sur la langue française*, and poems in imitation of the Spanish ballads. — JEAN-FRANÇOIS DE LA HARPE (1739–1803), of Paris, likewise a disciple of VOLTAIRE, began with successful tragedies, as *Warwick* (1763) and *Philoctète* (1783), after SOPHOCLES, and pronounced emphatic *Éloges*. In the *Lycée* (1799–1805) — lectures delivered at that institution — he founds oral literary criticism in France. He is an advocate of poetry and contributed to the national esteem for the authors of the seventeenth century. LA HARPE is the author of a *Correspondance littéraire* (1801–1807) and of commentaries on the theater of RACINE and VOLTAIRE. — FRIEDRICH MELCHIOR GRIMM (1723–1807), of Ratisbonne, owes his importance to his *Correspondance littéraire*, a bi-monthly

series of letters to prominent personages on French literature (1753-1790), and giving the most authentic account of the time. His example was much imitated. — Interest in the old literature was revived by the publication of the popular **epic romances** in the *Bibliothèque universelle des romans* (1775-1789), begun by LA VERGNE DE TRESSAN (1705-1783), and in the *Nouvelle bibliothèque des romans* (1798-1805). — A **philologist** was LA CURNE DE SAINTE-PALAYE (1697-1781), who left a manuscript of the first *Dictionnaire des antiquités françaises*. — DUSSIEUX published the first daily **newspaper**, the *Journal de Paris* (1777).

15. **Philosophy** continued materialistic. — CLAUDE-ADRIEN HELVÉTIUS (1715-1771), of Paris, opposed the views of MONTESQUIEU in his work *De l'esprit* (1758), the doctrine of selfishness. — PAUL HEINRICH DIETRICH VON HOLBACH (1721-1789), of Heidelsheim, assailed all existing relations in the *Système de la nature* (1770), in which the individual, the work of nature, should follow freely his nature. Political anarchy was one of its consequences. — The mathematician, CARITAT DE CONDORCET (1743-1794), in the *Esquisse d'un tableau historique des progrès de l'esprit humain* (1794), showed the historical development of the human mind. — CONSTANTIN-FRANÇOIS DE CHASSEBŒUF-VOLNEY (1758-1820), the last of the Encyclopedists, applied materialism to moral science in the *Catéchisme d'un citoyen français* (1793), and to historical events in the *Ruines*. He also, among other treatises, wrote a scheme of a world-language. — The best philosopher of the century is a follower in part of LOCKE, the abbot ÉTIENNE BONNOT DE MABLY-CON-

DILLAC (1715–1780). In the *Essai sur l'origine des connaissances humaines* (1746), the *Traité des systèmes* (1749), and the *Traité des sensations* (1754), he derives all knowledge from sensual perception. His style is clear and attractive.

16. **Oratory** was revived by the Revolution and found a tribune in the National Assembly. Of the many harangues of the period the *Discours* of GABRIEL-HONORÉ DE RIQUETTI-MIRABEAU (1749–1791) preserve still, in their rough style and incorrect expression, their force and brilliancy. — MIRABEAU is also the author of political treatises, as the *Essai sur le despotisme* (1776) and *De la monarchie prussienne* (1788).

17. **Fiction** produced little of lasting value. — DIDEROT followed CRÉBILLON in the *Bijoux indiscrets* (1748). A polemic, but influenced by RICHARDSON, is the *Religieuse* (1760), a psychological study. The *Neveu de Rameau* (1760), in dialogue form, assails vices and theorizes on music. Other stories, the *Petits papiers*, are remarkable for style and finish. — MARMONTEL, guided by the English school, wrote the *Contes moraux* (1761) for the *Mercure*, keen in observation; the historical but argumentative novels, *Bélisaire* (1767) and the *Incas* (1777), declamatory against fanaticism; and the *Nouveaux contes moraux* (1801). — JEAN-JACQUES BARTHÉLEMY (1716–1795) puts in the form of a novel, the *Voyage du jeune Anacharsis en Grèce* (1788), his knowledge of the manners and life of ancient Greece. The work incited scientific research. — JACQUES-HENRI BERNARDIN DE SAINT-PIERRE (1737–1814), of Le Havre, was a disciple of ROUSSEAU in his sentimentality and love of nature. This influence, given

free play by extensive travel, appeared in the *Voyage à l'Isle de France* (1773) and in the *Études de la nature* (1789), which include the idyll, *Paul et Virginie*. The natural innocence and happiness of man, removed from civilization and left to the savage state, is here unfolded in romantic descriptions and emotional phrases. Its overdelicacy and excessive sentiment were not felt by the ideal tendency of the time. It is the only enduring novel of the period. Of a similar nature is the story, the *Chaumière indienne* (1790). The *Harmonies de la nature* (1796) continue the *Études*. SAINT-PIERRE is the medium of communication between ROUSSEAU and Romanticism. — JEAN-PIERRE CLARIS DE FLORIAN (1755–1794) wrote the pastoral novels, *Galatée* (1783) and *Estelle* (1788). His historical romances, *Numa Pompilius* (1786), *Gonzalve de Cordoue* (1791), after PEREZ DE HITA, and *Guillaume Tell* (1794) were too sentimental. His comedies, stories, and *Fables* (1792), after LA FONTAINE, were better received. — ARNAUD BERQUIN (1749–1791), a writer of idylls and ballads, gained reputation by the *Ami des enfants* (1782), after WEISSE, and other books for children. — RESTIF DE LA BRETONNE (1734–1806) was a voluminous writer of coarse tales, distinguished for observation of manners. In satire he follows CYRANO. He is much imitated in later literature.

PART VI.

The Nineteenth Century. 1801–.

CHAPTER XVI.

FIRST PERIOD. 1801-1848. POETRY. THE DRAMA.

1. **Poetry.** The Classical School: CHARLES DE CHÊNEDOLLÉ, 1769–1833; LOUIS-PIERRE-MARIE-FRANÇOIS BAOUR-LORMIAN, 1770–1854; MARC-ANTOINE-MADELEINE DÉSAUGIERS, 1772–1827; PIERRE-JEAN DE BÉRANGER, 1780–1857; CHARLES-HUBERT MILLEVOYE, 1782–1816; PIERRE-ANTOINE LEBRUN, 1785–1873. The Romantic School: ALPHONSE MARIE-LOUIS DE LAMARTINE, 1790–1869; ÉMILE DESCHAMPS, 1791–1871; ALFRED DE VIGNY, 1799–1863; VICTOR-MARIE HUGO, 1802–1885; AUGUSTE BARBIER, 1805–1882; ALFRED DE MUSSET, 1810–1857; THÉOPHILE GAUTIER, 1811–1872.
2. **Drama.** Classical tragedy: LOUIS-JEAN-NÉPOMUCÈNE LEMERCIER, 1773–1840; ALEXANDRE SOUMET, 1788–1845; JEAN-FRANÇOIS-CASIMIR DELAVIGNE, 1794–1843. Classical comedy: FRANÇOIS ANDRIEUX, 1759–1833; LOUIS-BENOÎT PICARD, 1769–1828. The Romantic theater: HUGO; ALEXANDRE DUMAS, 1803–1870; DE VIGNY; AUGUSTIN-EUGÈNE SCRIBE, 1791–1861; DE MUSSET. Classical reaction: DELPHINE GAY, 1805–1855; FRANÇOIS PONSARD, 1814–1867.

1. Characteristics of the Nineteenth Century; Periods. — The literature of the nineteenth century is the outcome of the social and political revolution of 1789. Opening the French mind to the thought of neighboring peoples, English and German writers were widely imitated. The transference of power to the third estate, and ultimately to the laborer and artisan, gave a new field for study and a new reading public. — The literary revolution began with Rousseau. It was fulfilled in spirit with Chateaubriand, in form with Hugo. The principles which prevailed were to regard more the thought of the productions, their likeness to nature, rather than fidelity to fixed rules of expression. Standards of style wavered. The taste of the moment guided the best authors. Beauty in form and nobility in sentiment were absent. — Two distinct periods separate the works of the century. The first extends from *Atala* (1801) to the death of Chateaubriand (1848), which year saw also a further change in society and government. The second is not yet ended. — The first period is subdivided in poetry and drama. From 1801 to 1820 — the years of the writings of Chateaubriand — diminished and deteriorated by the absolutism of the Revolution, of Napoleon, and of Louis XVIII., they remained within the old forms, and presented, as did the costume and art of the time, the figures of antiquity. On the other hand, the prose, more faithful to the masses, showed in its intense catholicism in religion and literature, the desire for new and broader modes of thought, which culminated in the reform of the Romantic movement (1820-1848).

2. **Poetry** in the forms marked out by Boileau was continued in a romantic spirit by Charles de Chênedollé (1769-1833), who, in his love for nature and

emotional expression, was guided by SAINT-PIERRE and CHATEAUBRIAND. — LOUIS-PIERRE-MARIE-FRANÇOIS BAOUR-LORMIAN (1770-1854), a writer of tragedies and an enemy of the Romantic movement, attempted epic poetry in the *Atlantide* and the *Retour de la religion*, but is best known for his translations of the *Gerusalemme liberata* and of *Ossian*. — PIERRE-ANTOINE LEBRUN (1785-1873) celebrated the military glory of the Empire in various odes, as *Ode à la grande armée* (1805) and *Poème lyrique sur la mort de Napoléon* (1821). He produced *Marie Stuart* (1820), after SCHILLER, and described travels in the poem, *Voyage en Grèce* (1828). — **Descriptive** poetry was cultivated by CHARLES-HUBERT MILLEVOYE (1782-1816), in the *Plaisirs d'un poète, Charlemagne à Pavie*, and the elegy, *Chute des feuilles*.

3. **Popular Poetry** received a literary finish in the *chansons* of MARC-ANTOINE-MADELEINE DÉSAUGIERS (1772-1827), the head of the *Caveau moderne* and a vaudevillist. His songs are mainly on love and wine. — The family poet, who was also patriotic and jovial, was PIERRE-JEAN DE BÉRANGER (1780-1857), of Paris. Beginning with general themes, he continues after the Restoration with political and satirical songs, attacking the government and extolling the Empire, which owes much of the notions of its glory to BÉRANGER. His popularity is still great. His letters are fine specimens of prose.

4. **The Romantic Lyric.** — The essence of Romanticism was freedom in literature. Opposition to rules and theories and attacks on the classical forms were the main features of the movement. The writers sought in the art of the Middle Ages and in the poetry of the

Pléiade their inspiration. — Less important was the influence of the Catholic reaction in France. — The language was enriched with new and obsolete words. Color, life, and sonorousness were aimed at in expression. The versification was rid of the prosaic element, poetical terms were revived or invented, the rules for the cæsura and overflow disregarded, and a multiplicity of verse sought after. — The Romantic school began with the study of foreign literature. It first appeared in journalism, the *Muse française*, to which the *Globe* (1824-1832), founded by PAUL DUBOIS, succeeded. The club of the reformers, the *Cénacle*, was first led by CHATEAUBRIAND, afterwards by NODIER.

5. ALPHONSE MARIE-LOUIS DE LAMARTINE (1790-1869), of Mâcon, forms the transition between the new ideas and their new forms. Like CHATEAUBRIAND his chief characteristics are admiration for religion and nature. His favorite reading was found in Italian authors, MILTON, *Ossian* and his French predecessors. PARNY influenced his first poems. The *Méditations poétiques* (1820), reposing on personal experience and rendered in pure and harmonious verse, revealed the new spirit though still in the old dress. The *Lac* is perhaps the most finished elegy in French literature. — The *Nouvelles Méditations* (1823) and the *Harmonies poétiques et religieuses* (1829) are along the lines marked out by CHATEAUBRIAND and show the same excellence of style and sentiment. — A project of a Christian epic resulted in the episodes, *Jocelyn* (1836), the best long poem of LAMARTINE, and the *Chute d'un ange* (1838), a failure through negligence of expression and dilution of thought. — The *Recueille-*

ments poétiques (1839) and detached works, as the *Mort de Socrate* (1823), and the *Dernier chant du pèlerinage de Childe Harold* (1825), after BYRON, show the merits of LAMARTINE, harmony and purity, and his defects, excessive facility and vagueness. — His prose works, as the *Voyage en Orient* (1835), after CHATEAUBRIAND, the *Histoire des Girondins* (1847), a prose epic, the success and political influence of which was enormous, and the story *Graziella* (1852), an idyll of Naples, are lively in narration and poetical in style. A vast amount of historical sketches, biography, and criticism of slight value contributed to destroy the literary reputation of the poet. — LAMARTINE was also eminent as an orator. In his *Discours de réception* (1830), at the Academy, he appeared as mediator between the old and new schools of poetry.

6. VICTOR-MARIE HUGO (1802–1885), of Besançon, the leader of the Romantic school, seeks only outward material in royalty and Christianity. His genuine inspiration comes from literary opposition to the seventeenth century classics and the ideas of the Encyclopedists. Putting himself forward as the mouthpiece of his age, he aims to express its inspirations and emotions. A poet of the *Jeux floraux* (1818), his *Odes* (1822) show force and beauty. In the *Odes et ballades* (1826), from the Middle Ages, and the *Orientales* (1829), on Eastern subjects, he reveals his nature in the color and brilliancy of his language, in the strangeness of his images, and in the variety of his measures. Rich rime is revived, and the rhythm often drowns the thought. — Social and political subjects are replaced by those of the household

and family in the *Feuilles d'automne* (1831), the *Chants du crépuscule* (1835), the *Voix intérieures* (1837), and the *Rayons et les ombres* (1840). — Political, against the Second Empire, are the *Châtiments* (1852), after D'AUBIGNÉ. The *Contemplations* (1856), on his own life, on the poor, and on nature, were followed by his most ambitious undertaking, an epic of humanity, the *Légende des siècles* (1859, 1877), which for depth of thought, for variety and nobility of expression and richness of similes and verse, is the best work of HUGO. A collection of graceful pastorals are the *Chansons des rues et des bois* (1865). The *Quatre vents de l'esprit* (1881) contain many fine pieces. The posthumous poetry of HUGO, as *Toute la lyre*, shows both the qualities and defects of his previous work. The latter arise from poverty of thought, from a striving for rhetorical effect, and from extravagance in metaphors and language.

7. ALFRED DE MUSSET (1810–1857), of Paris, the third great poet of the century, began as an extreme Romanticist in idea and form, as in the *Contes d'Espagne et d'Italie* (1830). Later his original talent brings him back to classicism. Reflecting the idle and wasted side of life in the Byronian manner, he publishes several collections of poems, as *Un spectacle dans un fauteuil* (1832), in which is *Namouna*, after BYRON's *Don Juan*. *Rolla* (1833) is in the same vein of weary disgust of life. — A broader style and deeper thought are found in the four *Nuits* (1835–1836), inspired by an unfortunate passion for GEORGE SAND. Various poems of the first rank, as the *Lettre à Lamartine* and the *Stances à la Malibran*, followed. — MUSSET is peculiarly the poet of youth.

Save these last works his poems are limited in scope and immature. But he is intense in the expression of personal pain and passion. His verse has the harmony of LAMARTINE together with his own lightness and conciseness.

8. **Minor Poets of the Romantic School.** — The work of ÉMILE DESCHAMPS (1791-1871), of Bourges, was to introduce foreign literature. He translated GOETHE's plays, SCHILLER's poems, and SHAKSPERE's dramas. His *Études françaises et étrangères* (1829-1835) copy the forms of foreign lyrics with an excessive use of feminine rimes. — His brother, ANTONY (1800-1869), translated PETRARCH and DANTE. — MARCELINE DESBORDES-VALMORE (1787-1859) wrote elegies and descriptive poems of much feeling and grace. — More inspiration is shown by ALFRED DE VIGNY (1799-1863), of Loches. A disciple of CHÉNIER and a friend of HUGO, his *Poèmes antiques et modernes* (1822-1826) are unusual for their philosophic thought, pure style, and graceful expression. Didactic and descriptive are the *Destinées* of his later years. His best single works are *Moïse* and *Éloa* of his first attempts. — AUGUSTE BARBIER (1805-1882), of Paris, is best known for his *Iambes* (1831), imitated in form from CHÉNIER. They are satires against the vices and greed of the time. Later, foreign subjects were treated by BARBIER, as *Il pianto* (1833), on Italy, and *Lazare* (1841), on the English laborer. Lighter are his *Chansons et odelettes* (1851) and *Silves et rimes légères* (1872). — A poet of nature is AUGUSTE BRIZEUX (1806-1858), of Lorient, whose idylls, *Marie* (1831) and the *Bretons* (1845), written at first in Celtic, are delicate and

simple scenes of rural life. — Hégésippe Moreau (1810–1838), of Paris, in the *Myosotis* (1838), a collection of elegies, describes his unfortunate career and his misery.

9. Théophile Gautier (1811–1872), of Tarbes, is the most faithful follower and imitator of Hugo. His vocation of artist influenced his choice of picturesque and colored language. His *Premières poésies* (1830), after the *Orientales*, are addressed to the senses alone. His *Émaux et camées*, clear-cut, finely polished, leave little to be desired from the artistic standpoint. He is the leader of the school of art for art and the head of the *Parnassiens*.

10. **Classical Tragedy**, upheld by the genius of Talma (1763–1826), was cultivated by Louis-Jean-Népomucène Lemercier (1773–1840), the author of the scientific epic, the *Atlantiade*, and of the satirical epic, the *Panhypocrisiade* (1819). His best tragedy was *Agamemnon* (1797). In *Christophe Colomb* (1809) the three unities are disregarded. Mediæval history furnishes the subject of later plays, as *Frédégonde et Brunehaut* (1821). Original and vigorous, Lemercier approaches the views of the Romantic school. — Victor-Joseph Étienne de Jouy (1764–1846) wrote *Bélisaire* (1818) and *Sylla* (1821), of slight interest. — Antoine-Vincent Arnault (1766–1834) extolled Bonaparte, after the *Vénitiens* (1799), in *Scipion* (1804) and *Germanicus* (1817). He was also a moral poet and fabulist. — Alexandre Soumet (1788–1845) shows the influence of the reform in *Jeanne d'Arc* (1825), after Schiller, in *Une Fête de Néron* (1830) and *Norma* (1831).

11. **More Romantic** is Jean-François-Casimir Dela-

VIGNE (1794–1843), the poet of the political *Messéniennes* (1818) against the Restoration. Purely classical are his *Vêpres siciliennes* (1819). The *Paria* (1821), Romantic in theme, is followed by *Marino Faliero* (1829), after BYRON. *Louis XI.* (1832) and the *Énfants d'Édouard* (1833), both still popular, show the absorbing tendency of the new school. DELAVIGNE wrote also comedies, at first in the old patterns, as the *Comédiens* (1821) and the *Princesse Aurélie* (1828), afterwards, as *Don Juan d'Autriche* (1835), imitating SCRIBE, with whom he also collaborated. The versification and facility of DELAVIGNE do not compensate for his lack of invention. — JACQUES-ARSÈNE-POLYCARPE-FRANÇOIS ANCELOT (1794–1854) produced a highly successful tragedy, *Louis IX.* (1819), imitated SCHILLER in *Fiesque* (1824), wrote dramas, vaudevilles, comedies, an epic poem, a novel, and the *Épîtres familières*, a collection of satires.

12. **Classical Comedy** is represented by FRANÇOIS-GUILLAUME ANDRIEUX (1759–1833), of Melun, whose *Étourdis* (1787) is his best play. His *Contes* are also distinguished for their wit and grace. — LOUIS-BENOÎT PICARD (1769–1828) is amusing and witty in *Médiocre et rampant* (1797), the *Petite ville* (1801) or the *Marionnettes* (1806). But he lacks style and is superficial. His novels are forgotten. — MICHEL-THÉODORE LECLERQ (1777–1851) followed CARMONTELLE in his *Proverbes dramatiques* (1823, 1836).

13. **The Romantic Drama**, like the poetry, so far as it is in verse, was inspired by the same notions of opposition. In subject, however, it aimed at the imitation of the English stage and attempted, like the *drame bourgeois*

of DIDEROT, to draw nearer to life. The fusion of the comic and the tragic, the violation of the unities, and the introduction of monologues are the principal features. Its language is both popular and noble; its rhythm both regular and broken, the alexandrine is varied, and lyric measures are frequent. The manifesto of the school is the preface of *Cromwell* (1827).

14. VICTOR HUGO, after presenting his views in *Cromwell*, which was never acted, produced, in imitation of the English drama, *Hernani* (1829). The triumph of this play over the opposition of the classicists led to *Marion Delorme* (1831), the *Roi s'amuse* (1832), *Lucrèce Borgia* (1833), *Marie Tudor* (1833), *Angelo* (1835), *Ruy Blas* (1838), next to *Hernani* in merit, and the *Burgraves* (1843), a decided failure. *Torquemada* (1882) is his last play. — The theater of HUGO is his weakest point. His violation of the traditional laws of composition and versification was not counterbalanced by sufficient vigor of thought or dramatic skill. The comic side is too often vulgar, and his conception of the real too trifling or grotesque.

15. ALEXANDRE DUMAS (1803–1870), of Villers-Cotterets, followed English and German models in his plays, original or dramatized from his novels. *Christine de Suède* (1829), *Henri III. et sa cour* (1829), in the taste of the time and full of life, were successful in spite of their defects of action and of historical exactness. *Antony* (1831) and the *Tour de Nesle* (1833) are cruel and bloody, as are the remaining tragedies. In his comedies, as *Kean* (1836) and *Mlle. de Belle-Isle* (1839), DUMAS employs the same methods of surprises and unconnected

development of plot. In his knowledge of the stage and in dramatic instinct he is the best of the school. — ALFRED DE VIGNY translated from SHAKSPERE, *Shylock* (1828) and *Othello* (1829). His historical plays, the *Maréchale d'Ancre* (1831) and *Chatterton* (1835) are less exaggerated than those of HUGO or DUMAS. — The main defect of the Romantic drama is unreality. The truth sought after is lacking. The characters, feebly sketched, speak invariably the sentiments of the author, which derive not from observation, but from imagination. Melancholy is the main trait of the hero.

16. **The Comedy** of the time is neither classical nor Romantic. — Its great exponent, AUGUSTIN-EUGÈNE SCRIBE (1791–1861), of Paris, the author of some four hundred pieces, is renowned mainly for his skill in construction. Beginning with farces, as *Une nuit de corps de garde*, he tried high comedy in the successful *Mariage d'argent* (1827), against the prevailing avarice, and in *Avant, Pendant et Après* (1828), a political trilogy in favor of the government. Besides many vaudevilles, he wrote comedies of note, as *Bertrand et Raton* (1833) and *Adrienne Lecouvreur* (1849), for Rachel. SCRIBE is the best librettist of France, as the *Dame Blanche*, *Masaniello*, *Fra Diavolo* and the operas of Meyerbeer demonstrate. — ALFRED DE MUSSET produced, for reading, various short dramas, as the *Nuit vénitienne* (1830), the *Caprices de Marianne* (1833), *Lorenzaccio* (1834), more ambitious, and the *Chandelier* (1835). His dramatized proverbs, as *Il ne faut jurer de rien*, *On ne badine pas avec l'amour*, and *Il faut qu'une porte soit ouverte ou fermée*, are perhaps the most charming short plays in French literature,

resembling those of MARIVAUX, but stronger, more pathetic, and highly poetical. — PROSPER MÉRIMÉE (1803–1870), of Paris, introduced Romantic notions in a collection of dramas, the *Théâtre de Clara Gazul* (1825), rather realistic in nature.

17. **Classical reaction in tragedy** was brought about by the improbabilities and exaggerations of the Romantic drama. — Incited by Élisabeth Rachel (1821–1858), who revived (1838) CORNEILLE and RACINE with great success, DELPHINE GAY DE GIRARDIN (1805–1855), of Aachen, a follower of LAMARTINE in odes and elegies, wrote *Judith* (1843) and *Cléopâtre* (1847). In comedy she imitated MOLIÈRE in *Lady Tartuffe* (1853) and produced the still popular *La joie fait peur* (1859). — FRANÇOIS PONSARD (1814–1867), of Vienne, opposed the Romanticists in *Lucrèce* (1843), written for Rachel, which established his reputation. *Agnès de Méranie* (1846) and *Charlotte Corday* (1850) were taken from French history. The popular taste changing, PONSARD produces comedies of the ideal, didactic kind, as *Honneur et l'argent* (1853), the *Bourse* (1856), the *Lion amoureux* (1866), and *Galilée* (1867).

THE NINETEENTH CENTURY. 1801–.

CHAPTER XVII.

FIRST PERIOD. 1801-1848. PROSE.

Prose. FRANÇOIS-RENÉ DE CHATEAUBRIAND, 1768–1848. Political treatises: LOUIS-GABRIEL-AMBROISE DE BONALD, 1753–1840; JOSEPH-MARIE DE MAISTRE, 1754–1821; HUGUES-FÉLICITÉ-ROBERT DE LAMENNAIS, 1782–1854. Social treatises: CLAUDE-HENRI DE SAINT-SIMON, 1760–1825; FRANÇOIS-MARIE-CHARLES FOURIER, 1772–1837; PIERRE-JOSEPH PROUDHON, 1809–1865. Essays: JOSEPH JOUBERT, 1754–1824; PAUL-LOUIS COURIER, 1772–1825. History: AIMABLE-GUILLAUME-PROSPER BRUGIÈRE DE BARANTE, 1783–1866; FRANÇOIS-PIERRE-GUILLAUME GUIZOT, 1787–1874; AUGUSTIN THIERRY, 1795–1856; FRANÇOIS-AUGUSTE-ALEXIS MIGNET, 1796–1884; LOUIS-ADOLPHE THIERS, 1797–1877; JULES MICHELET, 1798–1874; ALEXIS CLÉREL DE TOCQUEVILLE, 1805–1859. Literary history and criticism: FRANÇOIS-JUSTE-MARIE RAYNOUARD, 1761–1836; ABEL-FRANÇOIS VILLEMAIN, 1790–1870; CHARLES-AUGUSTIN SAINTE-BEUVE, 1804–1869. Philosophy: PIERRE-PAUL ROYER-COLLARD, 1763–1845; VICTOR COUSIN, 1792–1867; AUGUSTE COMTE, 1798–1857. Oratory: JEAN-BAPTISTE-HENRI LACORDAIRE, 1802–1861. Fiction; Ideal: MME. DE STAËL, 1766–1817; HUGO; DE VIGNY; DUMAS; DE MUSSET; GAUTIER; GEORGE SAND, 1804–1876; ÉMILE SOUVESTRE, 1806–1854; GÉRARD DE NERVAL, 1808–1854; JULES SANDEAU, 1811–1883. Realistic: MARIE-HENRI BEYLE (STENDHAL), 1783–1842; PROSPER MÉRIMÉE, 1803–1870; HONORÉ DE

BALZAC, 1799–1850; FRÉDÉRIC SOULIÉ, 1800–1847; EUGÈNE SUE, 1804–1857; JULES JANIN, 1804–1874; CHARLES DE BERNARD, 1805–1850.

1. **The Prose** of the period was affected by the Romantic movement in its vocabulary and style. The simple, concise, logical phrase gave way before the enthusiasm of new ideas and new modes of expression and left the sentence wavering and obscure. — The dominating spirit is that of ROUSSEAU and of the Encyclopedists. In politics and social science many theories are advocated. History is philosophically cultivated. Criticism is given a new and objective base. Oratory is advanced to a higher plane and invades the schools. Fiction undergoes a great revival and extension and becomes again the leading popular branch of literature.

2. FRANÇOIS-RENÉ DE CHATEAUBRIAND (1768–1848), of St. Malo, is the leader and inspirer of his generation. In him the worship of nature is united with the religious enthusiasm of the Catholic reaction. Attempts at poetry were followed by the skeptical *Essai historique, politique et moral sur les révolutions* (1797), in which he represents humanity as turning hopelessly in an endless circle. — His true vein, strengthened by travel in American forests, appears in *Atala* (1801), a tale of nature, melancholy, and suicide. It forms an episode of the *Génie du Christianisme* (1802), a defense of Christianity from the artistic and literary standpoint, and a eulogy of the Middle Ages. Sentimental rather than dogmatic, bold in its attacks on infidelity, the new thought expressed in a colored and figurative language, the vividness of description and the warmth of its literary expo-

sition assured the work the sympathy of the times it represented. Another episode, *René*, is the romance of the savage life of its restless, melancholy hero. In these fictions is seen the disciple of ROUSSEAU and SAINT-PIERRE. The *Dernier des Abencerages* (1807), after PEREZ DE HITA, was followed by the *Martyrs* (1809), a sequel, in novel form, to the *Génie*. — The style of modern travels was set by the *Itinéraire de Paris à Jérusalem* (1810). Various political writings, the *Natchez* (1826) — a sequel to *René*, — the autobiographical *Mémoires d'outre tombe* (1811-1833) and the *Études historiques* (1831) are his remaining works. — The main defect of CHATEAUBRIAND is lack of plan. He reflects his epoch. He forms the transition and is the chief inspirer of the Romantic movement.

3. **Political and Religious Treatises.** — Among the political writers LOUIS-GABRIEL-AMBROISE DE BONALD (1753-1840) opposed the Revolution in various essays, as the *Théorie du pouvoir civil et religieux* (1796). His views are summed up in the *Législation primitive* (1802). Weak thinking and a severe and firm style are his characteristics. — To the same party belongs JOSEPH-MARIE DE MAISTRE (1754-1821), of Chambéry. The *Considérations sur la France* (1796), against the doctrines of the eighteenth century, the *Essai sur le principe générateur des constitutions politiques* (1810), in favor of an unlimited monarchy, and *Du pape* (1819), advocating the supreme spiritual and temporal authority of the pontiff, were followed by the *Soirées de Saint-Pétersbourg* (1821), philosophical conversations on evil and its punishment, and by various posthumous works. DE MAISTRE resem-

bles ROUSSEAU in his dogmatism and eloquence. — From a purely **religious** point of view the abbot HUGUES-FÉLICITÉ-ROBERT DE LAMENNAIS (1782–1854), of St. Malo, defends the church in the *Réflexions sur l'état de l'église en France* (1808) and in the *Essai sur l'indifférence* (1817–1823), an eloquent attack on skepticism and in favor of the absolute theocracy of the pope. The rights of the latter he had shown historically in the *Traditions de l'église* (1814). The *Apologie* (1821) defends the privileges of the church. The essay, *De la religion* (1825–1826), is against Gallican independence. His journal, the *Avenir* (1830), supported the same democratic opinions. These were further advocated in the *Paroles d'un croyant* (1833), in Biblical style. Other treatises against Rome and in favor of socialism, as *De l'esclave moderne* (1840) and *Esquisse d'une philosophie* (1841–1846), based on common consent, reveal theistic notions. Ardent declamation and mysticism are the chief qualities of LAMENNAIS. — LOUIS VEUILLOT (1813–1883) was the Ultramontane champion in the journal, *Univers*, in clerical novels, and in keen but often coarse pamphlets. — BENJAMIN CONSTANT (1767–1830), an orator of note, led the liberals in politics and religion. His numerous writings and orations and his philosophical work, *De la religion* (1824–1830), were supplemented by novels, as *Adolphe* (1816), and a tragedy, *Waldstein*.

4. **Political Economy** is represented by the numerous works of JEAN-BAPTISTE SAY (1767–1832) of the school of ADAM SMITH. — Industrial socialism is upheld by CLAUDE-HENRI DE SAINT-SIMON (1760–1825), in the *Réorganisation de la société européenne* (1814) and other

writings. — Social reform is demanded by FRANÇOIS-MARIE-CHARLES FOURIER (1772–1837) in the *Théorie de quatre mouvements* (1808) and later treatises. — Private property is attacked in *Qu'est-ce que la propriété ?* (1840) and the *Système des contradictions économiques* (1846) of PIERRE-JOSEPH PROUDHON (1809–1865).

5. **The Essays** of JOSEPH JOUBERT (1754–1824), of Montignac, consist of *Pensées* and *Maximes* on various subjects, highly polished, concise and classical. — PAUL-LOUIS COURIER (1772–1825), of Paris, a student of Greek and of the sixteenth century, satirized the Restoration in pamphlets of exquisite irony and extremely artistic style.

6. **History** of the descriptive kind is seen in the *Histoire des ducs de Bourgogne* (1824–1828) of AIMABLE-GUILLAUME-PROSPER BRUGIÈRE DE BARANTE (1783–1866), who opposed centralization in other works, as the essay *Des communes et de l'aristocratie* (1821) and the *Histoire de la Convention* (1852–1853). His *Tableau de la littérature française au XVIIIe siècle* (1809) advocates national themes and contains well-grounded judgments. — **Philosophical history** is found in the numerous productions of FRANÇOIS-PIERRE-GUILLAUME GUIZOT (1787–1874), of Nîmes. His lectures at the Sorbonne on the history of civilization were published as *Cours d'histoire moderne* (1828–1830). The *Histoire de la révolution d'Angleterre* (1826–1828), the *Collection de mémoires* (1823–1835), the *Vie de Washington* (1839), *Mémoires* (1858–1868), and the *Histoire de France* (1870–1875) are among his most important works. The broad style and easy eloquence of GUIZOT attracted imitators, as did his

method of historical investigation. — Among them FRAN-ÇOIS-AUGUSTE-ALEXIS MIGNET (1796 – 1884), of Aix, gained celebrity by the *Histoire de la Révolution française* (1824), which centers around the third estate. Various studies and biographies, as the *Histoire de Marie Stuart* (1851) and *Portraits et notices* of past colleagues, are distinguished for their keenness of insight and brilliancy of style. — LOUIS-ADOLPHE THIERS (1797 – 1877), of Marseille, an eminent orator, wrote a *Histoire de la Révolution française* (1823–1827), somewhat epic in character, but is best known for the *Histoire du Consulat et de l'Empire* (1843–1863), precise and clear. — A work of social science is *De la démocratie en Amérique* (1835), by ALEXIS CLÉREL DE TOCQUEVILLE (1805–1859), to which his *Ancien régime et la Révolution* (1856) is hardly inferior. — The head of the **descriptive school** is AUGUSTIN THIERRY (1795–1856), of Blois, who produced, with more criticism than BARANTE, the *Histoire de la conquête de l'Angleterre* (1825), the *Lettres sur l'histoire de France* (1827), the *Récits des temps mérovingiens* (1840) and the *Tiers-État* (1853). — JULES MICHELET (1798–1874), of Paris, a deeply poetical nature, displays more partisanship and fancy than historical accuracy in the *Histoire de France* (1837–1867), the *Histoire de la Révolution française* (1847–1853), and various essays, remarkable for their abrupt and picturesque style. — EDGAR QUINET (1803–1875), of Bourg, philosophizes on history and religion in numerous writings, as the *Génie des religions* (1842) and the *Révolutions d'Italie* (1848). He is also a poet and an admirer of the mediæval literature. His bent is mystical. — HENRI MARTIN (1810–1884) resumes the results of the investigators in the standard *Histoire de France* (1833-1836). — Minor historians abound.

7. **Literary History and Criticism.** — Incited by the new historical research, FRANÇOIS-JUSTE-MARIE RAYNOUARD (1761-1836), of Brignoles, the author of tragedies, as the *Templiers* (1805), turned his attention to Provençal linguistics. The *Éléments de la grammaire romane* (1816), the *Choix de poésies originales des Troubadours* (1816-1821), and the *Lexique roman* (1838-1844), together with other publications, established his reputation. — The South of France was also the object of the historical and literary studies of CLAUDE FAURIEL (1772-1844), whose *Histoire de la poésie provenḁle* (1846) is best known. — JEAN-CHARLES-LÉONARD SIMONDE DE SISMONDI (1773-1842), of Geneva, attracted attention by various historical works, as the *Histoire des Français* (1821-1844), and by *De la littérature du midi de l'Europe* (1839). — ABEL-FRANÇOIS VILLEMAIN (1790-1870), of Paris, began the criticism of literature from the historical standpoint. His lectures, published as the *Cours de littérature française* (1828-1838), were supplemented by many literary and historical essays. — The most prominent follower of VILLEMAIN is FRANÇOIS-AUGUSTE SAINT-MARC GIRARDIN (1801-1873), the author of the *Cours de littérature dramatique* (1843) and of *La Fontaine et les fabulistes* (1867).

8. CHARLES-AUGUSTIN SAINTE-BEUVE (1804-1869), of Boulogne-sur-Mer, the critic of the Romantic school, reaches the highest point of the historical method. Beginning with articles in the *Globe*, united in the *Tableau de la poésie française au seizième siècle* (1828, enlarged

1838 by the *Théâtre*), he proved the former independence of the rules of MALHERBE. He continued with various poems and a novel, *Volupté* (1834). A study of the Jansenists resulted in the *Histoire de Port-Royal* (1840). Under the head of *Portraits littéraires* (1832–1839), *Portraits contemporains* (1846), *Causeries du lundi* (1851–1862), *Nouveaux lundis* (1863–1869), and other titles, he collected many studies and sketches which form a history of French literature from the sixteenth century. Isolated works, as *Chateaubriand et son groupe littéraire* (1860), complete the journal articles. The method of SAINTE-BEUVE was to study an author in connection with his surroundings. — JEAN-MARIE-NAPOLÉON-DÉSIRÉ NISARD (1806–1888) upholds the dogmatic, subjective criticism of the **old school** in his *Histoire de la littérature française* (1844–1861), remarkable for its rigid application of æsthetic principles.

9. **Philosophy** passes from the materialistic to the ideal school in the writings of MAINE DE BIRAN (1766–1824). — The doctrines of the Scottish school were adopted by the celebrated orator, PIERRE-PAUL ROYER-COLLARD (1763–1845). — VICTOR COUSIN (1792–1867), of Paris, is eclectic and superficial. His *Cours d'histoire de la philosophie* (1827), his *Fragments philosophiques* (1826), and *Du vrai, du beau et du bien* (1836) are noted for their firm and pure style. COUSIN attained more lasting reputation in his literary-historical essays, as *Jacqueline Pascal* (1842), *Mme. de Longueville* (1853), and the *Société française au XVIIe siècle* (1858). — The great philosopher of the period is AUGUSTE COMTE (1798–1857), whose positivism is expounded in the *Cours de*

philosophie positive (1839 – 1842) and the *Système de politique positive* (1851–1854).

10. **Oratory** counts many illustrious names, as PIERRE-ANTOINE BERRYER (1790–1868), a lawyer and political orator. — The Dominican, JEAN-BAPTISTE-HENRI LACORDAIRE (1802–1861), at first associated with LAMENNAIS, is the greatest preacher of the century. His *Conférences* (1835–1850) treat also of political and social questions.

11. **Ideal Fiction.** — A co-worker with CHATEAUBRIAND in preparing Romanticism (which word she introduced) was ANNE-LOUISE-GERMAINE NECKER DE STAËL (1766–1817), of Paris. The influence of ROUSSEAU is seen in dramas, as *Jane Gray;* stories, as *Mirza;* and the *Lettres sur le caractère et les écrits de J.-J. Rousseau* (1788). Various political pamphlets preceded the demand for a new poetry, after *Ossian* and *Werther,* in *De la littérature considérée dans ses rapports avec les institutions sociales* (1800). The ideal novel, *Delphine* (1802), is against social forms and their harmful influence on the individual. *Corinne* (1807), likewise inspired by her own life, revealed Italian art and literature to France. In *De l'Allemagne* (1810) the German people in its life and education is compared from its own standpoint with the French. The effect of this work on the popular spirit was decisive. Various political treatises and memoirs are posthumous. — Poetical and sensitive, MME. DE STAËL is unequal in her writings. Her main merit was in opening the French mind to foreign influences. — The **classical ideal novel** was continued by MME. DE GENLIS (1746–1830); by JOSEPH FIÉVÉE (1767–1839), the author of the *Dot de Suzette;* by ÉTIENNE PIVERT

DE SÉNANCOUR (1770-1846), whose *Obermann* (1804) is a series of melancholy letters on moral themes and on nature; and by SOPHIE GAY (1776-1852) who, like SÉNANCOUR, shows the new movement in various works, as *Anatolie* (1815). — More observation and reality are found in the stories, after STERNE, of XAVIER DE MAISTRE (1764-1852). His *Voyage autour de ma chambre* (1794), *Lépreux de la cité d'Aoste*, and the *Prisonniers du Caucase*, excel in narrative and emotional style. — CHARLES-EMMANUEL NODIER (1780-1844) begins with sentimental and idyllic novels, as *Stella* (1802) and the *Peintre de Saltzbourg* (1803). His later works are a mixture of classicism and Romanticism, as *Smarra* (1821) and *Trilby* (1822). He also attempted linguistics and literary history.

12. **The Romantic Fiction** is characterized by a striving for the grotesque, the fantastical, and the terrible, and by a brilliant and colored style. — VICTOR HUGO reveals all the faults of the school in the unreal and bloody *Han d'Islande* (1823) and *Bug-Jargal* (1825). The successful *Notre-Dame de Paris* (1831) combines the qualities of imaginative construction with a local study of the fifteenth century. Its broad and rapid style and picturesque narrative made it the leading novel of the decade. It argues against religious dogmas. The *Misérables* (1862), the best work of HUGO, advocates the cause of the poor. The *Travailleurs de la mer* (1866) relates man's struggles against nature. The *Homme qui rit* (1869), an extravagant romance, was followed by one more moderate, *Quatre-vingt-treize* (1874). Other prose works, of a social, political, and literary nature, as the

Dernier jour d'un condamné (1829) and *Histoire d'un crime*, present the same mingling of gigantic and puny thoughts and phrases.

13. **The Historical Novel of** SCOTT is imitated in the *Cinq-Mars* (1826) and *Stello* (1832) of ALFRED DE VIGNY. — ALEXANDRE DUMAS turned his attention to fiction and produced numerous novels, with slight fidelity to history. The plots were his own, the composition often the work of others. Fanciful, vigorous, and lively, his most popular romances are the *Trois mousquetaires* (1844), *Monte-Cristo* (1844–1845), and *Vingt ans après* (1845). Entertaining and keen are the *Impressions de voyage* (1833–1841) of DUMAS.

14. AMANTINE-AURORE DUDEVANT (1804–1876), of Paris, called GEORGE SAND, is the leader of the ideal school of ROUSSEAU. Beginning with SANDEAU in *Rose et Blanche* (1831), she continued, in *Indiana* (1832), the narrative of her own experience. *Lélia* (1833) is also a plea for social freedom. Under the influence of LAMENNAIS she produced a series of democratic novels, as *Mauprat* (1837). Her musical surroundings inspired *Consuelo* (1842–1843), and the *Comtesse de Rudolstadt* (1843–1845). Her most enduring works are pastorals, as the *Mare au diable* (1846), *François le Champi* (1849), and the *Petite Fadette* (1849). Various dramas, as the *Mariage de Victorine* (1851), after SEDAINE, and memoirs, belong to her later years. Great invention, emotion, and inspiration, united with a superior style, often too fluent, are her qualities. — The sentiment of MME. SAND for the poor was the theme of LÉON GOZLAN (1803–1866) in the *Notaire de Chantilly* (1836), and other narratives and

plays. — ÉMILE SOUVESTRE (1806–1854), of Morlaix, is the author of socialistic plays and novels, as the *Confessions d'un ouvrier* and *Un philosophe sous les toits* (1851). — GÉRARD LABRUNIE (1808–1854), of Paris, called DE NERVAL, wrote poems, dramas, translated *Faust* and produced stories, as *Filles du feu* and the *Bohême galante*, of much beauty and originality. — JULES SANDEAU (1811–1883), of Aubusson, described provincial life in the *Docteur Herbeau* (1841), *Mlle. de la Seiglière* (1848) and *Jean de Thommeray* (1873). Many of his stories were dramatized. — XAVIER BONIFACE (1798–1865), called SAINTINE, noted as a dramatist, produced *Picciola* (1836), the best of his novels.

15. ALFRED DE MUSSET belongs to the Romantic school in the unreal *Confessions d'un enfant du siècle* (1836) and in various stories, as the *Fils du Titien, Frédéric et Bernerette* and *Margot* (1838). — THÉOPHILE GAUTIER exhibits his sensuous leanings in *Mlle. de Maupin* (1835). Various tales of the same order and the historical novel *Capitaine Fracasse* (1863), after SCARRON, with exact and witty relations of travel, and criticisms on art and literature, are preserved by their faultless form.

16. **The Realistic Novel** of the century begins with the psychological studies of MARIE-HENRI BEYLE (1783–1842), of Grenoble, called STENDHAL. Criticisms on art and literature preceded the novel *Armance* (1827), a sarcastic picture of Parisian society. The *Rouge et le noir* (1830) and the *Chartreuse de Parme* (1839) are bitter and powerful sketches of evil. — The immediate follower of BEYLE was the great stylist, PROSPER MÉRIMÉE, also a former Romanticist. His stories, as *Colomba*

(1841), the best known, and *Carmen* (1847), are unexcelled in observation, wit, and simplicity of style. His posthumous *Lettres à une inconnue* (1873) are personal and vigorous, though unsympathetic.

17. HONORÉ DE BALZAC (1799–1850), of Tours, began with unsuccessful tragedies, as *Cromwell*, and romances. He won the public with the historical novel, the *Dernier Chouan* (1829), but turned immediately, under STENDHAL's influence, to the life of the time. He saw, as the leading motive in society, avarice. After the *Contes drolatiques* (1830), in the old *gaulois* style, and studies of married life, in the *Physiologie du mariage* (1831), he paints the greed of money in the *Peau de chagrin* (1831), one of his best works. Observing all sides of humanity, he calls his productions the Human Comedy, and divides them into scenes from Private life, Provincial life, Parisian life, Political life, Military life, Country life. He writes also novels under the titles of *Études philosophiques* and *Études analytiques*. Of the ninety-eight known, the *Recherche de l'absolu* (1834), *Eugénie Grandet* (1834), and the *Père Goriot* (1835) are the best. His drama, *Vautrin* (1840), and comedy, *Mercadet* (1851), were well received. Together with LAMENNAIS, DUMAS, and GEORGE SAND, he founded the *Société des Gens de Lettres* (1837). — BALZAC is the genuine head of the moderate realistic school, and shows both its merits and defects. Seeking types true to life, he often saw only the repulsive and vicious. He is both simple and sophistical in his exposition. His style, abrupt and broad, is poor on the whole. His attention to details becomes wearisome. The influence of BALZAC on subsequent fiction is over-

whelming, both at home and abroad. He still remains the greatest French novelist.

18. **Minor Writers of the Realistic School** include the voluminous PAUL DE KOCK (1794-1871). — CHARLES DE BERNARD (1805-1850) excels in witty and agreeable tales, as the *Paravent* (1839), and in the longer *Gerfaut* (1838) and the *Peau du lion* (1841). Satire against the liberals pervades them. — Satire, but against the Romantic school, is also the substance of *Jérôme Paturot à la recherche d'une position sociale* (1843), a study of misfortune by LOUIS REYBAUD (1799-1879). — A pleasing writer is RODOLPHE TOEPFFER (1799-1846), of Geneva, the author of *Nouvelles génevoises* (1841) and *Rosa et Gertrude* (1846).

19. **Naturalist Novels**, so called from their description solely of the evil side of life, were written by FRÉDÉRIC SOULIÉ (1800-1847), of Foix, a dramatist, and an enemy of the educated classes, which he satirizes in the *Vicomte de Béziers* (1834), the *Conseiller d'état* (1835), and the *Forgerons* (1842). — EUGÈNE SUE (1804-1857), of Paris, imitated COOPER in narratives, as *Atar-Gull* (1831), and DUMAS, as *Arthur* (1838). From the people he took his *Mystères de Paris* (1842-1843) and the *Juif errant* (1844-1845), which were translated into all the languages of Europe. With SUE vice is ever triumphant, and cruelty the leading motive. — JULES JANIN (1804-1874), of St. Étienne, better known as a critic, as the *Histoire de la littérature dramatique* (1858), produced many stories of hardship and crime, as the *Âne mort* (1829), *Barnave* (1831), more historical, and the *Chemin de traverse* (1836).

THE NINETEENTH CENTURY. 1801–.

CHAPTER XVIII.

SECOND PERIOD. 1848–.

1. **Poetry.** VICTOR DE LAPRADE, 1812–1884. The Parnassians: CHARLES-MARIE LECONTE DE LISLE, 1818–; CHARLES BAUDELAIRE, 1821–1867; THÉODORE FAULLAIN DE BANVILLE, 1820–; RENÉ-FRANÇOIS-ARMAND SULLY-PRUDHOMME, 1839–; FRANÇOIS COPPÉE, 1843–.
2. **Drama.** *Drame:* ALEXANDRE DUMAS *fils*, 1824–; VICTORIEN SARDOU, 1831–. Comedy: EUGÈNE LABICHE, 1815–1888; ÉMILE AUGIER, 1820–; ÉDOUARD PAILLERON, 1834–.
3. **Prose.** History and politics: LUDOVIC VITET, 1802–1873; CHARLES FORBES DE MONTALEMBERT, 1810–1870; ÉDOUARD DE LABOULAYE, 1811–1883; VICTOR DURUY, 1811–; LOUIS BLANC, 1813–1882; ERNEST RENAN, 1823–. Literary history and criticism: MAXIMILIEN-PAUL-ÉMILE LITTRÉ, 1801–1881; HIPPOLYTE TAINE, 1828–. Social and economic treatises: MAXIME DUCAMP, 1822–; LUCIEN-ANATOLE PRÉVOST-PARADOL, 1829–1870. Fiction; Ideal: OCTAVE FEUILLET, 1812–; VICTOR CHERBULIEZ, 1832–. Realistic: GUSTAVE FLAUBERT, 1821–1880; ALPHONSE DAUDET, 1840–. Naturalist: EDMOND (1822–) and JULES (1830–1870) DE GONCOURT; ÉMILE ZOLA, 1840–.

1. **Features of the Period.**—The literature of France since the death of CHATEAUBRIAND and the social change brought about by the revolution of 1848, sees no prevail-

ing standard or school. As a reaction to Romanticism real life in content and simplicity in form are sought after. Individualism is everywhere. The practical side of things and a scientific attention to detail are combined with a general eclecticism. — The language suffers from the introduction of neologisms and foreign words, though the democratic spirit shows at present a reversion to the language of the people. — In poetry, Romantic extravagance gives way to the school of art-for-art, and later to domestic and popular themes. — In drama, tragedy is almost entirely replaced by the *drame:* the union of tragedy and comedy, modified and refined, attempted by HUGO. Comedy returns to the principles of MOLIÈRE. In both the rules of the unities again appear. — In prose, science displaces literature. The study of linguistics assumes importance. Fiction tends towards naturalism and prepares a reaction towards didactic romances, after the Russian school. Over-delicacy of style and affected analyses sap its vigor.

2. Poetry; The Parnassians. — The great writers of the Romantic school still survive in works and influence. — A follower of LAMARTINE is VICTOR DE LAPRADE (1812–1884), of Montbrison, whose *Psyché* (1841), *Symphonies* (1855), *Pernette* (1868), and the *Livre d'un père* are philosophical and religious. — GAUTIER alone is the founder of a school, the *Parnassiens*, distinguished for word-painting and rhythm. Their manifesto was a collection of poems, the *Parnasse contemporain* (1866). — Among the Parnassians are CHARLES-MARIE LECONTE DE LISLE (1818-), of Réunion. His *Poèmes antiques* (1852), *Poèmes barbares* (1862), and translations from the Greek, as the *Iliad* (1866), Æschylus (1872), and Sophocles (1877), are remarkable for form and diction. — Charles Baudelaire (1821-1867), more original, represents naturalism in poetry. The *Fleurs du mal* (1857) is his best work. He belonged to the opium-eating writers, and translated Poe and De Quincey. — Théodore Faullain de Banville (1820-), a critic, writer of comedies and stories, as the *Pauvres Saltimbanques* (1853), imitated Musset in the *Cariatides* (1842), and later Gautier. His *Odes funambulesques* (1859), *Ballades joyeuses* (1873), and the *Occidentales* (1875) show a return to the forms of pre-Renaissance poetry. His *Petit traité de poésie française* (1872) embodies the doctrines of the school. — Joséphin Soulary (1815-), more Romantic, cultivated the sonnet in *Sonnets humoristiques* (1858) and other collections.

3. René - François - Armand Sully - Prudhomme (1839-) began as a Parnassian, in *Stances et poèmes* (1865). His later works are profoundly philosophical, as *Justice* (1878) and *Bonheur*, and represent a classical reaction. — François Coppée (1843-), of Paris, was likewise a Parnassian, but turned his verse to the praise of humble living and fireside scenes, as the *Humbles* (1871) and *Arrière-saison* (1888). His best work is found in his plays, as the *Passant* (1869), the *Luthier de Crémone* (1876), and *Severo Torelli* (1883). His *Contes rapides* (1888) are admirable examples of story-writing. — Paul Déroulède has a temporary reputation as a patriotic poet. — Jean Richepin is a naturalist, after the manner of Villon, as in the *Chanson des gueux*, and is a successful dramatist.

4. **The** *Drame.* — This legacy of the Romantic school was taken up by ALEXANDRE DUMAS *fils* (1824–) in the best serious plays of the period. The mixed society of the Second Empire furnished him the theme of the novel, the *Dame aux camélias* (1848), which he dramatized (1852), and of the plays, *Diane de Lys* (1853), also from a novel (1852), and the *Demi-monde* (1855). Becoming philosophical, DUMAS advocates legal and social reforms in the *Fils naturel* (1858), the *Idées de Mme. Aubray* (1867), and *Monsieur Alphonse* (1873). Simplicity of action, brilliancy of dialogue, and a return to the classical stage are the qualities of DUMAS. His novels, as the *Affaire Clémenceau* (1866), are against existing social abuses. He is also known as the author of pamphlets on divorce. — VICTORIEN SARDOU (1831–), of Paris, less original than DUMAS, continues the work of SCRIBE. The *Pattes de mouche* (1861), the *Famille Benoîton* (1865), *Rabagas* (1872), and *Daniel Rochat* (1880) are superior in thought to his later comedies and *drames*. SARDOU excels in dramatic construction and theatrical display. — HENRI DE BORNIER (1825–) approaches tragedy in the *Fille de Roland* (1872), a patriotic play.

5. **Comedy.** — Many of the best plays of SARDOU are comedies, satires on the vices of the time. — ÉMILE AUGIER (1820–1889), of Valence, a follower of PONSARD in classical comedy, wrote the *Ciguë* (1844), the *Aventurière* (1848), *Gabrielle* (1851), and the less serious *Gendre de M. Poirier* (1854). The *Fils de Giboyer* (1862) was answered by VEUILLOT in the *Fond de Giboyer*. The *Fourchambault* (1878) was also a success. The subjects

are taken from life, and the form is witty and elegant. — EUGÈNE LABICHE (1815–1888), of Paris, excels in the farce. The *Chapeau de paille d'Italie* (1851) and the *Voyage de M. Perrichon* (1860) are highly amusing and free from coarseness. — ÉDOUARD PAILLERON (1834–), of Paris, the author of the satirical poems, the *Parasites* (1861) and *Amours et haines* (1868), followed at first PONSARD, but achieved success in light and graceful irony, as the *Monde où l'on s'amuse* (1868) and the *Monde où l'on s'ennuie* (1881). — ERNEST LEGOUVÉ (1807–), of Paris, wrote plays, treatises in behalf of the higher position of woman, and collaborated with SCRIBE in *Adrienne Lecouvreur*. — OCTAVE FEUILLET (1822–), of St. Lô, wrote comedies, as *Montjoye* (1863), but won popularity by his many *Proverbes*, in the manner of MUSSET. — HENRI MEILHAC (1832–), of Paris, collaborated with LUDOVIC HALÉVY in many amusing farces which furnished themes to Offenbach, as *Orphée aux enfers* (1861), and the *Vie parisienne* (1866), and in *Froufrou* (1869).

6. **Prose.** — **Political Essays** and plays form the most important part of the work of the journalist, ÉMILE DE GIRARDIN (1806–1881). — LUDOVIC VITET (1802–1873), the author of numerous historical dramas (1826–1829), wrote various economic essays. He is best known, however, for his *Études sur l'histoire de l'art* (1864). — CHARLES FORBES DE MONTALEMBERT (1810–1870), of London, associated with LAMENNAIS, defended the church in various pamphlets and historical treatises, as the *Moines d'occident* (1860–1867). — HENRI ROCHEFORT (1830–), of Paris, the journalist, bitterly attacked the Second Empire and his later political foes.

7. **History** became more detailed and less literary after the great historians had passed away. — ÉDOUARD DE LABOULAYE (1811–1883), of Paris, satirized the Second Empire in the novel, *Paris en Amérique* (1862). Besides travels, stories, and political studies, he is the author of a *Histoire des États-Unis*. — VICTOR DURUY (1811–) paid especial attention to ancient history, as in his chief work, the *Histoire des Romains*. He also produced short histories of Greece, Rome, France, the mediæval and modern epochs. — LOUIS BLANC (1813–1882), of Madrid, shows a socialist leaning in the *Histoire de dix ans* (1841–1846) and the *Histoire de la Révolution française* (1847–1862).

8. ERNEST RENAN (1823–), of Tréguier, is rather a historical critic than a historian. His *Histoire des langues sémitiques* (1855) was followed by a study of *Averroës* (1853), the *Études d'histoire religieuse* (1857), the *Livre de Job* (1859), and the *Cantique des cantiques* (1860). Adopting the views of the German school, his *Vie de Jésus* (1863) attracted wide attention by its dramatic exposition and vivid description. Other essays on the New Testament and religious dogmas, as *Saint Paul* (1869), and the *Église chrétienne* (1878), were marked by the same qualities of style. The *Dialogues et fragments philosophiques* (1876) contain perhaps the most enduring prose of the century. *Marc-Aurèle* (1882) and the *Histoire d'Israël* (1888) are philosophical essays of great brilliancy. In literary studies and theatrical pieces RENAN displays also his critical keenness and affable irony.

9. **Literary History** and linguistics are the most im-

portant subjects treated by MAXIMILIEN-PAUL-ÉMILE LITTRÉ (1801–1881), of Paris, a follower of COMTE. The *Analyse raisonné du cours de philosophie* (1845) and *Auguste Comte et la philosophie positive* (1863) are among his philosophical essays. The *Histoire de la langue française* (1862) was followed by his great work, the *Dictionnaire de la langue française* (1863–1872) and various articles on philosophy, politics, and language. — JEAN-JACQUES AMPÈRE (1800–1864) attempted the history of mediæval literature, as the *Histoire de la littérature française au moyen âge* (1841), but is more valuable for his influence than for his research. His later works are essays on history and literature, remarkable for style. — PAULIN PARIS (1800–1881), less literary but more scientific, advanced the study of mediæval poetry by his contributions to the *Histoire littéraire* and his version of the *Romans de la Table ronde* (1872–1877).

10. **Criticism** is represented by HIPPOLYTE-ADOLPHE TAINE (1828–), of Vouziers, a disciple of SAINTE-BEUVE. The latter's method he developed into the rules of determining an author's work by his race, surroundings, and epoch. These he applied in the *Histoire de la littérature anglaise* (1864). Other literary studies are *Sur les fables de Lafontaine* (1853), and *Sur Tite-Live* (1856). Travels, lectures on art, as *Philosophie de l'art en Italie* (1867) and *en Grèce* (1869), essays on philosophy, and a partisan *Origines de la France contemporaine*, reveal great activity. — PAUL DE SAINT-VICTOR (1827–1881), the author of *Hommes et Dieux*, pays more attention to style than to accuracy. — A follower of SAINTE-BEUVE was EDMOND SCHÉRER (1815–1888). — Of the living critics of French

literature, FERDINAND BRUNETIÈRE, ÉMILE FAGUET, and PAUL STAPFER are noted for power and breadth.

11. **Studies of Economics**, as *Paris, ses organes, ses fonctions et sa vie* (1869–1875), were pursued by MAXIME DUCAMP (1822–), of Paris. Besides various travels in the East he celebrates man's conquest of matter in numerous poems, as the *Chants modernes* (1855). He is also a novelist. — LUCIEN-ANATOLE PRÉVOST-PARADOL (1829–1870), of Paris, treats of social evils in *Du rôle de la famille dans l'éducation* (1857), and other moral and political essays, as *France nouvelle* (1868). Of critical import are his *Études sur les moralistes français* (1864).

12. **Ideal Fiction.** — OCTAVE FEUILLET imitated at first DUMAS, but afterwards adopted a more refined, though sensuous manner. The *Roman d'un jeune homme pauvre* (1858) was dramatized. His two best works are *M. de Camors* (1867) and *Julie de Trécœur* (1872), both pathetic and melancholy. The *Journal d'une femme* (1878) shows also the best qualities of the author's style, pure and graceful. — HENRI MURGER (1822–1861), of Paris, describes the Latin Quarter in the *Vie de Bohême* (1848), the *Pays latin* (1852), and the *Buveurs d'eau* (1856), series of pleasing and vivid sketches. — ÉMILE ERCKMANN (1822–) and ALEXANDRE CHATRIAN (1826–) imitated HOFFMANN, as in *Contes de la montagne* (1860), based on Alsatian life. Their first successful novel was the *Illustre docteur Mathéus* (1859). This was followed by stories of the wars of the Revolution and Empire, as *Madame Thérèse* (1863), *Histoire d'un conscrit de 1813* (1864), *Waterloo* (1865), and the *Blocus* (1867), all from the peasant's standpoint. Their influence in disposing

the mass of the nation for peace was great. Some of their tales were dramatized with success, as *Ami Fritz* (1864), on village life. Their later works represent Alsatian patriotism, as the *Rantzau* (1882). — EDMOND ABOUT (1828–1885), of Dieuze, the journalist, began with stories and novels, based on his foreign travels. *Tolla* (1855), the *Roi des montagnes* (1856), and *Germaine* (1857) are his best works. Witty and amusing are the *Homme à l'oreille cassée* (1862) and the *Nez d'un notaire* (1862). — VICTOR CHERBULIEZ (1832–), of Geneva, a follower of GEORGE SAND, displays much dramatic force in the *Comte Kostia* (1863), the *Roman d'une honnête femme* (1866), and the *Aventure de Ladislas Bolski* (1869). *Meta Holdenis* is witty and ironical. CHERBULIEZ is the author also of essays on art and politics. — LUDOVIC HALÉVY (1834–), of Paris, is unexcelled in the keen and polished satire of his stories, as *Monsieur et Madame Cardinal*. Of his novels the best known is *Abbé Constantin*.

13. **Realistic Fiction** entered on a new phase with the novels of GUSTAVE FLAUBERT (1821–1880), of Rouen. His master-piece, *Madame Bovary* (1857), a study of provincial life, recalls BALZAC in observation and GAUTIER in style, while in construction it is superior to either. *Salammbô* (1862), a study in archæology, contains fine descriptions. The *Éducation sentimentale* (1869) is philosophical but rambling. The *Tentation de St. Antoine* (1874) is a fantastical narrative. *Trois Contes* (1877) contain some of the author's best work. *Bouvard et Pécuchet* (1881), unfinished, is disheartening in its coldness and pessimism. FLAUBERT in his later writings becomes over-erudite and finical in style.

14. ALPHONSE DAUDET (1840–), of Nîmes, tried at first poetry and stories for the *Figaro*, as his admirable *Lettres de mon moulin* (1863–), on the life of Provence. Theatrical pieces were followed by an autobiographical romance, the *Petit chose* (1866), and by the stories, *Contes du lundi* (1868–), of great charm and delicacy. Tales of the war and plays, as the *Arlésienne* (1872), preceded perhaps his best novel, *Fromont jeune et Risler aîné* (1874), remarkable for observation and composition and its sadness of tone. The *Nabab* (1877) is highly dramatic, while *Numa Roumestan* (1881) is broader in plan and insight. The later works of DAUDET show a falling-off in thought and style. A painstaking artist, his observation is too often narrow and special.

15. **Naturalism in Fiction** has formed for itself a school which proceeds by scientific methods and documentary evidence, limited as yet to the evils of life. At its head are the brothers EDMOND (1822–) and JULES (1830–1870). DE GONCOURT, who became known by studies on the art and society of the eighteenth century. In fiction they descend from FLAUBERT. *Sœur Philomène* (1861), *Renée Mauperin* (1864), remarkable for its dialogue, and *Germinie Lacertreux* (1865) are all sad and pessimistic.

16. ÉMILE ZOLA (1840–), of Italian origin, was at first a hack-writer, but won the populace in the *Mystères de Marseille* (1867), of no literary merit. *Thérèse Raquin* (1867), in his better manner, was succeeded by a series of naturalist novels, the *Rougon-Macquart* (1871–), describing the decadence of a family through its various members. The best work of the series is the *Assommoir* (1877), which

in scope and force is unequalled in French literature. *Germinal* (1885) has an epic tone. — ZOLA excels in combination of detail, in picturesque and sensuous language, and in sweep of diction. Unnecessarily coarse and repulsive, his work is less faithful to life than that of the realistic school, which he however surpasses in exuberance of imagination.

17. **Minor Writers** in vogue include ANTOINE-GUSTAVE DROZ (1832–), the author of delicate and witty society tales, as *Monsieur, Madame et Bébé* (1866); PAUL BOURGET, a disciple of STENDHAL in psychological analysis, as the *Cruelle énigme* (1885); GUY DE MAUPASSANT, who is superior in stories of the naturalist school, though often showing the pleasant side of life; and PIERRE LOTI (JULIEN VIAUD), whose tales of the Breton sailors and sketches of Japan are remarkable for style and artistic appreciation.

INDEX.

About. E., 232s.
Academy. French, 124, 128ss, 129, 136, 143, 161, 170, 172, 202.
Adam, 149s.
Adam de la Halle, 58s, 59s.
Addison, 182.
Adelaide. Queen, 13, 14.
Adenet le Roi, 53s, 54.
Adgar, 42.
Ælred, 60.
Æschylus, 226.
Aimeri de Narbonne, 18.
Alamanni. L., 96.
Alarcon, 134.
Albéric of Briançon, 22s.
Alberich, 20.
Aleschans, 13.
Alexander the Great, 21ss, 72.
Alexandre, 22s, 54, 88.
Alexandre. La Vengeance d', 22s.
Alexandre du Pont, 56s.
Alexandre de Bernai, 22.
Alexandreïs, 22.
Alexis. G., 76s.
Alexis. La Vie de St., 13.
Alice. Queen, 48.
Alione d'Asti. G., 92s.
Allegory, 45ss.
Amadis des Gaules, 100s, 121, 142, 143, 144, 146.
Ambroise, 38.
Ami et Amile, 20, 61, 69.
Aminta. See Tasso.
Ampère. J-J., 229s.

Amyot. J., 114ss, 118, 121.
Anacreon, 105, 186.
Ancelot. J-A-P-F., 206s.
Ancients and Moderns. Quarrel of, 151, 169, 171, 172, 177.
André de Coutances, 44, 47.
André de la Vigne, 84, 85s, 94–95.
André le Chapelain, 43, 46, 79.
Andrieux. F-G., 206s.
Ange et l'Ermite. L', 43.
Anger, 41.
Anglais. La Chartre aux, 56–57.
Anglais. La Paix aux, 56.
Anue de Gonzague, 162.
Anne of Brittany, 85.
Apollonius of Tyre, 20.
Apôtres. Actes des, 82s, 95, 98.
Apuleius, 150.
Ariosto, 65, 94, 112, 113, 150, 152.
Aristophanes, 110–111, 157.
Aristotle, 70, 96, 109, 193.
Arnauld. A., 139s.
Arnault. A-V., 205s.
Arras, 48, 49.
Assomption de Notre Dame. L', 83–84.
Assonance, 5.
Astrée. L'. See D'Urfé.
Atala. See Chateaubriand.
Aucassin et Nicolette, 34.
Audefroi le Bâtard, 47s.
Audigier, 53.
Augier. É., 227–228.
Augustin. St., 15, 70.

Avignon, 70.
Bacon. F., 192.
Baïf. J-A. de, 102, 105-106, 113.
Baïf. L. de, 96s, 104.
Ballade, 68s.
Ballette, 59s.
Balsac. R. de, 87-88.
Balzac. H. de, 222-223, 232.
Balzac. J-L. Guez de, 127, 138ss, 159, 163.
Banville. T. Faullain de, 226s.
Baour-Lormian. L-P-M-F., 200s.
Barante. G-P. Brugière de, 214s, 215.
Barbier. A., 204s.
Barbieri, 152.
Barclay. J., 133, 143s, 145s.
Barlaam et Josaphat, 41.
Barthélemy. J-J., 196s.
Basoche. The, 85s.
Basselin. O., 81s, 110.
Bastard de Bouillon. Le, 54.
Bataille, 45s.
Bataille de carême et de charnage. La, 45.
Batteux. C., 193s.
Baude. H., 85s.
Baudelaire. C., 226s.
Baudouin d'Avesnes, 60.
Baudouin de Condé, 57s.
Baudouin de Sebourg, 54.
Baudri de Bourgueil, 38.
Bayard, 96.
Bayle. P., 169-170.
Beatrice. Empress, 32.
Beaumarchais. P-A. Caron de, 185, 188-189.
Becket. Thomas, 42.
Bede, 14.
Béjart. Mad., 152.
Belleau. R., 102, 105s, 113.
Belle Doette, 14.
Belloy. P-L. de, 189s.
Benedict, 13.

Benoît de Ste-More, 22ss, 26, 32, 38. See *Troie*.
Bonserade. I. de, 127s.
Béranger. P-J. de, 200s.
Berçuire. P., 70s.
Bergerac. S. Cyrano de, 146-147, 197.
Bernard. C. de, 223s.
Bernard. St., 51.
Berni, 125.
Bernier, 36.
Béroalde de Verville, 141s.
Béroul, 26.
Berquin. A., 197s.
Berryer. P-A., 218s.
Bertaut. J., 109s.
Bertrand of Bar-sur-Aube, 18s.
Bestiaries, 14s.
Bèze. T. de, 110s, 117.
Bibbiena, 96.
Bible. The, 50, 70, 96, 140.
Bien avisé, mal avisé, 83.
Bien boire, 84.
Billaut. A., 129s.
Blanc. L., 229s.
Blanchet. P., 85s.
Blason, 93s.
Blondel de Nesle, 49s.
Boccaccio, 23, 34, 55, 89, 94, 99, 150.
Bodel. J., 18, 49s, 58.
Bodin. J., 116s.
Boëthius, 43, 60, 67.
Boileau. É., 61.
Boileau. N. Despréaux, 141, 150-151, 155, 157, 158, 166, 172, 175, 199.
Boisrobert. F. le Métel de, 126-127, 128, 133.
Bojardo, 173.
Bonald. L-G-A. de, 212s.
Bonet. H., 71s.
Bornier. H. de, 227s.
Bossuet. J-B., 162-163, 171, 179.
Boucher. J., 117s.
Bouchet. G., 141s.

Bouchet. J., 92-93.
Boucicaut. Le Livre des faits du maréchal de, 72.
Bouhours. D., 162s.
Bourdaloue. L., 163s, 171.
Bourget. P., 234s.
Bourgogne. Hôtel de, 95, 110, 133, 153, 154, 156.
Boursault. E., 155s, 156.
Bozon. N., 56s.
Brantôme. P. de Bourdeilles de, 115s.
Brébeuf. G. de, 129s.
Brécourt. G. Marcoureau de, 156.
Brendan. Le Voyage de Saint, 13.
Brisebarre. J., 64.
Brizeux. A., 204-205.
Brueys. D-A. de, 167s.
Brun de la Montagne, 64.
Brunetière, F., 231.
Brunetto Latino, 47, 61s.
Brutus, 24.
Buchanan, 96.
Buddha, 41.
Buffon. C. L. Leclerc de, 194s.
Burgundy, 76, 77, 78.
Burgundy. Duke of, 150, 170.
Bussy-Rabutin. R. de, 159s, 160.
Buttet. M-C. de, 107s.
Byron, 107, 202, 203, 206.
Calvin (Cauvin). J., 97ss, 117.
Campistron. J. Galbert de, 168s.
Camus. J-P., 143s.
Caquets de l'accouchée. Les, 141-142.
Carduino, 28.
Carmontelle. L. Carrogis de, 188s, 206.
Castro, G. de, 134.
Cato, 43, 65.
Caveau. The, 178, 200.
Caxton, 47.
Caylus, Mme. de, 179s.
Cénacle. The, 201.

Cent Ballades. Le Livre des, 67-68, 78.
Cent Nouvelles nouvelles. Les, 89s, 97, 98, 121, 150.
Chamfort, S-R-N., 193s.
Chanson, 48s, 200.
Chanson de croisade, 15s, 48.
Chanson de geste, 11.
Chanson. Sotte, 59.
Chant royal, 68s, 74.
Chapelain. J., 128s, 133.
Chapuzeau. S., 155s.
Chardri, 41s.
Charité. La, 83.
Charlemagne, 10, 18, 19, 39, 162.
Charles the Bald, 10, 19.
Charles the Bold, 75, 86, 87.
Charles the Infant, 20.
Charles V., 63, 66, 67, 70s, 71, 91.
Charles VI., 63, 66, 71.
Charles VII., 78.
Charles VIII., 87, 91.
Charles IX., 107, 117.
Charles d'Anjou, 58.
Charles d'Orléans, 77-78.
Charles Martel, 10, 18, 19.
Charroi de Nîmes. Le, 13.
Charron. P., 121s.
Chartier. A., 75, 77, 78-79, 81.
Chasse du cerf. La, 58.
Chassignet. J-B., 109s.
Chastellain. G., 75, 77s, 85, 86s, 87s, 92.
Chastiement des dames. Le, 57.
Chastiement d'un père à son fils. Le, 35.
Chateaubriand. F-R. de, 174, 185, 186, 199, 200, 201, 202, 211-212, 218, 224.
Châtelain de Couci. Le, 54.
Châtelain de Couci. G., 49s.
Châtelaine de Vergi. La, 33.
Châtelet. The, 93.
Chatrian. A., 231-232.

Chaucer, 23, 65, 67.
Chaulieu. G. Amfrye de, 166s.
Chênedollé. C. de, 199-200.
Chénier. A-M. de, 79, 125, 185, 186-187, 190, 204.
Chénier. M-J. de, 190s.
Cherbuliez. V., 232s.
Chesterfield, 180, 181.
Chétifs. Les, 21.
Chevalier au cygne. Le, 21, 69.
Chrétien. F., 117s.
Chrétien de Troies, 26-28, 29, 30, 43, 48.
Christine de Pisan, 67s, 71s, 72s.
Chronique saintongeaise. La, 50.
Chronique scandaleuse. La, 87.
Chronique de Reims. La. See *Récits*.
Chroniques de Saint-Denis. Les, 60s, 71.
Chroniques gargantuines. Les, 98.
Cicero, 96.
Cigognini, 153.
Claris et Laris, 54.
Clef d'amour. Le, 43.
Clerville, 145.
Clovis, 9.
Cochon. P., 86s.
Code. The, 60, 76.
Coke. J., 87.
Colin Muset, 56s.
Collerye. R. de, 93s.
Colletet, G., 128s, 133.
Collin d'Harleville. J-F., 188s.
Combat des Trente. Le, 63s.
Comédie des Tuileries. La, 133.
Comédie française, 154, 166.
Comédie larmoyante, 178s.
Comines. P. de, 74, 87s.
Comte, A., 217-218, 230.
Comte de Poitiers. Le, 34.
Condé. Prince of, 162, 163.
Condillac. É. Bonnot de Mably-, 195-196.

Condorcet. M-J-A-N. Caritat de, 195s.
Confidante. The, 113.
Conrart. V., 128s.
Constant. B., 213s.
Constant l'empereur, 61.
Conon de Béthune, 48s.
Contes du monde aventureux. Les, 121s.
Conti. Prince of, 171.
Cooper, 223.
Coppée. F., 226s.
Coq-à-l'âne, 93s.
Coquillart. G., 76s, 85, 93.
Corneille. P., 123, 127, 128, 131, 132, 133, 134-136, 137, 152, 154, 156, 157, 158, 168, 169, 209.
Corneille. T., 155, 156-157.
Correspondance littéraire. La, 194-195.
Courier. P-L., 214s.
Cousin. V., 217s.
Coutumiers, 51.
Crébillon. C-P. Jolyot de, 182s, 196.
Crébillon. P. Jolyot de, 168s, 176.
Cretin. G. (Dubois), 76, 77s, 92, 93.
Crusades. The, 4, 19, 37s, 38.
Cuvelier, 64.
Cuvier. Le, 84s.
Dagobert, 10, 18.
D'Aguesseau. H-F., 181s.
D'Alembert. J. Le Rond, 192s.
Dancourt. F. Carton, 167s.
Dance of Death. See *Macabré*.
Danse des femmes. La, 75.
Danse des hommes. La, 74.
Dante, 193, 204.
Dares, 23.
D'Aubignac. F. Hédelin, 141s.
D'Aubigné. T-A., 107-108, 116s, 145, 203.
Daudet. A., 233s.
D'Aulnoy. M-C., 171s.
Dauphin. The, 162, 171.

INDEX. 239

Daurat. J. (Dinemandy), 102s.
Débat, 45s, 74.
Débat des hérauts. Le, 87s.
Débat du corps et de l'âme. Le, 45, 46.
Débat du vin et de l'eau. Le, 45.
De Brosses. C., 193s.
Decameron. See Boccaccio.
Delavigne. J-F-C., 205–206.
Delille. J., 47, 187s.
Della Casa, 125.
De Quincey, 226.
Déroulède. P., 226s.
Désaugiers, M-A-M., 200s.
Desbordes-Valmore. M., 204s.
Descartes. R., 137, 138–139, 147, 150, 160, 161, 162, 169.
Deschamps. A., 204s.
Deschamps. É., 204s.
Deschamps. E., 65, 66–67, 69s.
Descort, 47.
Des Essarts. N. Herberay, 100s.
Deshoulières. A., 149s.
Desmarets. J., 132–133.
Des Périers. J. Bonaventure, 99s.
Desportes. P., 109s, 125.
Destouches. P. Néricault, 177s.
De Thou. J-A., 116s.
Dialogus of Gregory I., 41.
Dictys, 23.
Diderot. D., 178, 180, 187–188, 189, 191–192, 193, 196s, 207.
Diodorus, 114.
Disciplina clericalis, 35.
Dit, 45s, 74, 84.
Dit des trois morts et trois vifs. Le, 45, 57, 74.
Dolet. É., 96s, 99.
Dolopathos, 35.
Don Quixote, 145.
Doon de Mayence, 88.
Dorat. C-J., 185s.
Drame, 225s.
Drame bourgeois, 178s, 206.

Droz. A-G., 234s.
Du Bartas. G. de Salluste, 47, 107ss, 108.
Du Bellay. J., 91, 102s, 103s, 104–105.
Du Boccage. M-A. Fiquet, 185s.
Dubois. J. (Sylvius), 100s.
Dubois. P-F., 201.
Ducamp. M., 231s.
Ducis. J-F., 189–190.
Duclos. C. Pinot, 193s.
Dufresny. C. Rivière, 166s.
Dumas. A., 207–208, 220s, 222, 223, 231.
Dumas. A. *fils*, 227s.
Dupleix, S., 140s.
Duplessis-Mornay. P., 115s.
Durant. G., 117s.
D'Urfé. H., 126, 128, 130, 132, 137, 142ss, 143, 145.
Durmart le Gallois, 28s.
Duruy. V., 229s.
Du Ryer. P., 133s, 137.
D'Ussieux. L., 195s.
Du Vair. G., 116–117, 118.
Échiquier d'amour. L', 79.
Eilhart von Oberg, 26.
Eleanor. Queen, 22, 24, 48.
Élie, 43.
Empereur qui tua son neveu. L', 84s.
Empire. First, 200, 231.
Empire. Second, 203, 227.
Encyclopædia. The, 180, 188, 190, 191–192, 194, 195, 202, 211.
Énéas. Roman d', 23s.
Eneid. See Vergil.
Enfant juif. L', 43.
Enfants de Maintenant. Les, 83.
Enfants sans souci. The, 85s.
England, 64, 72, 161, 179, 180.
England. Queen of, 162.
Entrée d'Espagne. L', 65.
Epictetus, 140.

Épitre farcie, 41s.
Erckmann. É., 231-232.
Ernoul, 51.
Escoufle. Roman de l', 88.
Esop, 35, 36.
Estampie, 59.
Estienne. C., 96.
Estienne. H., 118-119.
Estienne. R., 100s, 118s.
Établissements de St. Louis. Les, 61.
États du monde. Les, 44.
Étienne de Fougères, 44.
Étienne de Jouy. V-J., 205s.
Eulalia. Sequence on St., 6.
Euripides, 134, 157, 158.
Évangile des femmes. L', 44.
Everat, 46.
Fableau, 12, 35s, 84, 89.
Fabre d'Églantine. P-F-N., 189s.
Faguet. É., 231.
Faits des Romains. Les, 50.
Farce, 59, 83, 84s, 111, 113.
Fatrasie, 54, 59, 84, 93.
Fauchet. C., 119-120.
Faur de Pibrac. G. du, 110s.
Faure. A., 110s.
Fauriel. C., 216s.
Faust. See Gœthe.
Favart. C-S., 188s.
Fénelon. F. de La Mothe, 163, 170-171.
Feuillet. O., 228s, 231s.
Fierabras, 88.
Fiévée. J., 218.
Figaro. Le, 233.
Flaubert. G., 232s, 233.
Fléchier. E., 149, 163s.
Fleury. C., 169s.
Floire et Blanchefleur, 33, 34.
Floire et Jeanne, 61.
Floovent, 10.
Florian. J-P. Claris de, 197s.
Folklore, 34s.

Fontenelle. B. le Bovier de, 169s.
Foulque de Candie, 13.
Fouquet, 149, 153, 160.
Fourier. F-M-C., 214s.
Fous. The, 85s.
Fous. La Fête des, 84.
Franc archer de Bagnolet. Le, 85s.
Francis I., 63, 91, 92, 93, 95, 100.
Francus, 23.
Froissart. J., 63, 67s, 72s.
Furetière. A., 161-162, 164s.
Gab, 12.
Gace Brulé, 49s.
Gace de la Bigne, 66s.
Galen, 97.
Galien le Rétoré, 88.
Galland. A., 172s.
Garçon et de l'aveugle. Du, 59.
Garnier. R., 112-113, 130.
Garnier de Pont-Ste-Maxence, 42.
Gassendi. P., 152.
Gautier. Th., 146, 205s, 221s, 225, 226, 232.
Gautier-Garguille (Hugues Guéru), 133.
Gautier d'Arras, 32s, 33s.
Gautier de Bibelesworth, 61s.
Gautier de Châtillon, 22s.
Gautier de Coinci, 42s, 47, 49.
Gautier de Metz, 47s.
Gay, S., 219s.
Gay de Girardin, D., 209s.
Gazette de France. La, 140s.
Gelée. J., 55s.
Genlis. Mme. de, 218.
Gens de Lettres. La Société des, 222.
Geoffrei of Paris, 55s.
Geoffrei Gaimar, 24s, 38.
Geoffrey of Monmouth, 24s, 25, 29, 30, 38.
Gerbert de Montreuil, 29, 34.
Germany, 64, 92, 188, 191, 193, 218.
Gerson. J., 71s.

Gerusalemme liberata. See Tasso.
Gervaise, 47.
Gesta Romanorum, 43, 99.
Geste des ducs de Bourgogne. La, 64.
Gilbert. N-J-L., 186s.
Giliberti, 153.
Gilles le Muisit, 66s.
Girard d'Amiens, 53, 54s.
Girard de Fratte, 19.
Girard de Roussillon, 18, 19.
Girard de Roussillon, 19, 63, 88.
Girard de Vienne, 18, 20.
Girardin. É. de, 228.
Giraud de Barri, 60.
Globe. Le, 201s, 216.
Glossaries, 61.
Godfrey of Bouillon, 21.
Godwin. F., 146.
Goethe, 37, 204, 218, 221.
Gombauld. J. Ogier de, 126s, 133, 143s.
Gomberville. M. Leroy de, 143–144.
Goncourt. E. de, 233s.
Goncourt, J. de, 233s.
Gongorism, 123s, 126.
Gottfried von Strassburg, 26.
Goujet. C-P., 183s.
Gozlan. L., 220-221.
Graindor de Douai, 21.
Grant mal fist Adam, 44.
Greban. A., 82s.
Greban. S., 82s.
Grégoire. La Vie de St., 13.
Gresset. J-B-L., 176s.
Grévin. J., 112s, 113.
Grignan. Mme. de, 159.
Grimm. F. M., 194–195.
Gringore. P., 84, 85–86, 93.
Griselidis. L'Histoire de, 69.
Gros-Guillaume (Robert Guérin), 133.
Guarin. F., 77s.
Guerin de Monglane, 88.

Guevara, 172.
Gui de Cambrai, 22, 41.
Gui de Warwick, 33.
Guiart. G., 55.
Guiart des Moulins, 59.
Guido Colonna, 23, 83, 87.
Guilebert de Berneville, 58.
Guillaume au Court Nez, 11.
Guillaume de Deguilleville, 65s.
Guillaume de Dole, 33, 34, 61.
Guillaume de Lorris, 46s, 57, 58.
Guillaume de Palerme, 32.
Guillaume de Saint-André, 64.
Guillaume de Saint-Pair, 38.
Guillaume d'Orange, 11, 13, 18.
Guillaume le Clerc, 45, 46.
Guillaume le Maréchal. La Vie de, 38s.
Guiot de Provins, 44.
Guirlande de Julie. La, 127–128.
Guiron, 25.
Guizot, F-P-G., 214–215.
Guzman de Alfarache, 121.
Haakon. King, 64.
Halévy. L., 222, 232s.
Hamilton. A., 172s.
Hardy. A., 131ss, 132, 135, 137.
Hartmann von Aue, 30.
Heine, 80.
Heinrich der Glichezare, 37.
Heinrich von Veldeke, 23.
Hélinand, 44–45.
Heliodorus, 114, 144.
Helvétius. C-A., 195s.
Henri d'Andeli, 36, 45.
Henri de Valenciennes, 50.
Henrietta of England, 157, 162.
Henry II., 106, 115.
Henry III., 118.
Henry IV., 108, 110, 115s, 119, 127, 140, 175.
Henry III. of Brabant, 58.
Herbert, 35.
Herbort von Fritzlar, 23.

Herenc. Baudet, 87s.
Herman de Valenciennes, 42, 46.
Hesiod, 106.
Hesselin. D., 87s.
Hilary, 49.
Hippocrates, 97.
Histoire littéraire. L', 183s, 230.
Histoires de Baudouin. Les, 60.
Hita. Perez de, 145, 163, 197, 212.
Hoffmann, 231.
Holbach. P. H. Dietrich von, 195s.
Holy Grail. The, 21, 26, 29ss.
Homer, 23, 85, 96, 107, 177, 226.
Honorius, 47.
Horace, 103, 109, 125, 151, 175.
Horn, 20.
Hotman. F., 117s.
Housse partie. La, 36.
Huet. P-D., 164s.
Hugo. V-M., 18, 19, 108, 199, 202-203, 204, 205, 207s, 208, 219-220, 225.
Huguenot, 95.
Huon de Bordeaux, 20-21, 88.
Huon de Méri, 46.
Ignaure, 25, 54.
Iliad. See Homer.
Image du Monde. L', 47, 61.
Imitation de Jésus-Christ. L', 135.
Ingénue. The, 135, 167.
Innocent III., 50, 76.
Institutes. The, 60.
Isengrimus, 37.
Isopets, 36s.
Italy, 13, 64ss, 91, 94, 187, 193, 204, 218.
Jacot de Forest, 50.
Jacques d'Amiens, 43.
Jacques de Baisieu, 57.
Jacques de Longuyon, 54.
Jacques de Vitri, 43.
Jakemon Sakesep, 54.
James I., 130.
Jamyn. A., 107s.

Janin. J., 223s.
Jean d'Anjou, 89.
Jean d'Arkel, 70s.
Jean d'Arras, 72s.
Jean de Bateri, 65.
Jean de Bric, 71s.
Jean de Condé, 55, 57.
Jean de Dammartin, 54s, 88.
Jean de Haute-Seille, 35.
Jean de le Mote, 64.
Jean de Lescurel, 66s.
Jean de Meun, 47, 57, 58, 60s, 63, 67. See *Rose. Roman de la*,
Jean de Paris, 88s.
Jean des Prés, 64s, 72.
Jean de Thuin, 50.
Jean le Marchant, 42.
Jean le Venelais 22.
Jeanne d'Albret, 107.
Jérusalem. Assises de, 51.
Jérusalem. Chanson de, 21.
Jérusalem. Complainte de, 44.
Jérusalem. Description de, 51.
Jérusalem. Saint Voyage de, 72.
Jeu parti, 78s.
Jeux à vendre, 67s.
Jeux floraux, 112, 188, 189, 202.
Joan of Arc, 67, 128, 175.
Jodelle. É., 102, 108, 110-111, 130.
John of Bohemia, 66.
John the Good, 65, 66, 70.
Joinville. J. de, 60s.
Jonah. Homily on, 6.
Jongleurs. The, 10-11, 12.
Joseph of Arimathea, 29.
Josephus, 76.
Joubert. J., 214s.
Jourdain de Blaie, 20, 33.
Jourdain Fantosme, 38.
Journal de Paris. Le, 195.
Journal d'un bourgeois de Paris. Le, 87.
Juvenal, 125, 186.
Karlamagnus Saga, 64.

Kock. P. de, 223.
Konrad, 12.
Labé. L. (Charly), 106s.
Labiche. E., 228s.
La Boétie. É. de, 116s, 120.
Laboulaye. É. de, 229s.
La Bruyère. J. de, 160–161, 165, 167.
La Calprenède. G. de Costes de, 137, 144ss.
La Chaussée. P-C. Nivelle de, 178s, 187.
Lacordaire. J-B-H., 218s.
La Fare. C-A., 166s.
La Fayette. M-M. de, 163–164, 167, 171.
La Fontaine. J. de, 94, 149–150, 151, 154, 164, 172, 185, 197.
La Force. Mlle. de, 171.
La Fosse d'Aubigny. A. de, 168s.
La Grange-Chancel. F-J. de, 168.
La Harpe. J-F. de, 194s.
Lai. The lyric, 47, 68s.
Lai. The narrative, 25.
Lamartine. A-M-L. de, 186, 201–202, 204, 209, 225.
Lambert le Tort, 22.
Lamennais. H-F-R. de, 213s, 218, 220, 222, 228.
La Mettrie. J. Offray de, 181–182.
La Motte. A. Houdart de, 177s.
Lamprecht, 22.
Lancelot, 29–30.
Langage. La Manière de, 72.
Lannel. J. de, 146s.
La Noue. F. de, 115s.
La Péruse. J. de, 112s.
Lapidaries, 14, 47.
La Popelinière. L. de, 116s.
Laprade. V. de, 225s.
Larivey. P., 113–114, 121s, 154.
La Rochefoucauld. F. de, 159, 160s, 163.
La Salle. A. de, 88–89.

La Taille. J. de, 112s.
Lazarillo de Tormes, 59, 121.
Le Bel. J., 70, 72s.
Lebrun. P-A., 200s.
Lebrun. P-D. Échouard-, 185s.
Leclerq. M-T., 206s.
Leconte de Lisle. C-M., 225–226.
Le Fèvre. J., 65–66.
Lefèvre d'Étaples. J., 96s.
Lefranc de Pompignan. J-J., 185s.
Léger. *La Vie de St.*, 6.
Le Gouais. C., 56.
Legouvé. E., 228s.
Legrand, M-A., 167s.
Le Houx. J., 81, 110s.
Le Maire de Belges. J., 76s, 77, 86–87, 92, 104.
Lemercier. L-J-N., 205s.
Lenglet du Fresnoy. N., 183s.
Leroy. P., 117s.
Lesage. A-R., 172–173, 182.
Lessing, 55.
L'Estoile. C. de, 133s.
L'Estoile. P. de, 115s, 133.
Le Tellier. M., 162.
Letourneur. P., 189.
L'Hospital. M. de, 117s.
Littré. M-P-É., 230s.
Livre des histoires. Le, 50.
Livy, 70, 134, 135.
Locke, 175, 191, 195.
Lohengrin, 21.
Longueville. Mme. de, 141.
Longus, 114.
Lope de Vega, 134.
Lorens, 61.
Loret. J., 141s.
Lorraine. Duchess of, 58.
Loti. P. (J. Viaud), 234.
Louis I., 10, 18.
Louis IX., 18.
Louis XI., 77, 83, 87.
Louis XII., 74, 76, 85, 95.
Louis XIII., 138.

244 INDEX.

Louis XIV., 123s, 124, 149, 151, 157, 159, 162, 165, 170, 171, 178.
Louis XV., 192.
Louis XVIII., 199.
Louis. Le Couronnement de, 18.
Louis. Roi, 12.
Louise of Savoy, 93.
Louvet. J., 95.
Loyal serviteur. Le, 96–97.
Lucan, 50, 112, 129, 134.
Lucian, 99.
Ludwigslied, 12.
Lulli, 135, 150, 152, 154.
Lybeas Disconus, 28.
Lydgate, 23.
Mabillon. J., 169.
Mably. G. Bonnot de, 192–193.
Macabré. La Danse de, 74s, 81.
Macé de la Charité, 58.
Machaut. G. de, 63, 65, 66s, 68, 78.
Macrobius, 46.
Mademoiselle. The Great, 149.
Magny. O. de, 106s.
Maillart. O., 88.
Maine de Biran. F-P-G., 217.
Mainet, 18.
Maintenon. Mme. de, 158, 168–169, 179.
Mairet. J. de, 132s, 133, 135.
Maistre. J. de, 212–213.
Maistre. X. de, 219s.
Malebranche. N. de, 161s, 170.
Malherbe. F. de, 91, 102, 109, 123, 124–125, 126, 127, 150, 166, 175, 217.
Malory, 30.
Mancini. Marie, 150.
Mandeville. Sir J., 72s.
Manuscripts, 6, 12.
Marais. M., 179s.
Marais. Theater of the, 131, 132.
Marbodius, 14, 105.
Marco Polo, 61s, 72.
Mareschal. A., 146s.
Margaret of Anjou, 86.

Margaret of Austria, 76.
Margaret of Lorraine, 150.
Margaret of Navarre, 94s, 95, 97s, 99s, 105.
Margaret of Savoy, 107.
Margaret of Valois, 115s.
Maria Theresa, 162.
Marie de France, 25s, 32, 36, 42.
Marino, 123.
Marivaux. P. Carlet de Chamblain de, 177s, 182s, 209.
Marivaudage, 177.
Marmontel. J-F., 194s, 196s.
Marot. C., 93–94, 95, 100, 103, 106, 108, 110, 125.
Marot. J. (des Mares), 80–81, 93.
Marotic, 94s.
Martial de Paris (d'Auvergne), 79s.
Martin. H., 215–216.
Martin le Franc, 75–76.
Mary of Champagne, 27, 46, 48, 49.
Mary of Cleves, 88.
Mary Stuart, 103, 112.
Mascaron. J., 163s.
Massillon. J-B., 171s.
Matheolus, 66.
Mathieu. P., 110s, 112s.
Maucroix. F. de, 149s, 150.
Maupassant. G. de, 234.
Maurice de Sully, 51s.
Maximilian I., 76.
Maynard. F. de, 126s.
Medici. C. de', 96.
Medici. L. de', 114.
Medici. M. de', 143.
Medicis. The, 91.
Meigret. L., 100s.
Meilhac. H., 228s.
Mélusine, 72.
Ménage. G., 141s.
Ménippée. La Satire, 117s.
Mennessier, 29.
Menot. M., 88.
Mercadé. E., 82s.

Mercure français. Le, 140.
Mercure galant. Le, 149, 156.
Mérimée. P., 209s, 221–222.
Meschinot. J., 75s, 76.
Metz, 50.
Meyerbeer, 208.
Mézerai. F. Eudes de, 140s.
Michaut. P., 75s.
Michel. J., 82s.
Michelet. J., 215s.
Mignet. F-A-A., 215s.
Miles de Nanteuil, 33.
Mille et une nuits. Les, 172.
Millet. J. (Milet), 82–83.
Millevoye. C-H. de, 200s.
Milton, 107, 176, 185, 201.
Mirabeau. G-H. de Riquetti-, 196s.
Miracles, 16s, 69s, 82.
Moetjens. *Recueil* of, 172.
Molière (J-B. Poquelin), 20, 36, 84, 114, 123, 134, 135, 151, 152–155, 156, 157, 166, 167, 209, 225.
Molina. Tirso de, 153.
Molinet. J., 76s, 77, 92, 93.
Monchrestien. A. de, 130s.
Mondor, 133.
Monluc. B. de, 115s.
Monologue, 84s.
Montaigne. M. de, 116, 120–121, 140, 160.
Montalembert. C. Forbes de, 228s.
Montalvo, 100.
Montausier. Mme. de, 163.
Montemayor, 121, 142.
Montesquieu. C. de Secondat de, 161, 163, 180–181, 195.
Montfleury. A-J., 156s.
Montreux. N. de, 121s.
Mont-St-Michel. La Chronique du, 86s.
Moore, 107.
Moralité, 83–84.
Moreau. H., 205s.
Moreto, 153.

Mort. Les Vers de la, 44–45, 74.
Motet, 47s.
Motteville. Mme. de, 159s.
Mousket. P., 39s.
Moyen de parvenir. Le, 141s.
Muret, 96, 112.
Murger. H., 231s.
Muse française. La, 200.
Muse historique. La, 141s.
Musset. A. de, 80, 203–204, 208–209, 221s, 226, 228.
Mysteries, 15s, 69, 82–83, 95.
Napoleon, 190, 199, 205.
Navagero, 105.
Nemo. Les grands et merveilleux faits de St., 85.
Nennius, 24, 27.
Nerbonesi. I, 13.
Nerval. G. de (Labrunie), 221s.
Neuville. Le Siége de, 53.
Newton, 175, 176.
Nicodemus. Gospel of, 29.
Nicolas de la Chesnaye, 84s.
Nicolas de Senlis, 50.
Nicolas of Troyes, 98–99.
Nicole. P., 160s.
Niccolò da Verona, 64–65.
Nisard. J-M-N-D., 217s.
Nithard, 5.
Nodier. C-E., 201, 219s.
Noël du Fail, 99s.
Normandy, 2, 51, 109.
Norway, 64.
Oaths of Strassburg. The, 5–6.
Odyssey. See Homer.
Offenbach, 228.
Oger, 19.
Oger. Les Enfances d', 19, 53.
Oger le Danois, 19.
Ogier. F., 132.
Olivet. P-J. Thoulier d', 183s.
Olivier de la Marche, 87s.
Opera, 161, 167. See Lulli.
Opéra-Comique. The, 188.

Operetta, 59.
Ordre de Chevalerie. L', 58.
Oresme. N., 70s.
Orior, 14.
Orléans. Mme. la Duchesse d', 169s.
Orléans. Le Siége d', 82.
Orpheus, 105.
Ossian, 200, 201, 218.
Otway, 168.
Ovid, 23, 27, 43, 46, 47, 56, 80, 134.
Pailleron. É., 228s.
Palais-Royal. Theater of the, 154, 157.
Palaprat. J., 167s.
Palissot de Montenoy. C., 188s.
Palissy. B., 117–118.
Palsgrave, 100.
Paon. Le Parfait du, 64.
Paon. Le Restor du, 64.
Paon. Les Vœux du, 54s, 64.
Paradise Lost. See Milton.
Paré. A., 118s.
Parfaict. C., 182–183.
Parfaict. F., 182–183.
Paris. G., 9.
Paris. P., 230s.
Parliament of Paris. The, 95, 103, 181.
Parnasse contemporain. Le, 225.
Parnassians. The, 205, 225s.
Parnell, 43.
Parny. É-D. Desforges de, 186s, 201.
Parténopeus de Blois, 34.
Pascal. B., 137, 139–140, 160.
Pasquier. É., 119s.
Passerat. J., 108s, 117s.
Passion. La, 82s.
Passion. La Confrérie de la, 83, 85, 95, 110.
Pastor Fido, 130.
Pastourelle, 14s, 47, 81.
Pathelin, 84s, 167.
Patin. G., 138s.
Patru. O., 161s, 162.

Pèlerinage de Charlemagne. Le, 12s, 88.
Pelletier. J., 118s.
Pellisson. P., 160s, 183.
Perceforest, 72.
Perrault. C., 172s.
Persius, 70.
Petit de Julleville. L., 132.
Petrarch, 63, 65, 70, 71, 94, 103, 104, 142, 204.
Petrus Alphonsus, 35.
Phaedrus, 36.
Philip Augustus, 2, 18.
Philip of Flanders, 28.
Philip the Bold, 61.
Philip the Good, 75, 86, 87, 88, 91.
Philippa. Queen, 64.
Philippe de Beaumanoir, 54s, 61.
Philippe de Maizières, 71s.
Philippe de Thaon, 14s.
Philippe de Vitri, 65s.
Picard. L-B., 206s.
Pierre de Provence, 88s.
Pierre d'Orgemont, 72s.
Pierre de St. Cloud, 22, 37.
Pilgrim's Progress, 65.
Pindar, 103.
Pippin, 10.
Piron. A., 178s.
Pithou. P., 117s.
Plato, 96, 99, 120, 158.
Plautus, 96, 105, 113, 136, 152, 154, 167.
Pléiade. The, 78, 83, 87, 91, 94, 102–103, 123, 125, 126, 201.
Pliny, 107, 125.
Plutarch, 111, 112, 114, 130, 191.
Poe, 146, 226.
Poème moral. Le, 45s.
Poggio, 89.
Poisson. R., 156.
Ponsard. F., 209s, 227, 228.
Pontalais. J. du (de l'Espine), 95s.
Pope, 176.

INDEX. 247

Port-Royal, 139, 157, 158, 160, 217.
Pradon. N., 157s.
Précieuses. The, 143, 144, 145, 151, 152, 153, 154, 160, 163, 168.
Précieux. See *Précieuses.*
Prévost d'Exiles. A-F., 182s.
Prévost-Paradol. L-A., 231s.
Princesse de Clèves. La. See La Fayette.
Priorat. J., 60.
Protestants, 93, 95, 104.
Provençal, 1, 2, 27, 47–48, 216.
Proudhon. P-J., 214s.
Prudentius, 45, 46.
Psalters, 16.
Pseudo-Callisthenes, 21.
Puis. The, 49, 59, 68, 74, 83, 85.
Quatrains moraux. Les, 110s.
Quesnay. F., 192s.
Quietism, 160, 163, 170.
Quinault. P., 135, 151–152, 154, 155, 156, 157.
Quinet. E., 215s.
Quintus Curtius, 22.
Quinze signes du jugement dernier. Les, 45.
Rabelais. F., 88, 97–98, 99, 121, 141, 146, 150.
Racan. H. de Bueil de, 126s, 130, 149.
Rachel. É., 208, 209.
Racine. J., 123, 130, 135, 141, 151, 156, 157–158, 168, 176, 194, 209.
Racine. L., 176s.
Raimbert of Paris, 19, 53.
Rainaud, 14.
Rambouillet. C. de Vivonne de, 127.
Rambouillet. Hôtel de, 124, 127–128, 142, 144, 162.
Ramée. P. de la (Ramus), 106, 118s, 120s.
Raoul de Cambrai, 20.
Raoul de Houdan, 28, 46–47, 56, 57.
Raoul de Presles, 70s.

Raoul le Fèvre, 87s.
Rapin. N., 117s.
Raulin. J., 88.
Raynal G-T-F., 193s.
Raynouard. F-J-M., 216s.
Récits d'un bourgeois de Valenciennes. Les, 72.
Récits d'un ménestrel de Reims. Les, 60s, 86.
Reclus de Molliens. B. le, 44s.
Reformation. The, 90s, 96, 97s, 107.
Refugee style, 97s.
Regency. The, 177, 178, 180.
Regnard. J-F., 114, 166–167.
Regnier. J., 74, 79s.
Régnier. M., 125s.
Régnier-Desmarets. F-S., 170s.
Reinke de vos, 37.
Renaissance. The, 90ss.
Renan. E., 229s.
Renard. Le Couronnement de, 55.
Renard. Roman de, 36–37, 55s.
Renard le Contrefait, 55.
Renard le Nouvel, 55.
Renaud, 32.
Renaud de Beaujeu, 28.
Renaud de Montauban, 19.
Renaudot. T., 140s.
René d'Anjou, 79s.
Restif de la Bretonne, 197s.
Restoration. The, 200, 206, 214.
Résurrection. La, 49.
Retz. J-F-P. de Gondi de, 159s.
Revolution. The, 175, 186, 189, 191, 196, 199, 212, 231.
Reybaud. L., 223s.
Reynaert de vos, 37.
Richard I., 49.
Richard d'Annebaut, 60.
Richard de Fournival, 47, 65.
Richard le Beau, 54.
Richardson, 196.
Richelieu, 123, 127, 128, 132, 133, 140.

Richepin. J., 226s.
Richeut, 36.
Rime, 68–69, 81s, 91–93, 202, 204. See Assonance and Versification.
Rivarol. A. de, 193s.
Robert de Blois, 57.
Robert de Boron, 29s, 30.
Robert de Brunne, 56.
Robert de Clari, 50.
Robert le Diable, 33, 69.
Rochefort. H., 228.
Roger Bontemps, 93.
Rois. Les Quatre Livres des, 50.
Rojas. F. de, 146, 156.
Roland, 11–12, 18, 19, 88.
Rollin. C., 181s.
Romance, 14s, 32s, 47, 48.
Romans. La Bibliothèque des, 20, 195.
Romans. La Nouvelle Bibliothèque des, 195.
Romans d'aventure, 31–34, 88, 100.
Romanticism, 109, 197, 199, 200–205, 206–208, 209, 211, 212, 216, 218, 219, 221, 223, 225, 227.
Romeo and Juliet. Story of, 443.
Romulus, 36s.
Rondeau, 58s, 59, 68s.
Ronsard. P. de, 102, 103–104, 105–106, 107, 108, 109, 110, 125.
Rose. Roman de la, 46s, 57–58, 63, 65, 67, 71, 74, 75, 76, 78s, 79, 93. See also, *Guillaume de Dole*.
Rose. Dit de la, 46.
Rotrou. J., 133, 136s, 157.
Rotrouenge, 47–48.
Roucher. J-A., 187s.
Rouget de L'Isle. J., 186s.
Round Table. The, 24, 25–26. See P. Paris.
Rousseau. J-B., 166s, 185.
Rousseau. J-J., 144, 175, 188, 190–191, 196, 197, 199, 211, 212, 213, 218, 220.

Royer-Collard. P.-P., 217.
Rustebeuf, 55s, 56s, 59s, 80.
Rusticiano of Pisa, 30s, 61s.
Sablé. Mme. de, 160.
Sablière. Mme. de la, 150.
Sacy. Le Maistre de, 140s.
Sagon. F., 93.
Saint-Amant. M-A, de Gérard de, 129s.
Saint-Cyr, 158, 168.
Sainte-Beuve. C-A. de, 216–217, 230.
Sainte-Palaye. J-B. de La Curne de, 195s.
Saint-Évremond. C. de St-Denis de, 161s.
Saint-Gelais. M. de, 94s, 103.
Saint-Gelais. O. de, 80s, 94.
Saint graal. Le, 30.
Saint graal. La Quête du, 30.
Saintine. X. (Bouiface), 221s.
Saint-Lambert. C-F. de, 187s.
Saint-Marc Girardin. F-A., 216s.
Saint-Pierre. J-H. Bernardin de, 196–197, 200, 212.
Saint-Réal. C. Vichard de, 168.
Saint-Simon. C-H. de, 213–214.
Saint-Simon. L. de Rouvray de, 178s.
Saint-Victor. P. de, 230s.
Saisnes. Les, 18.
Sales. St-F. de, 137–138, 143.
Salon. Annual, 192. Social; see Rambouillet. Hôtel de,
Salut d'amour, 48.
Samson de Nanteuil, 46.
Sand. G. (A-A. Dudevant), 203, 220s, 222, 232.
Sandeau. J., 220, 221s.
Sannazaro, 105, 121.
Sappho, 186.
Saracens, 10, 11, 18.
Sardou. V., 227s.
Sarrazin. J., 60.
Savetier Calbain. Le, 84.

Say. J-B., 213.
Scaliger. J-C., 112, 118, 131, 136.
Scarron. P., 129s, 146s, 188, 221.
Schelandre. J. de. (Daniel d'Anchères),.131-132.
Schérer. E., 230.
Schiller, 168, 200, 204, 205, 206.
Scott, 220.
Scribe. A-E., 206, 208s, 227, 228.
Scudéry. G. de, 137s.
Scudéry. M. de, 137, 144-145, 152, 163.
Sebonde, 120.
Secchi, 152.
Sedaine. M-J., 188s, 220.
Segrais. J. de, 149s.
Sénancour. É. Pivert de, 218-219.
Seneca, 70, 102, 111-112, 113, 134, 135, 157.
Sénecé. A. Bauderon de, 166s.
Sept Sages. Les, 35s.
Sermon joyeux, 84s.
Serres. O. de, 118s.
Serventois, 48s.
Sévigné. M. de Rabutin-Chantal de, 159-160.
Seyssel. C. de, 88s.
Shaftesbury, 191.
Shakspere, 20, 23, 34, 189-190, 204, 208.
Sibilet. T., 100s.
Sidrac. Le Livre de, 61.
Simon, 22.
Sismondi. J-C-L. Simonde de, 216s.
Smith. Adam, 213.
Somme du Roi. Le, 61..
Somnium Scipionis, 46.
Song of Solomon, 14.
Sonnet. The, 94-95.
Sophocles, 96, 105, 158, 194, 226.
Sorbonne. The, 93, 96.
Sorel. C., 145-146, 164.
Sots. The, 84, 85s.
Sottie, 84s.

Sotties de Genève. Les, 95-96.
Soubrette. The, 134.
Soulary. J., 226s.
Soulié. F., 223s.
Soumet. A., 205s.
Souvestre. É., 221s.
Spain, 64, 91s, 145, 187, 194 (ballads).
Spenser, 104.
Sponsus, 16.
Staal-Delaunay. Mme. de, 178-179.
Staël. A-L-G. Necker de, 218s.
Stapfer. P., 231.
Statius, 23.
Stendhal. (M-H. Beyle), 221s, 222, 234.
Sterne, 219.
Straparola, 121.
Sue. E., 223s.
Sully. M. de Béthune de, 140s.
Sully-Prudhomme. R-F-A., 226s.
Swift, 146.
Switzerland, 186.
Symposium. See Plato.
Tabarin, 133.
Tacitus, 157.
Tahureau. J., 109.
Taine. H-A., 230s.
Tallemant des Réaux. G., 159s.
Talma, 205.
Tansillo, 124.
Tasso, 65, 107, 121, 130, 150, 152, 200.
Tavola Ritonda, 29.
Tençon, 48s.
Terence, 96, 105, 113, 149, 152, 153.
Testament. Le Vieux, 82s.
Thaïs. La Vie de Ste, 45.
Thèbes. Roman de, 23-24
Theognis, 106.
Théologastres. Les, 96s.
Théophile de Viau, 125-126, 130, 145s.
Theophrastus, 160.
Thibaut of Navarre, 49s.
Thierry. A., 215s.

Thiers. L-A., 215s.
Thomas, 26.
Thomson, 187.
Thyard. P. de, 102, 106s.
Tocqueville. A-C-H. Clérel de, 215s.
Toepffer. R., 223s.
Tombeur de Notre Dame. Le, 43s.
Tory. G., 100s.
Tressan. L-É. de La Vergne de, 195s.
Triolet, 68s.
Trissino, 94, 130.
Tristan l' Hermite, 132s, 146s.
Tristran, 29.
Troie. Roman de, 22-23, 87.
Troilus, 72.
Turenne, 163.
Turgot. A-R-J., 192s.
Turlupin, 133.
Turpin. Le, 50.
Uhland, 19, 54.
Ulysses, 85, 170.
Univers. L', 213.
Vaudeville, 189.
Vaugelas. C. Favre de, 110, 127, 141s, 161.
Vauquelin de la Fresnaye. J., 108-109.
Vauvenargues. L. de Clapiers, 181s.
Vegetius, 60.
Vendôme. Princes of, 166.
Vergil, 23, 35, 80, 106, 111, 129, 158, 175, 187.
Verne. J., 146.
Versification, 5s, 12s, 14-15, 47-48, 58-59, 67, 68-69, 74; 81s, 106, 107, 124s, 126, 130, 187, 201.
Veuillot. L., 213s, 227.
Vies des Pères. Les, 41s.

Vigny. A. de, 204s, 208s, 220s.
Vilain mire. Le, 36s, 153.
Villehardouin. G. de, 50s.
Villemain. A-F., 216s.
Villiers. P. de, 153, 161.
Villon. (F. de Moncorbier), 56, 74, 79-80, 93, 94, 108, 125, 150, 226.
Violette. Roman de la, 34.
Vire. Vaux de, 81s, 110s.
Vireli, 59.
Vitae Patrum, 56.
Vitet. L., 228s.
Vivien. La Chevalerie de, 13.
Vizé. J. Donneau de, 155-156.
Voiture. V., 127s, 138, 159.
Volney. C-F. de Chasseboeuf-, 195s.
Voltaire. (F-M. Arouet), 43, 123, 168, 174, 175-176, 176-177, 178s, 179-180, 182s, 188, 189, 190, 191, 194.
Vrai anneau. Le, 55-56.
Wace, 24s, 38s, 41s, 42s.
Watriquet de Couvin, 57.
Wauquelin. J., 88s.
Weber. C-M. von, 20.
Weisse, 197.
Werther. See Goethe.
Wieland, 20.
Wilham de Wadington, 56s.
Wilkins. J., 146.
William the Conqueror. Laws of, 51.
Wirnt von Gravenberg, 28.
Wolfram von Eschenbach, 13, 21, 30.
Xenophon, 96.
Yolande of Flanders, 32, 50.
Zola. É., 233-234.

www.ingramcontent.com/pod-product-compliance
Lightning Source LLC
Chambersburg PA
CBHW021357230426
43666CB00006B/555